Value and Prices in Russian Economic Thought

This book explores the Russian synthesis that occurred in Russian economic thought between 1890 and 1920. This includes all the attempts at synthesis between classical political economy and marginalism; the labour theory of value and marginal utility; and value and prices. The various ways in which Russian economists have approached these issues have generally been addressed in a piecemeal fashion in the history of economic thought literature. This book returns to the primary sources in the Russian language, translating many into English for the first time, and offers the first comprehensive history of the Russian synthesis.

The book first examines the origins of the Russian synthesis by determining the condition of reception in Russia of the various theories of value involved: the classical theories of value of Ricardo and Marx on one side; the marginalist theories of prices of Menger, Walras and Jevons on the other. It then reconstructs the three generations of the Russian synthesis: the first (Tugan-Baranovsky), the second, the mathematicians (Dmitriev, Bortkiewicz, Shaposhnikov, Slutsky, etc.) and the last (Yurovsky), with an emphasis on Tugan-Baranovsky's initial impetus.

This volume is suitable for those studying economic theory and philosophy as well as those interested in the history of economic thought.

François Allisson is a Lecturer in History of Economic Thought at the Centre Walras Pareto, University of Lausanne, Switzerland.

Routledge Studies in the History of Economics

Value and Prices in Russian Economic Thought

A journey inside the Russian synthesis, 1890–1920

François Allisson

Routledge
Taylor & Francis Group

LONDON AND NEW YORK

First published 2015
by Routledge

2 Park Square, Milton Park, Abingdon, Oxfordshire OX14 4RN
52 Vanderbilt Avenue, New York, NY 10017

Routledge is an imprint of the Taylor & Francis Group, an informa business

First issued in paperback 2019

Copyright © 2015 François Allisson

The right of François Allisson to be identified as author of this work has
been asserted by him in accordance with the Copyright, Designs and
Patent Act 1988.

All rights reserved. No part of this book may be reprinted or reproduced or
utilised in any form or by any electronic, mechanical, or other means, now
known or hereafter invented, including photocopying and recording, or in
any information storage or retrieval system, without permission in writing
from the publishers.

Notice:
Product or corporate names may be trademarks or registered trademarks,
and are used only for identification and explanation without intent to
infringe.

British Library Cataloguing in Publication Data
A catalogue record for this book is available from the British Library

Library of Congress Cataloging in Publication Data
Allisson, François.
Value and prices in Russian economic thought: a journey inside the
Russian synthesis, 1890-1920 / Francois Allisson.
    pages cm
    1. Russia–Economic policy–1861–1917. 2. Russia–Economic
    conditions–1861-1917. 3. Marginality, Social–Russia. 4. Labor theory
    of value–Russia. 5. Tugan-Baranovskii, M. I. (Mikhail Ivanovich),
    1865–1919. 6. Economic history. I. Title.
    HC334.5.A45 2015
    338.5'21094709034–dc23   2014048165

ISBN: 978-1-138-83977-9 (hbk)
ISBN: 978-0-367-87195-6 (pbk)

Typeset in Times New Roman
by Wearset Ltd, Boldon, Tyne and Wear

To my beloved parents and family
To Sylvia

Contents

Tables

Acknowledgements

The editors of *Œconomia* and *The History of Economic Thought* are acknowledged for their permissions to reproduce the following previously published materials:

'Tugan-Baranovsky on Socialism: From Utopia to the Economic Plan', *Œconomia (History | Methodology | Philosophy)*, 4(1): 35–53, 2014.
'Reception of Walras' Theory of Exchange and Theory of Production in Russia', *The History of Economic Thought*, 51(1): 19–35, 2009.

I am also grateful to the Scientific Research Museum of the Academy of Arts of Russia, St Petersburg, for their authorisation to reproduce Kustodiev's Merchant (1918). For their precious remarks, support and encouragement during the genesis of this book, I would like to thank my PhD supervisor Pascal Bridel, the members of my PhD committee – Richard Arena, Vladimir Avtonomov, Roberto Baranzini, Jean-Pierre Potier and Alessandro Villa, the whole editorial staff at Routledge and their three anonymous referees, as well as my colleagues and friends at the Centre Walras-Pareto – Amanar Akhabbar, Joanna Bauvert, Michele Bee, Juan Manuel Blanco, Nicolas Brisset, Melek Cihangir, Francesca Dal Degan, Maxime Desmarais-Tremblay, Nicolas Eyguesier, Antoine Missemer, Thomas Mueller, Pelin Sekerler Richiardi and Sophie Swaton, and elsewhere – Graham Austing, Vincent Barnett, Daniele Besomi, Annie L. Cot, Irina Eliseeva, Daniel Gombau, Shuichi Kojima, Jérôme Lallement, Danila Raskov, Yannick Rochat, Leonid Shirokorad, Yuri Tulupenko and Joachim Zweynert.

Note to the reader

This book is a revised version of my doctoral dissertation, written under the supervision of Prof. Pascal Bridel, and defended in 2012 at the University of Lausanne, Switzerland. The dissertation was awarded the Prix de la Société Académique Vaudoise in 2012, and the History of Economics Society's Joseph Dorfman Best Dissertation Prize in 2013.

All quotations from the Russian have been translated by the author, unless a translation in English was readily available. Titles of books and articles originally written in Russian have been translated into English in the text, but the original title in Russian may always be found in a transliterated form in the References.

Boris Mikhailovich KUSTODIEV (1878–1927).
Merchant (Old man counting money) 1918 (Oil, 88.5 × 70 cm).
© Scientific Research Museum of the Academy of Arts of Russia, St Petersburg, Russia,
2015.

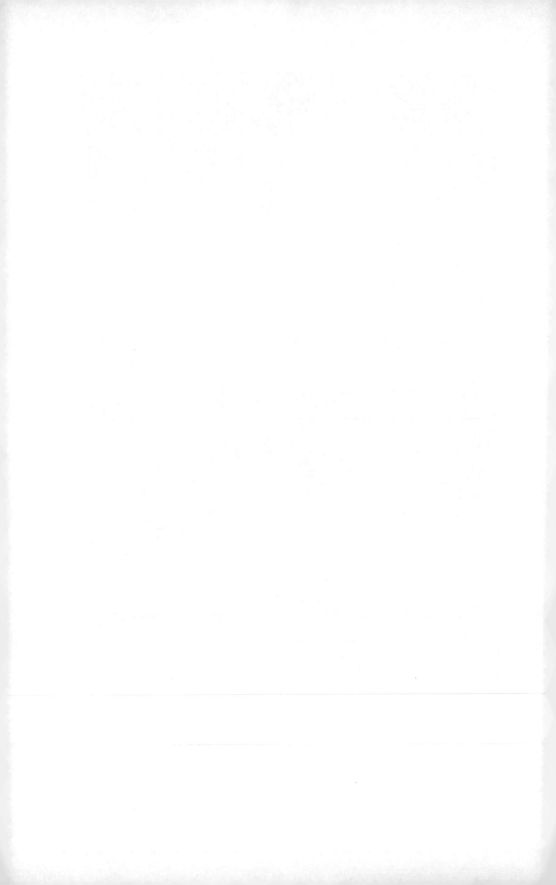

Introduction

The subject 'Value and prices in Russian economic thought (1890–1920)' should evoke several names and debates in the reader's mind. For a long time, Western scholars have been aware that the Russian economists Tugan-Baranovsky and Bortkiewicz were active participants in the Marxian transformation problem, that the mathematical models of Dmitriev prefigured neoricardian-based models and that many Russian economists were either supporters of the Marxian labour theory of value or revisionists. Moreover, these ideas were preparing the ground for Soviet planning. Russian scholars additionally knew that this period was the time of the introduction of marginalism in Russia, and that, during this period, economists were active in thinking about the relationship of ethics to economic theory. All these issues are well covered in the existing literature.[1]

But there is a big gap that this book intends to fill. The existing literature handles these pieces separately, although they are part of a single, more general, history. All these issues (the labour theory of value, marginalism, the Marxian transformation problem, planning, ethics, mathematical economics) were part of what this book calls the *Russian synthesis*.

The term 'Russian synthesis' in this book covers all the attempts at synthesis between classical political economy and marginalism, between the labour theory of value and marginal utility, and between value and prices that occurred in Russian economic thought between 1890 and 1920, and that embraces the whole set of issues evoked above.

This book is the first comprehensive history of the Russian synthesis. It has always surprised me that such a story has not yet been written. Several good reasons, both in terms of the scarce availability of sources and of ideological restrictions, may account for a reasonable delay of several decades. But it is now urgent to remedy the situation before the protagonists of the Russian synthesis are definitely classified under the wrong labels in the pantheon of economic thought.

To accomplish this task, it has seldom been sufficient to gather together the various existing studies on aspects of this story. It has been necessary to return to the primary sources in the Russian language. The most important part of the primary literature has never been translated, and in recent years only some of them have been republished in Russian. The secondary literature has been surveyed in the languages that are familiar (Russian, English and French) or almost familiar (German) to me, and which are hopefully the most pertinent to the present investigation. In addition, and in order to increase my familiarity with the text, which was the objective of all of this, some archival sources were used. The analysis consists of careful chronological studies of the authors' writings and their evolution in their historical and intellectual context.

The ultimate objective of this book is to change opinion on 'value and prices in Russian economic thought' by setting the Russian synthesis at the centre of the debate.

The Russian synthesis

The Russian synthesis is the generic label given in this book to all attempts made at a synthesis in Russia. There is no 'school' of the Russian synthesis, but rather a tradition of economists engaged in similar investigations. The common ground of their investigation is the synthesis between classical political economy and marginalism. Some added a synthesis between value and prices, others even between a pure labour theory of value and marginal utility. There are as many syntheses as there are authors, but the latter are called here protagonists of the Russian synthesis, in the singular.

It should be noted that the synthesis at stake owes nothing to the synthesis often ascribed to Hegel's dialectic. It represents something simpler: a combination of different elements in order to get a whole; Tugan-Baranovsky even speaks of an 'organic synthesis'.

The Russian synthesis kept the notion of value next to that of prices. It adopted the marginal utility theory. It preserved a link between labour, value and prices. And it loosened the link between the theories of value and prices, and the theory of distribution. In the whole episode, the notion of prices was unchanged in most respects, but the definition of value underwent several transformations.[2] In these constructions, the theory of marginal utility, the costs of production theory *and* the labour theory of value were accommodated in several ways.

As a first step, this synthesis started in the Russian revisionism of Marxism. In the 1890s, some Russian economists, led by Tugan-Baranovsky, were trying to rescue Marx's theory of value in the context of the transformation problem. They identified a solution with a synthesis between the Marxian labour theory of value and marginalism. Marx's labour theory of value was at that time almost confounded with Ricardo's theory of value in Russia (see Chapter 2), and marginalism in Russia was at that time an exclusively Austrian phenomena (see Chapter 3). This was the birth of the Russian synthesis. In Europe, with the exception of the German Social Democratic journal, *Die neue Zeit*, the Russian synthesis found no echoes, but it gave birth to numerous debates in Russia.

As a second step, and building on this attempt at synthesis between Marx and Menger, new syntheses appeared, taking the mathematical form. Dmitriev, Bortkiewicz and Slutsky engaged themselves in the synthesis between Walras and Ricardo. And Shaposhnikov followed in their tracks. This second step saw the mathematization of Marx's and Ricardo's theories of value, and the integration of these production equations with Walras's exchange equations, forming a classico-marginalist general equilibrium. Hence, the Russian synthesis, which was first in Tugan-Baranovsky's hands a Marx–Menger synthesis, became a Ricardo–Walras synthesis, but with a Ricardo in whom a labour theory takes the place of the traditional costs of production theory of value. This last point eventually changed with Yurovsky's final episode in the Russian synthesis.

The central claim of this book is that, in the fields of value and prices, the Russian synthesis, although it adopted marginal utility, remained essentially classical. The Russian attempts at syntheses demonstrated first and foremost a commitment to the holy classical link between labour and value. Second, they refused to choose, within the classical theory of value, between two variants – the labour theory of value and the costs of production theory – for they considered them as being one single theory with different domains of application. They were therefore attached to the wealth of *their* classical theory of value, which should be considered as yet another attempt at synthesis between Ricardo and Marx (see Chapters 2, 5 and 6). As to their synthesis between *their* classical theory of value and the marginalist theory of prices, the Russians always tried to keep a strong link between labour and value, while at the same time stressing the need to reduce the gap between value and prices.

The sources

The spatio-temporal horizon of the present history is defined as embracing the period 1890–1920, mainly in Russia. This decision is arbitrary and not entirely accurate. The date 1890 marks the rather belated importation of the theory of marginal utility to Russia, and the first attempt at synthesis, with Tugan-Baranovsky's 'Study on the Marginal Utility of Economic Goods as the Cause of their Value' (1890). But the nature of this investigation requires some incursions earlier into the nineteenth century, essentially to capture the Russian reception of the classical economists Ricardo and Marx. The date of 1920 is chosen in a somewhat provocative manner, crossing the traditional 1917 boundary, which is not relevant in this case. It allows us to evoke the last work devoted to the synthesis in the theory of value, Yurovsky's *Essays on Price Theory* (1919). And, incidentally, it coincides with the publication of the eighth edition of Marshall's *Principles of Economics*.

The same can be said about the geography, whose boundaries are variable. Russian economists are not writing exclusively in Russian for a Russian audience. Tugan-Baranovsky, for example, was born in the Ukraine, but spent most of his career in Russia. He published some of his works in Russian, a few in German, and even some in both languages. Bortkiewicz is a special case, difficult to consider as a Russian, as he spent most of his life in exile in Germany, and because of his Polish origins. But he nevertheless was brought up and educated in Russia and kept many contacts with Russians. He is therefore also included in this story as a Russian (although as a Western European Russian). It is therefore a useful abstraction to consider them all as part of a community of Russian economists.

The primary literature under investigation consists of the writings of the Russian economists Nikolay Ivanovich Ziber (1844–1888), Mikhail Ivanovich Tugan-Baranovsky (1865–1919), Nikolay Nikolaevich Shaposhnikov (1878–1939) and Leonid Naumovich Yurovsky (1884–1938). The first is chosen for its influential interpretation of Marx and Ricardo. The second is chosen as the founder of the tradition of the Russian synthesis. The third is chosen as the most representative protagonist of the Russian synthesis of the second – mathematical – generation. While Shaposhnikov's (and Yurovsky's) works are much less analytical than those of Dmitriev and Bortkiewicz, he is chosen from this second generation because he is the finest and most lucid observer of his contemporaries' theoretical developments. Shaposhnikov's writings on value and prices were essentially reviews of Dmitriev's works. Moreover, Shaposhnikov personally knew Bortkiewicz. Finally, Shaposhnikov was more conscious and explicit about the place of the Russian synthesis. A few more cases were also chosen, in order to support the claim that this was a Russian tradition: Slutsky, Stoliarov, Frank and Bilimovic. Finally, Yurovsky is chosen so that I can write a complete story of the Russian synthesis, up to its very end. It should be noted that some of their writings have been translated into European languages. But most of their writings on the synthesis (unlike their writings on the transformation debate) remain only in the Russian language.

There is a secondary literature dealing either with Tugan-Baranovsky's theory of value, or with some economists of the second, mathematical, generation of the Russian synthesis and these will be indicated in the text. But the literature on the theme of the synthesis, covering both Tugan-Baranovsky and the second generation (or at least some of its representatives), is scarce. They are four exceptions, but none provides a satisfying history of the synthesis. Gelesnoff provides a complete, but very short, account of the major publications on value theory from Tugan-Baranovsky, Dmitriev, Shaposhnikov, Bilimovic and Yurovsky (Gelesnoff 1927, 168–175). Already different is Seraphim's *Neuere russische Wert- und Kapitalzinstheorien* (1925), which analyses in detail Tugan-Baranovsky's contribution and that of some of his followers and the reactions of the critics in the Russian literature, but he does not reach the second generation. The critique of the synthesis by Howard and King (1995) provided interesting insights, but from the point of view of Marxist political economy. Recently, Kljukin (2007, 2010, 2014) was the first to embrace the whole range of Russian economists working on the synthesis, but with a focus on the circular representation of the economy, and not on the synthesis itself.

A collective investigation

This book pursues a tradition initiated by a few books written during the revival of the debates on the transformation problem in the 1970s in the aftermath of the Cambridge capital controversies and of the Ricardian resurgence as a result of

Sraffa. In these books, and especially in Gilles Dostaler's *Valeur et prix* (1978), the debate was translated into historical research on value and prices that led to the Russian economists of the period 1890–1920. Dostaler scrutinised the debates on the Marxian transformation *before* Bortkiewicz, convinced that crucial elements of the analysis were beyond his contemporaries' understanding and that Bortkiewicz's contribution to the transformation problem was retrospectively so influential that it concealed important parts of the debates that took place before him. And in doing so, he uncovered part of the Russian contribution to value and prices theory. With the same spirit in mind, it is shown in this book that several approaches to the theory of value and prices that were attempted by Russian economists between 1890 and 1920 were partly forgotten, in the shadow of Bortkiewicz's interpretation of the Marxian transformation debate. The importance of the Russian contributions to the Marxian transformation problem is not denied. But it is argued that they were only a small part of the overall original Russian contribution to the economic theory of value and prices: through the various platforms of conciliation found between labour and marginal utility. More generally, this book draws on the literature that originated in the 1970s and 1980s, supplemented by the recent new editions of the sources together with the renewed secondary literature published in the last two decades in contemporary Russia.

Before outlining the articulation of the present book, a few remarks are required. The focus of this book is, in Schumpeterian terms, on economic *analysis*. But at the same time, as the book deals with the circulation of analysis between Europe and Russia in a given historical context, the book deals with economic *thought* more broadly, with a core emphasis on economic analysis.

Three assumptions will be taken for granted in this book. First, the devotion to keeping a strong link between *human labour* and value is linked to the traditional anthropocentric Russian philosophy, which places the activity of human beings at the centre of everything, in this case, in production *and* in consumption, or in labour and in marginal utility. The proof is to be tracked down in the legacy of Russian Orthodoxy and in the basic socio-philosophical patterns of thought which are systematically analysed in Russian economic thought in Joachim Zweynert's magnum opus *Eine Geschichte des ökonomischen Denkens in Russland, 1805–1905* (2002). Second, the will to reduce the gap between value and prices can be construed as the predominance of practical (prices) over theoretical motivations (value), which can probably be traced to the very strong neo-Kantian current that invaded Russia in the 1890s (especially within Legal Marxists). Third, it is argued that the Russian quasi obsession for synthesis should be investigated in the realm of the *Russian soul* and the *Russian idea*; the Russian philosopher and theologian Berdiaev is probably the most fertile source for this.[3]

This book is not about all the theories of value and prices that are found in Russia during the period 1890–1920. It concentrates on the synthesis and, by doing this, it disregards all the concomitant works by Marxist scholars (Bukharin, Rubin), by marginalist authors (Woytinsky, Orzhencky), by theoreticians of prices of production (Charasoff). There is no intention either to reveal the existing filiation between the ideas and models of these Russian economists with those of Sraffa and later neoricardian or surplus approach economists.[4] Similarly, the book disregards monetary issues, as the protagonists of the Russian synthesis handled them separately.

Finally, it should be noted that Petr Nikolaevich Kljukin undertook in recent years the identification of a larger Russian 'analytic tradition', not only encompassing all the authors analysed in the present book (except for Ziber), but also including Charasoff, Kondratiev and Leontief, thus covering a longer time-span (1890–1935). His emphasis is on the development of analytical techniques in a circular flow approach. His books (Kljukin 2010; 2014) inevitably overlap with the present book, as they discuss different yet complementary objects.

Outline of the book

The history of the relations between value and prices in Russian economic thought between 1890 and 1920 – the story of the Russian synthesis – is outlined in this book in six chapters, conveniently divided into two parts.

The Russian synthesis between the labour theory of value and marginal utility is the result of multiple conditions: a specific intellectual context, specific developments within the discipline of economics, together with the authors' own intentions. The first part of this book (The origins of the Russian synthesis) intends to give an overview of the most relevant theoretical elements of that background. It is essential to capture the ingredients of the synthesis – classical political economy and marginalist theory – as they were understood in Russia by the protagonists of the synthesis. Therefore, Chapter 1 (The prehistory of the Russian synthesis) provides a theoretical introduction to the relation between value and prices in comparison with Europe. Chapter 2 (Classical political economy in Russia) focuses on the reception of the labour theory of value by Russian economists prior to Tugan-Baranovsky. This chapter dwells on the order of reading (Ricardo *after* Marx), and on the articulation between the notions of labour value and costs of production, notably through Ziber's influential interpretation. Chapter 3 (Marginalism in Russia) draws a map of the reception of marginalism from the 1890s onwards. It examines the relative influence of English, Austrian and Walrasian marginalist theories and their theories of exchange and production, as far as they were, or were not, involved. Taken together, these three chapters provide theoretical explanations of the genesis of the Russian synthesis, by pointing out in its Russian context from where the protagonists of the synthesis took the various parts of their theories of value and of prices.

The second part (The Russian synthesis) is devoted to the various syntheses, with a substantial interest in Tugan-Baranovsky's initial attempt. In order to understand it, his system of political economy is reconstructed, at the heart of which his synthesis takes a central meaning. To this purpose, Chapter 4 (Tugan-Baranovsky on capitalism and socialism) first retraces Tugan-Baranovsky's analysis of the capitalist mode of production from his theory of crises and cycles to his analysis of Russian industry. In parallel, his reconsideration of Marxist political economy, to which he first subscribed, is retraced until his rejection of Marx's notion of value. Then, starting with the background supplied by his reflections on utopia and science in his historical study of socialism, it evaluates Tugan-Baranovsky's positive theory of socialism, in which economic planning takes place according to his synthetic theory of value and prices. Chapter 5 (Tugan-Baranovsky's synthesis) then retraces the development of Tugan-Baranovsky's synthesis and shows that his analysis of the gap between value and prices provides the key notion of his economic typology between capitalism and socialism. Chapter 6 (The mathematicians' syntheses) analyses the evolution of Tugan-Baranovsky's initial synthesis at the hands of the first generation of Russian mathematical economists (Dmitriev, Bortkiewicz, Slutsky, Shaposhnikov, Yurovsky and a few others), with a particular emphasis on Shaposhnikov and Yurovsky.

Notes

1 On the Russian contribution to the Marxian transformation problem, see Dostaler (1978), Faccarello (1983) and Jorland (1995). On mathematical political economy in Russia, see Shukov (1988), Kljukin (2003) and Belykh (2007). On Russian 'neoricardians', see Nuti (1974), Schefold (1992), Marchionatti and Fiorini (2000), Schütte (2002), Gehrke and Kurz (2006) and Kljukin (2007). On Russian revisionists, see Kindersley (1962) and Howard and King (1989, chap. 10, 1990). On Soviet planning, see Zaubermann (1975) and Sutela (1984). On the introduction of marginalism in Russia, see Makasheva (2009). On the relation between ethics and economic theory, see Makasheva (2008).
2 Throughout this book, 'value' is most often kept in the singular, to underline the fact that if such an intrinsic truth exists, it should be unique; while 'prices' are most often kept in the plural, to indicate the manifold manifestations of this real phenomena.
3 See Berdiaev's *The Russian Idea* (1947). Berdiaev, Nikolay Alexandrovich (1874–1948) was a religious philosopher who, in the 1890s, offered a synthesis between revolutionary Marxism and Kant's idealist philosophy. Expelled in 1922 from Soviet Russia, he lived abroad, writing on philosophy, religion and Russia.
4 This has been done elsewhere. See for instance Nuti (1974), Schefold (1992), Marchionatti and Fiorini (2000), Schütte (2002), Gehrke and Kurz (2006), Belykh (2007) and Kljukin (2007).

References

Belykh, Andrej Akatovich. 2007. *Istoriâ Rossijskih èkonomiko-matematičeskih issledovanij (History of Russian Economic–Mathematical Investigations)*. Second edition. Moscow: LKI.
Berdiaev, Nicolas. 1947. *The Russian Idea*. London: G. Bless.
Dostaler, Gilles. 1978. *Valeur et prix. Histoire d'un débat*. Montréal: François Maspero, Presses Universitaires de Grenoble, Les presses de l'Université du Québec.
Faccarello, Gilbert. 1983. *Travail, valeur et prix: une critique de la théorie de la valeur*. Paris: Anthropos. Electronic ed., 2009, available at: http://ggjjff.free.fr/ (accessed on 16 July 2014).
Gehrke, Christian and Heinz D. Kurz. 2006. 'Sraffa on von Bortkiewicz: Reconstructing the Classical Theory of Value and Distribution'. *History of Political Economy*, 38(1): 91–149.

Gelesnoff, Wladimir Yakovlevich. 1927. 'Russland'. In Hans Mayer, Frank A. Fetter and Richard Reisch, eds, *Die Wirtschaftstheorie der Gegenwart*, vol. 1, 151–181. Vienna: Julius Springer.

Howard, Michael C. and John E. King. 1989. *A History of Marxian Economics: Volume I, 1883–1929*. London: Macmillan.

Howard, Michael C. and John E. King. 1990. 'Tugan-Baranovsky, Russian Revisionism and Marxian Political Economy'. In Donald E. Moggridge, ed., *Perspectives on the History of Economic Thought, Vol. III. Classicals, Marxians and Neo-Classicals*. Hants, England: Edward Elgar for the History of Economics Society.

Howard, Michael C. and John E. King. 1995. 'Value Theory and Russian Marxism before the Revolution'. In Ian Steedman, ed., *Socialism and Marginalism in Economics: 1870–1930*, 224–257. London: Routledge.

Jorland, Gérard. 1995. *Les paradoxes du capital*. Paris: Odile Jacob.

Kindersley, Richard. 1962. *The First Russian Revisionists: a Study of 'Legal Marxism' in Russia*. Oxford: Clarendon Press.

Kljukin, Petr Nikolaevich. 2003. 'Razvitie rossijskoj èkonomiko-matematičeskoj školy v pervoj treti 20 veka (Development of the Russian Economic–Mathematical School in the First Third of the Twentieth Century)'. In Y. V. Yakovec, ed., *Rossijskie èkonomičeskie školy (Russian Economic Schools)*, chap. 14, 256–307. Moscow: IFK-MFK.

Kljukin, Petr Nikolaevich. 2007. 'Reviziâ neorikardianskoj teorii cennosti i raspredeleniâ: novye svidetel'stva i novye gorizonty (Reconsideration of the Neoricardian Theory of Value and Distribution: New Evidences and Horizons)'. *Voprosy èkonomiki*, 5: 117–137.

Kljukin, Petr Nikolaevich. 2010. *Elementy teorii hozâjstvennogo krugooborota v trudah rossijskih èkonomistov-matematikov konca XIX – pervoj treti XX vv (Elements of a Theory of the Economic Circuit in the Works of Russian Mathematical Economists, End of XIX – First Third of XX Centuries)*. Moscow: Institute of Economics of the Russian Academy of Sciences.

Kljukin, Petr Nikolaevich. 2014. *Rossijskaâ tradicia èkonomičeskogo analiza, 1890–1935 (Russian Tradition of Economic Analysis, 1890–1935)*. Moscow: Institute of Economics of the Russian Academy of Sciences.

Makasheva, Natalia A. 2008. 'Searching for an Ethical Basis of Political Economy: Bulgakov and Tugan-Baranovsky'. In Vincent Barnett and Joachim Zweynert, eds, *Economics in Russia. Studies in Intellectual History*, chap. 6, 75–89. Aldershot, UK: Ashgate.

Makasheva, Natalia A. 2009. 'Kak maržinalizm prohodil v Rossiû? Dva èpizoda iz istorii (How Marginalism Settled in Russia? Two Episodes from History)'. *Terra economicus*, 7(3): 29–41.

Marchionatti, Roberto and Raffaella Fiorini. 2000. 'Between Walras and Ricardo. Ladislaus von Bortkiewicz and the Origin of Neo-Ricardian Theory'. *Revue européenne des sciences sociales*, 38(117): 173–191.

Marshall, Alfred. 1920. *Principles of Political Economy*. Eighth edition. London: Macmillan and Co.

Nuti, Domenico M. 1974. 'Introduction'. In V. K. Dmitriev, *Economic Essays on Value, Competition and Utility*, 7–28. London: Cambridge University Press.

Schefold, Bertram. 1992. 'V. K. Dmitriev: Ein russischer Neoricardianer'. In Heinz Rieter, ed., *Osteuropäische Dogmengeschichte*, vol. XII of Studien zur Entwicklung der ökonomischen Theorie, 91–110. Berlin: Duncker & Humblot.

Schütte, Frank. 2002. *Die ökonomischen Studien V. K. Dmitrievs*. Ph.D. diss., Technische Universität Chemnitz. Available at: http://monarch.qucosa.de/fileadmin/data/qucosa/documents/5136/data/start.html (accessed on 5 August 2014).

Seraphim, Hans-Jürgen. 1925. *Neuere russische Wert- und Kapitalzinstheorien.* Berlin and Leipzig: Gruyter.

Shukov, N. S. 1988. 'Mathematical Economics in Russia (1867–1917)'. *Matekon,* 24: 3–31.

Sutela, Pekka. 1984. *Socialism, Planning and Optimality: A Study in Soviet Economic Thought.* Helsinki: Finnish Society of Sciences and Letters.

Tugan-Baranovsky, Mikhail Ivanovich. 1890. 'Učenie o predel'noj poleznosti hozâjstvennyh blag kak pričina ih cennosti (Study on the Marginal Utility of Economic Goods as the Cause of their Value)'. *Ûridičeskij Vestnik,* XXII(10/2): 192–230.

Yurovsky, Leonid Naumovich. 1919. *Očerki po teorii ceny (Essays on Price Theory).* Saratov, Russia: Saratov University.

Zauberman, Alfred. 1975. *The Mathematical Revolution in Soviet Planning.* London: Oxford University Press.

Zweynert, Joachim. 2002. *Eine Geschichte des ökonomischen Denkens in Russland. 1805–1905.* Marburg, Germany: Metropolis Verlag.

Part I
The origins of the Russian synthesis

1 The prehistory of the Russian synthesis

> Value is, so to speak, the epigone of price, and the statement that they must be identical is a tautology.
>
> (Simmel [1900] 2004, 93)

The Russian synthesis was a peculiar understanding of the relations between value and prices between 1890 and 1920 in Russia. It was made possible through a given interpretation of the classical theory of value and with the importation of the new marginalist theory of prices. This chapter invites the reader on a detour of the possible relations that value and prices can have, before introducing this issue within the Russian political economy landscape.

More than a century ago, Vilfredo Pareto complained about the complete futility and even the harmfulness of the notion of *value* for economic science. He applied himself to demonstrating his claim against the classical economists and chiefly against Marx. He made fun of these economists who pretended that prices were only the concrete manifestations of the notion of value. In his own ironical words: 'After the incarnations of Buddha, we now have the incarnations of value! What can this mysterious entity really be?' (Pareto [1909] 2014, 122n). The only benefit of the notion of value, for Pareto, was to confuse the mind of the reader and hide the flaws of these theories, a claim that was made especially saliently in *Les systèmes socialistes* (Pareto 1902–1903, chap. 13). In other words, the metaphysical and therefore superfluous notion of value should be replaced once and for all by the positivist notion of prices:

> So many vague and sometimes contradictory meanings have thus been given to the term *value*, that it is better not to use it in the study of political economy. That is what Jevons did by using the expression *exchange ratio*; and it would be better still as did Walras, to use the concept of the price of a commodity B in terms of a commodity A.
>
> (Pareto [1909] 2014, 122)

Pareto further adds that general equilibrium is foreign to the idea that a single variable (even the utility or labour) may be the cause of prices (Pareto [1909]

2014, 123–124).[1] Therefore, as far as the theory of prices is concerned, Pareto had two expectations: first, the end of the controversies on the true cause of value; second, the disappearance of value in favour of prices. This would have accomplished, for him, the transition from the classical theory of value to a general equilibrium-based theory of prices.

The nature of the relation between value and prices

One century later, Pareto would be clearly disappointed. Not only has value not disappeared from economic theory, but the relation between value and prices was still at the heart of many theoretical debates that marked the twentieth century: the Marxian transformation problem, the socialist calculation debate, the non-substitution theorem, the Cambridge capital controversies. These debates were stimulated by several events that contributed to feed the controversies, among them, the rediscovery of Bortkiewicz's articles on the transformation problem and Sraffa's Ricardian revival.

The different points of view all implied a relation or absence of relation between value and prices and, in the background, an idea of the nature of the transition between the classical theory of value and the marginalist theory of prices. The consequence of the marginalist theory on the path of development of economic thought was especially debated: was there a marginalist revolution, or was it merely an evolution. This continuity vs rupture debate was discussed in a special issue of *History of Political Economy* (1972, no 2). As a clue that the classical economists were still alive, Ricardo was resuscitated in the 1950s–1960s, and Marx reappeared in times of crisis (and, if perhaps not better read, he was at least well reissued and sold, even in educational Japanese manga). Apparently, the classical theory of value was not yet buried.

The terms *value* and *prices* are often used as synonyms. After all, what a theory of value or a theory of prices tries to explain is the determinants of the ratio of a certain quantity of a good obtained in exchange for a quantity of another good. It is irrelevant at this stage to know if one of the two goods is money or whether the determinants of this ratio are to be found in the very fact of exchange, or in the process of production, or if they depend on specific social rules such as those regulating the distribution of the social output. What matters is that prices are such a ratio. However, several concepts of price are frequently distinguished within a single theoretical system. It is convenient to differentiate them by calling one *value* and the other *prices*. Various labelling strategies have been applied through time, but two of them are more frequently observed in the history of economic thought.[2] In the first – logical – strategy, prices are used to label the concepts that are closest to the prices actually observed in historically and spatially located markets; and value is used for more abstract and remote constructions of the mind. In the second – historical – strategy, the classical economists tended to favour the term 'value' (especially in the idiom 'labour value') and, since the marginalists, the term 'prices' has tended to dominate. Clearly, this terminology is only the result of an agreement, an implicit consensus. What matters is the content of these concepts and their rationale.

The primary function of a theory of prices is to explain an exchange ratio. Some concepts of prices (and above all value) may nevertheless serve other purposes, as it is the case in this book. Other typical purposes are the explanation of the coordination of economic activities, and the introduction of normative judgement in the process of valuation. Besides the analysis of the *nature* and the *cause* of prices, many economists also investigate its *measure*. It is therefore necessary to distinguish between attempts to determine absolute and relative prices. The quest for an absolute notion of prices (or value, as it was more often labelled) is contingent on the discovery of a standard of measure. This standard must be invariable in order to serve its purpose.[3] The standards adopted by economists were chosen for their allegedly near-invariability: labour, money (and other precious metals), corn (as a metaphor or approximation for real wages, and in the various models where corn was conceived as both input and output) and baskets of various commodities (real or theoretically constructed). This quest for an invariable standard of value was notably one of Ricardo's main preoccupations (see Mongin 2003).

Many economists confused the *cause* and the *measure* of value, often mixing them in their discourse, not specifying whether they had an absolute or a relative concept of prices in mind. In their turn, the theories investigating the causes of the (relative) ratio of exchange also took various forms. They have either been based on labour (incorporated or commanded), on costs of production, or on supply and demand (from its vaguest empirical perception to a complete theoretical formalisation of a partial or general equilibrium framework based – or not – on marginal utility).

The relationship between any two of these notions (e.g. market price with normal price, or market value with relative value, or relative value with absolute value, etc.) took various forms in the history of economic thought. Among the most remarkable:

• the *gravitation* of market price around natural price;
• the *transformation* of labour value into prices of production;
• and the *synthesis*, between labour value and marginal utility.

The last two are of interest in Russia's theoretical context.[4]

The Marxian transformation problem

The theory of value plays a central role in Marx's overall critique of political economy and of the understanding of the workings of a society characterised by a capitalist mode of production. In the present case, however, it is sufficient to keep in mind the following. The relation between value and prices in Marx's *Capital* is primarily concerned with revealing – behind the appearance of prices – that the origin of profit lies in surplus value, and therefore in the exploitation of workers by capitalists. To do this, Marx developed a system of value in volume I of *Capital* (1867), and a system of prices in volume III (1894). It is relevant to remember that, albeit published by Engels long after volume I (1867), volume III was composed prior to it. In this system of value, the value of a commodity is determined by the amount of socially necessary abstract labour time incorporated in that commodity during its process of production. This law of value applies to all commodities, including labour power, which appears as a special commodity under capitalism, alone able to generate surplus value. In order to survive, workers have to sell their labour power to the capitalists, and the capitalists benefit from the use value of this labour power. Surplus value appears during the production process as the difference between the value of the produced commodity (i.e. use value of labour power) and the value of labour power paid as wage (i.e. exchange value of labour power). The length of the labour day is greater than that necessary to reproduce labour-power, but the workers receive as a wage only that strict minimum. The resulting surplus labour time becomes unpaid labour and, albeit lawfully appropriated by capitalists, is the source of the exploitation of workers by capitalists, who benefit from this surplus value.

This allows Marx to express a rate of exploitation, defined as the ratio between surplus value and variable capital. It should be noted that, contrary to his predecessors who distinguished circulating from fixed capital, Marx distinguishes variable from constant capital. The former is constituted from labour power and is the sole creator of value. The latter, formed from the past product of labour (crystallised labour), only transmits its value to the commodity. In volume III, Marx tries to show how surplus value is distributed in the form of profits. This implies a shift from the system of value to the system of prices of production, and an attempt to explain the relation between the two systems. Marx suggests that the system of value is necessary for a genuine understanding of the system of prices. For him, the whole surplus value is socialised and then distributed among capitalists under the guise of profits, according to a uniform rate of profit proportional to their invested variable *and* constant capital. That uniform rate of profit is explained through the competition between capitalists.

In 1885, Engels published volume II of *Capital*, and announced that Marx provided a solution to the issue of the transformation of labour values into prices of production that would be published in the further volume of *Capital* that he was editing from Marx's drafts. In his foreword to volume II, Engels initiated a competition, later known as Engels's Prize Essay Competition, inviting every scholar to find Marx's solution. The solution was promised to appear within a few months, but it took almost a decade before Engels managed to publish volume III of *Capital*. In the meantime, various attempts were made to explain the existence of an average rate of profit (in the sphere of prices of production) that would be in harmony with the law of value and that would emerge from it. Many economists were sceptical of whether such a solution could exist and started to anticipate that volume I of *Capital*, based on the law of value, could be in contradiction to volume III. Nevertheless, several economists participated in this first round, such as Lexis, Schmidt, and Fireman.[5] When Engels eventually published volume III of *Capital* in 1894, Marx failed to convince his contemporaries, who definitely saw a contradiction between his assumption of a uniform rate of profit and his law of value. The issue was: why sectors with a lower organic composition of capital, and therefore generating a higher amount of surplus value, were to receive a comparatively lower amount of profit?

Many participants in the competition were disappointed. This was the starting point for transformation being seen as a problem. After 1894, many debates occurred between Marxists and non-Marxists, with the parallel development of revisionism within Marxism, notably in Germany, Italy and Russia. Engels himself was only involved in these debates for one year (he died in 1895) but he managed to produce an awkward defence of Marx, involving a historical interpretation of the law of value. The landmarks of these debates were provided by Böhm-Bawerk's critique of Marx and Hilferding's defence (see Sweezy 1949; Howard and King 1995a), until Bortkiewicz arrived in 1906 and 1907 with his long-lasting contributions to the transformation problem. Dostaler (1978) rightly showed that, despite the dazzling developments experienced by the transformation problem, Bortkiewicz's solutions shaped in a sustainable manner the nature and form that the debates would take after him.[6]

The Russian contributions to the Marxian transformation problem

Bortkiewicz's contribution was only the tip of the iceberg of the Russian contributions to the Marxian transformation problem, as remarkably showed in Gilles Dostaler's *Valeur et prix* (1978). Indeed, the works of the Russian economists Tugan-Baranovsky and Dmitriev are now frequently encountered in the literature dealing with the problem of the transformation of Marxian labour value into prices of production, including the issues of the nature and origin of profit, the tendency of the rate of profit to fall, the theory of distribution (notably the link or absence of a link between the labour theory of value and the theory of exploitation) and the use of Marx's schemes of reproduction for handling these various theoretical problems. The diffusion and integration of the works of these Russian economists into the theoretical debates of the Western literature is essentially due to Bortkiewicz's much commented on articles published in 1906–1907: 'Wertrechnung und Preisrechnung im Marxschen System' (1906–1907) and 'Zur Berichtigung der grundlegenden theoretischen Konstruktion von Marx im 3. Band des Kapital' (1907). Bortkiewicz explicitly acknowledged having drawn on the constructions of Tugan-Baranovsky and Dmitriev in these works.

From Tugan-Baranovsky's *Theoretische Grundlagen des Marxismus* (1905), Bortkiewicz used the solution to the 'inverse transformation problem', based on a numerical example of a revised version of Marx's schemes of simple reproduction.[7] He also looked, but with less interest, at Tugan-Baranovsky's criticism of Marx's theory on the tendency of the rate of profit to fall. From Dmitriev's *Economic Essays* ([1904] 1974), Bortkiewicz borrowed a handful of mathematical formulae, including a formulation of the Ricardian prices of production, the expression of the total amount of labour embodied in a commodity, and several expressions for the rate of profit. Drawing on Tugan-Baranovsky and Dmitriev, Bortkiewicz thus established what was to become the standard mathematical formulation of the transformation problem (1906–1907), and provided a general solution to it (1907).

Dmitriev, Tugan-Baranovsky and Bortkiewicz's contributions related to the transformation problem have thus been scrutinised in detail (Dostaler 1978; Jorland 1995; Faccarello 1983). But, for these Russian economists, these specific works on the transformation problem did not represent the conclusion of their investigations on value and prices theory. In fact, their specific works in Western economic literature only account for the starting point of their investigations. There is a rich tradition of value and prices theories in Russia which cannot be reduced to the well-known contributions of Tugan-Baranovsky, Dmitriev and Bortkiewicz on the transformation problem. And this tradition was engaged in another theoretical programme: the Russian synthesis between marginalism and the classical theory of value.

The other possible relation between value and prices examined here is their synthesis. The very idea of mixing the old classical theory of value with the new marginalist theory of price is not an exclusively Russian affair. The Russian synthesis has its peculiarities, but, before going further, it is time to see what was happening in Western Europe.

The synthesis in European economic thought

In the transformation framework, the system of value coexists with the system of prices, and the latter is subordinated to the former. In the synthesis framework, things are different. In the case of dialectics, the thesis and the antithesis both disappear to give a new and higher synthesis. In the case of the synthesis between the labour theory of value and marginal utility, however, it seems that both notions reflect a different aspect of the same phenomenon, like two different points of view. Both are necessary, and in a complementary relationship.

The synthesising trend between the classical theory of value and the marginalist theory of prices appeared in Europe from the 1890s onward. The marginalist revolution of the 1870s was mainly conceived *against* the classical theory of value. Then, starting from the 1890s, another approach appeared, which clearly dominated the debate from the 1920s onward: the conciliation between the classical and the marginalist theories. This conciliation movement took various forms, including the synthesis. It suggested an interpretation of continuity in the development of economic science from the classics to the marginalists, which partly explains the origin of the term *neo-classical* that replaced the more revolutionary *marginalist* appellation.

In theoretical terms, the conciliation or synthesis implied the renunciation of two claims: first, the marginalists' claim that everything can be reduced to reasoning on marginal utility, especially the prices of factors in the sphere of production (this imperialistic claim, which was in fact essentially an Austrian one, was rejected by those who were inclined to show a conciliatory approach); second, the classical claim of establishing too strong a link between labour and value. What the conciliation movement retained from the classical theory of value was only one of its variants, according to which normal value is determined by its long-term costs of production, measured as the sum of wages, profits and rent. This excludes Marx's theory of value and some of the interpretations of Ricardo's theory of value.

In England, Marshall offered such a conciliatory approach, according to which Ricardo and Jevons complemented each other. Despite Jevons's determination to let bygones be bygones,[8] this interpretation gained much influence in England and abroad. In France, Jevons was also considered to fill the gaps in Ricardo's nearly complete theory of value (Zouboulakis 1993, 154). In Italy, the conciliation of Marx with the writings of the 'Italian-Lausanne school' (Pareto, Pantaleoni) was not unusual (Leone, Labriola, Ricca Salerno). In Germany, where the debates were disguised under discussions on *Objektivismus* and *Subjektivismus*, the same reconciliation was offered by, for example, Dietzel and Bortkiewicz. Dietzel offered reconciliation between Ricardo and the Austrian *Grenznutzen* theory of prices, while Bortkiewicz offered attempts at synthesis between Ricardo and Walras (later in his life, however, Bortkiewicz proposed another synthesis, nearer to the Marshallian position, between Ricardo and Böhm-Bawerk – see Chapter 6). Within the Marxian revisionists, Bernstein proposed to fill the holes in the Marxian theory of value with marginalism. An overview of Bernstein's and Marshall's syntheses is now provided.

Eduard Bernstein, close to Ricardian socialists, was one of those Marxists who had been disappointed by the publication of volume III of Marx's *Capital*. He started to criticise several theoretical tenets of Marx's economic theories (for instance, the reduction of complex labour into simple abstract labour), which gave him the reputation of being the (world) leader in Marxism revisionism.

Bernstein considered that value is a metaphysical concept that owes nothing to reality, prices being the only real concept. Value can thus be of conceptual help, but certainly not in the discovery of exploitation, a concept that does not need to be abstractly proven, according to Bernstein, but that one can easily see in reality. Going further in the critique of the labour theory of value, he conceived of exchange relations as being governed by costs of production (allowing, like Engels, a historical dominance of the labour component).

Bernstein further explains that the labour theory of value analyses the commodity from the point of view of simple labour, making an abstraction of several important things, such as complex labour and utility. For its part, the theory of marginal utility, equally abstract and metaphysical, focuses its attention on utility while disregarding other components. And, recalling Marx's dual character of the commodity – use value and (exchange) value – he advocated supplementing the labour theory of value with marginal utility theory, in the spirit of Jevons and Böhm-Bawerk.

What seemed a heresy for orthodox Marxists like Kautsky or Luxemburg was for Bernstein only the continuation of Marx's work: after having spent some time on a particular abstraction (labour in volume I of *Capital*), it was time to take into account the social utility of commodities (volume III of *Capital*, supplemented by Bernstein's additions). This position was characterised more as conciliation than synthesis. This is best understood by Bernstein's own metaphor:

> Peter and Paul stand before a box filled with minerals. 'They are parallel-planed hemihedral crystal', says Peter. 'They are pyrites', says Paul.
>   Which of the two is right?
>   'Both are right', says the mineralogist. 'Peter's statement refers to form, Paul's to substance.' ... The same is true in the quarrel over value theory.
>
> (Bernstein 1899, translated by Gay 1962, 181)

Labour value and marginal utility are both useful devices in the understanding of prices. But Bernstein did not develop this conciliation or synthesis further, in contrast to what Marshall and the Russian synthesis will achieve. Indeed: 'beyond these hints at a synthesis between Marxism and marginalism Bernstein did not go' (Gay 1962, 182).[9]

For his part, Marshall's synthesis between Ricardo and Jevons – which had had the last word on this question by the 1920s – is most famously summed up in his scissors metaphor:

> We might as reasonably dispute whether it is the upper or the under blade of a pair of scissors that cuts a piece of paper, as whether value is governed by utility or costs of production. It is true that when one blade is held still, and the cutting is effected by moving the other, we may say with careless brevity that the cutting is done by the second; but the statement is not strictly accurate, and is to be excused only so long as it claims to be merely a popular and not a strictly scientific account of what happens.
>
> (Marshall 1920, Book V, chap. 3, §7)

One blade of the pair of scissors represents the short-period demand price, or market price, and focuses its attention on marginal utility. The other blade represents the long-period supply price, or normal price, and focuses on costs of production. In the very short period of time (demand prices), supply is considered as a given, and therefore only prices can adapt to demand. In the short period, however, supply can adapt to demand to the extent allowed by the present capacity of production (Marshall 1920, V, 5, §6). In the long period (supply prices), supply is capable of considerable adaptation to an anticipated demand, with changes in the infrastructure of production (Marshall 1920, V, 5, §7).

In other words, it is the equilibrium of demand and supply that governs value, with an emphasis on demand to explain market prices in short periods, and an emphasis on supply to explain normal prices in long periods. As such, it could be considered as the synthesis between the English classical and marginalist schools. But Marshall always maintained that he did not offer such a synthesis

(Zouboulakis 1993, 179). On the contrary, he insisted upon continuity – and therefore no need of synthesis – in the development of the English political economy. In his view, he achieved the construction for which Ricardo and J. S. Mill had provided most of the foundations, and which Jevons only completed. This interpretation is naturally more generous to Marshall than to Jevons.

Marshall considered that Ricardo had been unfairly accused of exclusively favouring costs of production at the expense of utility and demand in the explanation of value. Yet there are traces of demand and utility in chapter 1 of Ricardo's *Principles*, and even the germ of the idea of a distinction between total and final utility in chapter 20, 'Value and Riches' (see Marshall 1920, Appendix I, §1, on Ricardo's theory of value). Moreover, Ricardo's intentions were to show how false ideas about the influence of costs of production on value may lead to the wrong taxation policies. As appears from the following passage from Marshall's Appendix I on Ricardo's theory of value, Ricardo conducted his research in a (very Marshallian) *ceteris paribus* way, but unfortunately he forgot to state it explicitly:

> It would have been better if he had occasionally repeated the statement that the values of two commodities are to be regarded as in the long run proportionate to the amount of labour required for making them, only on the condition that other things are equal: i.e., that the labour employed in the two cases is equally skilled, and therefore equally highly paid; that it is assisted by proportionate amounts of capital, account being taken of the period of its investment; and that the rates of profits are equal.
>
> (Marshall 1920, Appendix I, §2)

The same applies to J. S. Mill, who was misinterpreted, according to Marshall, for his use of the expression *costs of production* to designate two different things: the efforts and abstinence of production (real costs), and its economic measure (money cost). The former should be called costs of production, the latter expenses of production. And when J. S. Mill wrote that value is regulated by the ratio of costs of production, only a reader who confuses *The Times* of New York and *The Times* of London may believe that Mill was in fact thinking of costs and not of expenses (Marshall 1876, 597–598). As in Ricardo's case, Marshall further asserts that had J. S. Mill spoken of the 'Law of Free Production and Average Demand' instead of the 'Law of Cost of Production', no controversies would have appeared. As for Jevons, Marshall does not play down his merits and even finds him some excuses for his alleged arrogance towards Ricardo and J. S. Mill in that the demand side was particularly neglected until the 1870s (Marshall 1920, Appendix I, §3). But he blames him for claiming that his new theory buries the older. He wrote: 'I hold that much of what Professor Jevons says about 'final utility' is contained, implicitly, at least, in J. S. Mill's account' (Marshall 1876, 599n). Marshall's achievement was to reconcile these many *ceteris paribus* (or *statical*) analyses of demand and supply in an all-encompassing general framework – his *Principles of Political Economy*, first published in 1890, with the last, eighth, edition published in 1920. Incidentally, this coincides with the Russian synthesis timespan.

The synthesis that took place in Russia, and that will be developed in the following chapters, was quite different from its European counterparts. To depict the spirit of the time, a brief introduction to the Russian debates on value and prices between 1870 and 1890 is given.

Political economy in Russia

Political economy was institutionalised early in Russia (Berelowitch 1986), which did not mean that it was independent from political authorities. Tugan-Baranovsky's case is significant in this respect. His nomination as professor took years to be confirmed by the Ministry of Education, and he was even temporarily exiled for political unreliability. Nevertheless, by the end of the nineteenth century, the teaching of political economy and of statistics in faculties of law was systematised. There were links between universities, local and central statisticians, the administration and learned societies. Universities were providing the expertise needed to pursue the reforms the country had been engaged in since the emancipation of the serfs in 1861.

There was in Russian economic thought a combination of various foreign influences (mainly, and in chronological order, French, English, German) with indigenous ideas. Often, foreign ideas were transformed to fit the perceived empirical local reality. Regardless of the group they belonged to (see below), economists read the Western literature as it came into the country. Often, the rapid or late importation of Western literature was either due to fashion, an official translation by the government or the presence or absence of censorship.

Smith was widely read at the beginning of the nineteenth century, subsequently followed by Malthus, Say, Sismondi, Saint-Simon, Proudhon, Fourier, etc. Economic ideas were strongly connected with philosophy in Russia, in several successive periods: romanticism, German idealism (Schelling and Hegel), materialism and, just before the twentieth century, neo-Kantianism. Economic ideas were also blended with other disciplines, especially orthodox religious thought but also with history and politics. Indeed, despite the early institutionalisation of the discipline of economics in Russia, it remained less of an autonomous discipline than in Western countries. This has been explained by historians of Russian thought by the obsessive Russian quest for universalism, a concept that lies at the core of the *Russian Idea* and which rejects the separation of theory from practice and the dissemination of knowledge into too loosely separated disciplines. As a matter of fact, Russian social scientists had a preference for applied issues over theoretical constructions. This explains the interest of Russian economists in historical investigations, the taste for statistical studies and, henceforth, the affinities with German historicism. Furthermore, they held sacred the importance of moral judgement in science, relegating positive issues well below normative and idealistic components of the economic discourse. It was only at the end of the nineteenth century that Russian economists started to free themselves from the necessity to apply moral judgement to social phenomena. Finally, Russian scientists favoured holistic approaches.[10]

That being said, it is time now for a review of the most important economists and groups of economists of the last part of the nineteenth century to provide an overview of the major forces involved: the Populists, the Marxists and the Historical Economists.

The Populists, or *narodniks*, were a considerable social movement born in the 1870s. They inherited much of their thought from the Slavophiles, supplemented with the writings of Marx. The Populists shared with the Slavophiles an unshakable faith in the Russian peasant, or *muzhik*:

> The Slavophiles believed in the people, in justice that belonged to the people, and for them the people was first and foremost the muzhik, who kept the Orthodox Faith and the national tenor of life. The Slavophiles were warm defenders of the Commune [i.e. obshchina], which they regarded as organic and as the original Russian structure of economic life among the peasantry, as all the *narodniks* thought. They were decided opponents of the ideas of Roman Law on property. They did not regard property as sacred and absolute; owners of property they regarded as stewards only. They repudiated Western, bourgeois, capitalist civilization.
>
> (Berdiaev 1960, 30)

Another great source of influence for the Populists was Chernyshevsky, whose motto is defined in his article 'Critique of Philosophical Prejudices Against Communal Ownership' (1858): the higher state of development is always similar to the original state in which the development started. According to him, since in Russia economic development started through a collective form of landownership (in the *obshchina*), it must end in this same form. Moreover, there is no necessity to go through all the stages of development: to the primitive, communism may immediately succeed the highest form of socialism.

The Populist literature from the 1870s onwards may be characterised as an attempt to combine the ideas of Chernyshevsky and Marx. The description of the painful consequences of capitalism in Marx's writings confirmed the Populist conviction that capitalism was not for Russia. Voroncov and Danielson, who were much more conservative than the revolutionary Chernyshevsky, had an ambitious theoretical programme. Under their pens, the Populist vision of the economic development of Russia became the following: capitalism is not only undesirable, but also impossible in Russia. The argument of shortage of international markets for technically backward Russian manufactured products was largely used to show that capitalism could not develop in Russia. Populists tried to prove with statistics that capitalism was not developing naturally in Russia as in Western countries, and that the industrialisation policy of the Imperial government was condemned to fail. This was for some to be taken as an advantage, to escape the painful stage described by Marx, and to go directly to the higher agrarian socialistic stage described by Chernyshevsky. These

Populist theses were most seriously disputed in the 1890s by their Marxist opponents.[11]

The Marxists. Before the Bolshevik 1917 revolution, Marxism covered wide and varied movements and trends. Almost every anti-Populist was a Marxist. This should not hide the fact that among so-called Marxists, only some were aware of any revolutionary dimension in Marxism, while many supporters of economic liberalism and industrialisation were ranked among Marxists.[12]

Marx found as nowhere else a remarkable circle of followers in Russia. In the 1870s, among the first readers of Marx, the talented Ziber provided a reading guide to *Capital* that replaced the original, the copies of which were sometimes extremely scarce. In the 1880s, the works of Marx were linked to a Russian social project started by Plekhanov. In the 1890s, Marxism was mainly used against the Populists for various political reasons (revolutionary, social-democrat, liberal). It was so trendy that it took the form of a religion, present in all spheres of society. The words of the Master were not supposed to be questioned. In the middle of the 1890s, however, some schisms appeared in Russian Marxism. So-called 'Legal Marxists', inspired by the German neo-Kantian philosophical current, proposed to revise Marx's doctrine, especially his materialist philosophy and theory of value. It is among these Legal Marxists that the Russian synthesis took form. Legal Marxists (among them Tugan-Baranovsky) were still fighting against the Populists alongside more 'orthodox' Marxists, such as Plekhanov and the up and coming Lenin. A few years later, in the early 1900s, a further division separated, within the orthodoxy, Bolsheviks from Mensheviks, according to the importance given, respectively, to the proletariat and to the peasants. Russian readings of Marx's theory of value are described below, in Chapter 2.

Historical Economists. The successive German historical schools, starting with *Kameralism* and going up to *Kathedersozialists* were highly prevalent in Russia, especially in the academic world. The affinity of Russian economists with the German historical school is easy to understand, especially in the case of Russians showing sympathy with the Populist vision of a singular path of Russian development. German economists, such as Roscher, Schmoller and Sombart, had a colossal reputation in Russia. The historical school's inductive method, as compared to the English classical school's more deductive method, inspired many economists in Russia to become statisticians also, to study the local conditions under which economic laws applied. But historicism was not an impermeable doctrine in Russia. It was more of a mindset (see Zweynert 2002, 3.6, 4.3 and 4.7; Barnett 2004; Sheptun 2005).

The most typical example of a Russian economist influenced by the German historical schools in the 1880s–1890s is A. I. Chuprov. Student and follower of Babst (the translator of Roscher in Russia), he was professor of political economy at the University of Moscow, where his manual of political economy was used by several generations of students. At the same time, he adopted Marx's theory of value, was an active promoter of *zemstvo* statistics (i.e. in local administration), and had sympathies with the Populists' doctrines. He is perhaps the most characteristic Russian economist of his time. Chuprov's example does not suggest that all Russian economists were historicists, but most of them shared an historical approach. There were of course other movements besides Populists, Marxists and Historicists, but they were marginal. They will be referred to as they are encountered. It can already be mentioned that there were anarchists, liberals, followers of early French socialists, and it should be noted that Ministers of Finance were more influenced by List and Smith than by Marx.

Supporters of the synthesis were located at the crossroads of these debates. Tugan-Baranovsky was a Legal Marxist struggling with the Populists (though later he had more affinities with agrarian and cooperative movements (see Chapter 4). He shares many historicist attitudes in his works concerning the use of history and statistics, but he is clearly more of a theoretician than his fellow economists. For his part, Shaposhnikov was born into another generation, that of the economist mathematicians, freed from the empirical ground of the German historical school, and already no longer concerned (at least up until the Bolshevik revolution) with these Populist/Marxist divides. Nevertheless, these divides were the broad environment in which the Russian synthesis was born.

The groups that have been reviewed in this section are primarily concerned with conceptions of economic development (and political concerns).[13] Behind these more visible debates, there was a rich tradition in value and prices theory in Russia.

Value and prices since 1870

This tradition has its beginnings in the 1870s and is associated with the pioneering figure of Ziber. Before the 1870s, most Russian economists were essentially following the teachings of Smith, Say, Storch, Sismondi, John Stuart Mill and von Thünen (the latter was particularly widely read in Russia, as compared to Western countries). An important exception might be observed, albeit it remained almost unnoticed until recently. In the 1850s, Vernadsky had already showed an awareness of the importance of Ricardo and Gossen in economic literature (Vernadsky 1858). With this exception in mind, it should be mentioned that Ricardo was almost absent from the debates until the 1870s, his reasoning being considered as too abstract for this audience (see Zweynert 2008). The 1870s were particularly rich in contributions on value and prices, with the appearance of Marx and Ricardo.

Marx's publication of the first volume of *Capital* in 1867 had already provoked several reactions in Russia, which were magnified by the publication of its successful Russian edition by Danielson in 1872 (3,000 copies were sold in a very short time).[14] The reactions were enthusiastic in the context of the debates concerning the potential advantage of being a backward economy in contrast to more advanced Western countries. Especially debated on a large scale were the description of capitalism, and the idea of stages (or a path) of economic development. The question of method attracted a smaller – more academic – audience (Resis 1970). However, even before the appearance of the Russian edition of

Marx's *Capital*, Ziber had already provided in 1871 a detailed account of Marx's economic theory, which was later to be praised by Marx himself (who learnt Russian in the meanwhile thanks to books and materials sent to him by Danielson). Further discussions took place in the late 1870s on Marx's labour theory of value, notably between Zhukovsky, Chicherin and Ziber, definitely putting Marx at the centre of the debates.

Ricardo's argument also entered the debate during the 1870s. But it should be stressed that while Marx and Ricardo were discovered together in Russia in the 1870s, the former was read by a larger public than the latter, who was confined to a narrower circle of academic economists. Unlike what happened in Britain and in other European countries, one can even confidently assert that most Russians, apart from a few pioneers, discovered Ricardo *after* Marx. More accurately, they read Ricardo according to Marx, through Marx's eyes.

In the early 1870s, however, Ricardo was discovered by some scholars. The issue of rent on land, and subsequently of value, attracted certain attention. In 1871, Fuks compared von Thünen's and Ricardo's theories of rent. The same year, Zhukovsky offered one of the first mathematical formulations of Ricardo's theory of rent. Also in 1871, Ziber provided a thoughtful interpretation of Ricardo's theory of value in his dissertation, *David Ricardo's Theory of Value and Capital*. Ziber subsequently offered the first Russian translation of Ricardo's *Principles of Political Economy and Taxation* (1873) and, later, an edition of Ricardo's *Works* (1882), based on McCulloch's edition. These annotated editions contributed to the dissemination of Ricardo's work.

Compared to the 1870s, the 1880s were a less agitated period as far as theoretical political economy was concerned. In some way, this is explained by the growing impact of the German historical school in Russia. For instance, the publication of volume II of Marx's *Capital* did not provoke many reactions (when compared to volume I, and, later, to volume III). The period is nevertheless characterised by a few noteworthy contributions, most of them coming surprisingly from Switzerland. Thus, from Bern, Ziber gave his final word on Ricardo and Marx in the enlarged version of his dissertation, *David Ricardo and Karl Marx in their Socio-Economic Researches* (1885), which, in various subsequent reprints, would become a classic, influential text. From Geneva, Plekhanov and his Emancipation of Labour Group, drawing on Ziber, gave birth to 'Russian Marxism', through which the future Bolsheviks and Mensheviks would learn their Marxism (Baron 1954).

Renewed interest in the theories of value and prices was heavily felt in the next decade, following the impetus given in the 1890s by the appearance in Russia of volume III of Marx's *Capital* and of the various early marginalist theories. The posthumous publication of volume III of Marx's *Capital* by Engels in 1894, and in Russian by Danielson in 1896, provoked many reactions, the most interesting of which was the Russian type of revisionism. For the first time, Russian economists were ahead of their German colleagues in a particular field: revision of Marxism.[15]

The introduction of marginalism in Russia took place at a time when the economic thinkers were absorbed in the classical theories (mostly Mill, Say and

Storch, but also belatedly Ricardo), the German historical school and Marx. However, the field was already prepared, as the works of von Thünen and, to a lesser extent, Gossen and Cournot, were already known in Russia, while some classical and historical economists, such as Say, Storch and Knies, all widely read in Russia, paid great tribute to the subjective notion of utility in their works. Unsurprisingly, the most circulated version of marginalism was Austrian, with Böhm-Bawerk as the most translated and quoted author. Jevonsian and Walrasian theories had a low profile until the number of mathematical economists grew, especially between the 1900s and the 1920s. Chapter 3 returns to the reactions sparked off by these theories.

With these elements, it is now possible to present a review of the various theories of value and prices in the three decades between 1890 and 1920. Most Russian economists shared a common education, understood as a mixture of classical political economy and the German historical school, together with a compulsory knowledge of Marx. They were interested in contemporary issues, concerned with agricultural economics, economic history and economic statistics; the most famous Russian economist to conform to this description is perhaps A. I. Chuprov (see above). However, there were many differences between them. As far as value and prices theories are concerned, the following groups can be identified: followers of the Classics, Marxists, Austrians, and proponents of the Synthesis.

The Classics. Until the 1890s, Russian economists had a privileged relationship with the classical theories of value. Ziber not only provided a convincing account of Ricardo's theory of value but also constructed a unifying picture of the Classical tradition, in which all Ricardo's predecessors could fit as pre-Ricardian economists. After the 1890s, however, fewer believed that the classical paradigm, as defined here, could stand the criticism conducted by the historical schools and the marginalists. Nevertheless, some points deserve to be remarked upon. First, an interpretation of the classics offered by Manuilov in *The Notion of Value According to the Economists of the Classical School* (1901) challenged Ziber's homogenising view by pointing out the great heterogeneity of classical theories from Smith to Ricardo and beyond. Second, Chicherin, albeit isolated in claiming liberalism in Russia, was well disposed towards the French liberal school, especially Bastiat. Finally, it should be remembered that the so-called Kiev school of political economy, which regularly provided Russia with ideas, professors and ministers, almost uniquely kept away from Marxism to profess a more 'classical truth'. (For a search for a definition of the Kiev school, see Sušjan 2010.) The strength of the classical school, beyond these specific economists, was its dominance in the education of economists in Russian universities.

The Marxists. Marxism attracted the crowd and many were disposed to publicly defend the Master: Plekhanov used Marx against Böhm-Bawerk, Bukharin against the Austrian subjective theory of value, Lenin against the Populists and so forth. At the same time, some Populists (and most evidently Danielson) were defending the Marxian labour theory of value against its detractors. But few actually contributed to analytically developing Marxism, and most of those who did were (or became) critics of Marx. In fact, the 1890s marked an intense period of activity by the Legal Marxists, this Russian branch of revisionism, inspired by neo-Kantianism. This group counted among its members Struve, Tugan-Baranovsky, Bulgakov, Frank and Berdiaev. They appeared favourable to Marxism at first, but their contributions very soon became critical, even destructive. It can be added that if there were many Marxists in Russia, there were only a few genuinely Marxian scholars: after Ziber in the 1870s, the next great Marxian scholar to renew the tradition is Rubin in the 1920s.

The Austrians. Encouraged by the growing subjectivism in Russian sociology (Mikhailovsky), a group of scholars adopted the theories of the Austrian school. Among these economists, the names of Gelesnoff, Zalesky, and Orzhencky are frequently found, together with a few others who felt affinities with the mathematical method in political economy, such as Woytinsky and Bilimovic. Under their guidance, the works of Menger, Philippovich and particularly Böhm-Bawerk were translated into Russian in the 1890s and 1900s. The theory of value based on subjective utility and questions of method were the main concerns for these Russian economists. However, as Dmitriev observed, they were also engaged in a reduction of political economy, and of the theory of value, to 'physical–chemical relations' (Dmitriev 1908, 24).

Besides these groups, the original position of Struve should be mentioned. In his *Economy and Price* (1913), he rejects all theories of value on the grounds that their authors take an abstract concept for reality. For him, value is nothing more than a metaphysical hypothesis without scientific signification (very much within a Paretian spirit). Only prices are real for him. At worst, an objective notion of value could be constructed on the basis of a statistical construction of prices. In this sense, value would depend on prices, and not the other way round. This approach led to a considerable reduction in the distance between value and prices, and resulted in investigations such as the comparison between various types of price (market vs administrative).

As can be seen from this account, the years 1890–1920 were part of a golden age of investigations of the theories of value and prices in Russia, which lasted until the end of the 1920s. The most original of these is that of the synthesis.

The prehistory of the Russian synthesis

Russian economic thought was characterised at the end of the nineteenth century by a plurality of schools. There was no leading school, such as the liberal school in France, the classical school in England, or the historical school in the German states. It will be further argued that the absence of a mainstream allowed the appearance of the Russian synthesis to take place more easily. Some trends dominated nevertheless: the historical school (for the methodology), the classical school (for the practical issues), and Marxism (for the labour theory of value).

With this background in mind, it is now possible to turn to the two ingredients of the synthesis as they were assimilated in Russia and as the protagonists of the Russian synthesis inherited them: the labour theory of value (Chapter 2) and the theory of marginal utility (Chapter 3). As will be seen, Tugan-Baranovsky was a major player in these debates (see Chapters 4 and 5), while Shaposhnikov and his colleagues inherited much from them (see Chapter 6).

Notes

1 Pareto had already expressed this idea in his very first lecture on pure economics at the University of Lausanne in 1893, when he replaced Léon Walras. See Baranzini and Bridel (1997).
2 In *Le détour de valeur* (1986), André Lapidus introduces the effective notion of the *champ d'évaluation* (evaluation field), to distinguish between these various concepts. See Lapidus (1986, 16, 45, 64–65, 85–86, 88 and 104–105).
3 An absolute measure of the prices of the commodities *a* and *b* (in terms of the invariable standard of measure *c*) would give at least two additional pieces of information that the relative exchange ratio $p_{a/b}$ does not: (1) to distinguish, at a given moment in time, which of the two commodities (if not both, and in which proportion) is responsible for a change in the relative prices $p_{a/b}$; and (2) to distinguish through time if a stable relative price $p_{a/b}$ is due to stable absolute prices p_a and p_b, or to an increase (or decrease) in both p_a and p_b in equal proportion.
4 The idea that the gravitational device is for most economists (with a very few exceptions) the central articulation between market prices and their theory of relative prices is the blueprint around which Bridel's anthology on *Price Theory* is organised. See the editor's introductions to the various texts (Bridel 2001, especially I: xiv–xvi, 27–28, 48–50, 112–113, 116–123; II: xii, 162–164; III: 97–99, 102–104; and IV: x–xviii).
5 The history of Engels's competition is well documented in Dostaler (1978, chap. 2), Jorland (1995, chap. 2) and Howard and King (1989, chap. 2). On Fireman, the winner consecrated by Engels, see Alcouffe *et al.* (2009).
6 Up until the 1970s, the debates between Marxists, neoricardians and neoclassical economists were conducted within Bortkiewicz's framework. A good survey of these contemporary debates is to be found in Jorland (1995, chap. 6). See Benetti and Cartelier (1975a, 1975b) for a good introduction to the issues at stake. Samuelson (1971) and Desai (1988) provide clear technical and interpretative insights. The end of the Bortkiewiczian monopoly on these debates, which occurred in the 1970s–1980s, gave birth to a much more varied literature, the survey of which is henceforth carried out by subgroups. Even today frequent reckless announcements appear of a definitive solution to the transformation problem, ending the controversies … until the next rejoinder. See Wright (2014) as an example.
7 The inverse transformation problem consists in finding a system of value and a rate of surplus value, on the basis of a given system of prices together with a given uniform rate of profit. Tugan-Baranovsky ignored fixed capital (the rate of rotation of constant and variable capital being of one year), but introduced varied organic compositions of capital. Furthermore, he respected the following constraints set by himself: (i) the system of prices *and* the system of value observe the conditions of simple reproduction; (ii) total profit is equal to total surplus value. The equality between total value and total prices, a condition frequently encountered in the literature answering Engels' competition, is not respected.
8 In Lausanne, Walras shared the same determination, although he arrived, in his theory of production, at a similar result: the equality between equilibrium prices of a good and its costs of production, understood as the sum of the equilibrium prices of the productive services of that good. For their part, Menger and his Austrian followers maintained that the former classical theory of value could be thrown away. On these two points, see Chapter 3.

9   On Bernstein's revisionism, see Angel (1961), Gay (1962), Dostaler (1978, chap. IV.A.1) and Howard and King (1989, chap. 4.II).
10 On the *Russian Idea*, see Berdiaev (1947). On its implication for the economic methodology, see Zweynert (2008).
11 On the thinkers qualified as Populists, see Venturi (2001). However, the scope, content and very existence of what is behind the label 'Populism' is controversial in the historiography. The standard account given by Walicki (1969) is challenged by the research of Richard Pipes (1964), who sees in Populism – in Russian, *Narodnichestvo* – a polemic historical reconstruction by its adversaries. On this debate, and on the role of Plekhanov in this reconstruction, see the careful historical inquiry of White (1996). Given that Tugan-Baranovsky was himself (at least at the beginning) an opponent to these Populists, we allow ourselves to use this term.
12 The Populists considered themselves genuine Marxists, and relegated what are called here Marxists under the label 'neo-Marxists'. The reader should not forget that Marx's translator in Russia, Danielson, was a leading Populist.
13 For a quick overview of the development of Russian economic thought in general, see Allisson (2015). A more comprehensive view is to be found in Kingston-Mann (1999), Zweynert (2002) and Barnett (2005). On the link between political economy and statistics in Russia, see Stanziani (1998) and Mespoulet (2001). Recent collective research on Russian economic thought includes Barnett and Zweynert (2008), Eliseeva and Dmitriev (2013), and Akhabbar and Allisson (2014).
14 Danielson completed a translation started by Bakunin (who gave up for reasons of personal incompatibility) and continued by Lopatin (who was arrested for trying to free Chernyshevsky from his forced exile). Danielson alone translated volumes II and III of *Capital* in 1885 and 1896, almost immediately after their publication in German, thanks to his active correspondence with Marx and, later, with Engels.
15 The reception in Russia of volume III of Marx's *Capital* and Russian revisionism (*Legal Marxism*) has been studied extensively by Kindersley (1962) and Howard and King (1989, chap. 7–10; 1995a; 1995b). It is noteworthy that Tugan-Baranovsky was the leading Russian revisionist and at the same time was ahead on crises and cycles theory (see Chapter 4).

References

Akhabbar, Amanar and François Allisson, eds. 2014. 'Russian Political Economy from Utopia to Social Engineering'. *Œconomia (History | Methodology | Philosophy)*, Special issues 4(1) and 4(2).

Alcouffe, Alain, Friedrun Quaas and Georg Quaas. 2009. 'La préhistoire du problème de la transformation'. In Alain Alcouffe and Claude Diebolt, eds, *La pensée économique allemande*, 309–337. Paris: Economica.

Allisson, François. 2015. 'Russia and Ukraine'. In Vincent Barnett, ed., *Routledge Handbook of the History of Global Economic Thought*, chap. 10, 102–110. London: Routledge.

Angel, Pierre. 1961. *Eduard Bernstein et l'évolution du socialisme allemand*. Paris: Marcel Didier.

Baranzini, Roberto and Pascal Bridel. 1997. 'On Pareto's First Lectures on Pure Economics at Lausanne'. *History of Economic Ideas*, V(3): 65–87.

Barnett, Vincent. 2004. 'Historical Political Economy in Russia, 1870–1913'. *European Journal for the History of Economic Thought*, 11(2): 231–253.

Barnett, Vincent. 2005. *A History of Russian Economic Thought*. London: Routledge.

Barnett, Vincent and Joachim Zweynert, eds. 2008. *Economics in Russia. Studies in Intellectual History*. Aldershot, UK: Ashgate.

Baron, Samuel H. 1954. 'Plekhanov and the Origins of Russian Marxism'. *Russian Review*, 13(1): 38–51.

Benetti, Carlo and Jean Cartelier. 1975a. 'Profit et exploitation: le problème de la transformation des valeurs en prix de production'. In Carlo Benetti, Claude Berthomieu and Jean Cartelier, eds, *Economie classique, Economic vulgaire*, 71–92. Paris and Grenoble: François Maspéro and Presses Universitaires de Grenoble.

Benetti, Carlo and Jean Cartelier. 1975b. 'Notes sur la littérature sur la transformation des valeurs en prix de production'. In Carlo Benetti, Claude Berthomieu and Jean Cartelier, eds, *Economie classique, Economic vulgaire*, 93–136. Paris and Grenoble: François Maspéro and Presses Universitaires de Grenoble.

Berdiaev, Nicolas. 1947. *The Russian Idea*. London: G. Bless.

Berdiaev, Nicolas. 1960. *The Origin of Russian Communism*. Ann Arbor, MI: University of Michigan Press.

Berelowitch, Wladimir. 1986. 'L'économie politique dans les universités russes au XIXe siècle (1804–1884)'. *Cahiers du Monde russe et soviétique*, XXVII(2): 137–152.

Bernstein, Eduard. 1899. 'Arbeitswert oder Nutzwert?' *Neue Zeit*, XVII(2): 548–549.

Bortkiewicz, Ladislaus von. 1906–1907. 'Wertrechnung und Preisrechnung im Marxschen System (I–II–III)'. *Archiv für Sozialwissenschaft und Sozialpolitik*, XXIII: 1–50; XXV: 10–51 and 445–488. Parts II and III transl. in English by J. Kahane. 1952. 'Value and Prices in the Marxian System'. *International Economic Papers*, 2: 5–60.

Bortkiewicz, Ladislaus von. 1907. 'Zur Berichtigung der grundlegenden theoretischen Konstruktion von Marx im 3. Band des Kapital'. *Jahrbücher für Nationalökonomie und Statistik*, 34: 319–335. Translated in English: 'On the Correction of Marx's Fundamental Theoretical Construction in the Third Volume of Capital'. In Paul M. Sweezy, ed., *Karl Marx and the Close of His System*, 199–221, 1949. New York: Kelley.

Bridel, Pascal. 2001. *The Foundations of Price Theory*. 6 vols. London: Pickering & Chatto.

Chernyshevsky, Nikolay Gavrilovich. 1858. 'Kritika filosofskih predubeždenij protiv obšinnogo vladeniâ (Critique of Philosophical Prejudices Against Communal Ownership)'. *Sovremennik*, 12. Translated in *Selected Philosophical Essays*, 1953. Moscow: Foreign Languages Publishing House.

Desai, Meghnad. 1988. 'The Transformation Problem'. *Journal of Economic Surveys*, 2(4): 295–333.

Dmitriev, Vladimir Karpovich. [1904] 1974. *Èkonomičeskie očerki (Economic Essays)*. Moscow: Rikhter. First essay published in 1898, Moscow: Moscow University. Second and third essays published in 1902, Moscow: Rikhter. English edition by Domenico Mario Nuti. 1974. London: Cambridge University Press.

Dmitriev, Vladimir Karpovich. 1908. 'Teoriâ cennosti. Obzor literatury na russkom âzyke (Value Theory. Review of the Literature in the Russian Language)'. *Kritičeskoe obozrenie*, VII: 12–26.

Dostaler, Gilles. 1978. *Valeur et prix. Histoire d'un débat*. Montréal: François Maspero, Presses Universitaires de Grenoble, Presses de l'Université du Québec.

Eliseeva, Irina Ilinichna and Anton Leonid Dmitriev, eds. 2013. *Vzaimosvâzi rossijskoj i evropejskoj èkonomičeskoj mysli: opyt Sankt-Peterburga. Očerki (Interconnection Between Russian and European Economic Thought: The Case of St Petersburg. Essays)*. St Petersburg: Nestor-Istoriâ.

Faccarello, Gilbert. 1983. *Travail, valeur et prix: une critique de la théorie de la valeur*. Paris: Anthropos. Electronic ed., 2009, available at: http://ggjjff.free.fr/ (accessed on 16 July 2014).

Gay, Peter. 1962. *The Dilemma of Democratic Socialism. Eduard Bernstein's Challenge to Marx*. New York: Collier Books.

Howard, Michael C. and John E. King. 1989. *A History of Marxian Economics: Volume I, 1883–1929*. London: Macmillan.

Howard, Michael C. and John E. King. 1995a. '"A Past and a Present, but no Abiding Future": The Critical Reception of Volume III of Capital, 1894–1900'. *History of Economic Ideas*, III(1): 27–69.

Howard, Michael C. and John E. King. 1995b. 'Value Theory and Russian Marxism Before the Revolution'. In Ian Steedman, ed., *Socialism and Marginalism in Economics: 1870–1930*, 224–257. London: Routledge.

Jorland, Gérard. 1995. *Les paradoxes du capital*. Paris: Odile Jacob.

Kindersley, Richard. 1962. *The First Russian Revisionists: a Study of 'Legal Marxism' in Russia*. Oxford: Clarendon Press.

Kingston-Mann, Esther. 1999. *In Search of the True West. Culture, Economics and Problems of Russian Development*. Princeton, NJ: Princeton University Press.

Lapidus, André. 1986. *Le détour de valeur*. Paris: Economica.

Manuilov, Aleksandr Apollonovich. 1901. *Ponâtie cennosti po učeniû èkonomistov klassičeskoj školy (The Notion of Value According to the Classical School of Economists)*. Moscow: Univ. Typ.

Marshall, Alfred. 1876. 'On Mr. Mill's Theory of Value'. *The Fortnightly Review*, 19(112): 591–602.

Marshall, Alfred. 1920. *Principles of Political Economy*. Eighth edition. London: Macmillan and Co.

Marx, Karl. 1867. *Capital. Volume 1*. London: Penguin. 1992. First Russian edition, 1872, translated by G. Lopatin and Nikolay Francevich Danielson. St Petersburg: Polâkov.

Marx, Karl. 1885. *Capital. Volume 2*. London: Penguin. 1993. First Russian edition, 1885, translated by Nikolay Francevich Danielson. St Petersburg: Polâkov.

Marx, Karl. 1894. *Capital. Volume 3*. London: Penguin. 1993. First Russian edition, 1896, translated by Nikolay Francevich Danielson. St Petersburg: Polâkov.

Mespoulet, Martine. 2001. *Statistique et révolution en Russie. Un compromis impossible (1880–1930)*. Rennes, France: Presses universitaires de Rennes.

Mongin, Philippe. 2003. 'On the Ricardian Problem of an Invariable Standard of Values'. In Heinz D. Kurz and Neri Salvadori, eds, *The Legacy of Piero Sraffa*, chap. 17. Cheltenham, UK: Edward Elgar.

Pareto, Vilfredo. 1902–1903. *Les systèmes socialistes*. 2 vols. Paris: V. Giard & E. Brière.

Pareto, Vilfredo. [1909] 2014. *Manual of Political Economy. A Critical and Variorum Edition*, edited by Aldo Montesano, Alberto Zanni, Luigino Bruni, John S. Chipman and Michael McLure. Oxford: Oxford University Press.

Pipes, Richard. 1964. 'Narodnichestvo: A Semantic Inquiry'. *Slavic Review*, 23(3): 441–458.

Resis, Albert. 1970. 'Das Kapital Comes to Russia'. *Slavic Review*, 29(2): 219–237.

Ricardo, David. 1873. *Sočineniâ Davida Rikardo Vyp. 1 (Works of David Ricardo Vol. 1)*. Translated by Nikolay Ivanovich Ziber. Kiev: Univ. Typ.

Ricardo, David. 1882. *Sočineniâ Davida Rikardo (Works of David Ricardo)*. Translated by Nikolay Ivanovich Ziber. St Petersburg: Panteleev.

Samuelson, Paul A. 1971. 'Understanding the Marxian Notion of Exploitation: A Summary of the So-Called Transformation Problem Between Marxian Values and Competitive Prices'. *Journal of Economic Literature*, 9(2): 399–431.

Sheptun, Alla. 2005. 'The German Historical School and Russian Economic Thought'. *Journal of Economic Studies*, 32(4): 349–372.

Simmel, Georg. [1900] 2004. *The Philosophy of Money*. Translated from the German third enlarged edition. London and New York: Routledge.

Stanziani, Alessandro. 1998. *L'économie en révolution: le cas russe. 1870–1930*. Paris: Albin Michel.

Struve, Petr Berngardovich. 1913. *Hozâjstvo i cena (Economy and Price)*. St Petersburg and Moscow: Šreder.

Sušjan, Andrej. 2010. 'Historicism and Neoclassicism in the Kiev School of Economics: The Case of Aleksander Bilimovich'. *Journal of the History of Economic Thought*, 32(2): 199–219.

Sweezy, Paul M., ed. 1949. *Karl Marx and the Close of His System by Eugen von Böhm-Bawerk and Böhm-Bawerk's Criticism of Marx by Rudolf Hilferding*. New York: Kelley.

Tugan-Baranovsky, Mikhail Ivanovich. 1905. *Theoretische Grundlagen des Marxismus*. Leipzig: Duncker & Humblot.

Venturi, Franco. 2001. *The Roots of Revolution: A History of the Populist and Socialist Movements in 19th Century Russia*. London: Phoenix Press. Original edition in Italian, 1952.

Vernadsky, Ivan Vasilevich. 1858. *Očerk istorii političeskoj èkonomii (Essay on the History of Political Economy)*. St Petersburg: Èkonomičeskij Ukazatel'.

Walicki, Andrzej. 1969. *The Controversy over Capitalism. Studies in the Social Philosophy of the Russian Populists*. Oxford: Clarendon Press.

White, James D. 1996. *Karl Marx and the Intellectual Origins of Dialectical Materialism*. London: Macmillan.

Wright, Ian. 2014. 'A Category-Mistake in the Classical Labour Theory of Value'. *Erasmus Journal for Philosophy and Economics*, 7(1): 27–55.

Ziber, Nikolay Ivanovich. 1871. *Teoriâ cennosti i kapitala Rikardo s nekotorymi iz pozdnejših dopolnenij i raz"âsnenij (David Ricardo's Theory of Value and Capital in Relation to the Latest Contributions and Interpretations)*. Kiev: Univ. Izv.

Ziber, Nikolay Ivanovich. 1885. *David Rikardo i Karl Marks v ih obŝestvenno-èkonomičeskih issledovaniâh (David Ricardo and Karl Marx in their Socio-Economic Researches)*. First edition. St Petersburg: Stasiulevich.

Zouboulakis, Michel. 1993. *La science économique à la recherche de ses fondements. La tradition épistémologique ricardienne, 1826–1891*. Paris: PUF.

Zweynert, Joachim. 2002. *Eine Geschichte des ökonomischen Denkens in Russland. 1805–1905*. Marburg, Germany: Metropolis Verlag.

Zweynert, Joachim. 2008. 'Between Reason and Historicity: Russian Academic Economics, 1800–1861'. In Vincent Barnett and Joachim Zweynert, eds, *Economics in Russia: Studies in Intellectual History*, chap. 5, 57–73. Aldershot, UK: Ashgate.

2 Classical political economy in Russia

The influence exerted by Ziber's interpretation of Ricardo might be a factor explaining the persistence of classical political economy in Russia, and the distinctive character of this intellectual tradition with respect to the 'modernised' form of classicism then prevailing in Britain under the influence of Mill and Marshall.

(Scazzieri 1987, 23)

Classical political economy has a long tradition in Russia, starting in the early nineteenth century. Within classical political economy, Russian economists were not primarily interested in value theory. They were instead entangled in more applied and urgent issues such as the consequences of enforced labour on economic development, the search for an optimal tariff policy, or the need for regulation of rural credit. And it is only from the 1870s onwards that the theory of value started to attract their attention. This can be explained in part by the gradual transformation of the methodology used by Russian economists towards more theoretical concerns during the first half of the nineteenth century.[1] But one can also see here the influence of the various reforms of the 1860s. The abolition of serfdom implied that labour acquired a value. As a consequence, the concept of wage, which was a theoretical notion borrowed from Western manuals of political economy, became an empirical notion. The same applied to land, which could (and most of the time should) be purchased by peasants from their former landlords. The ongoing redistribution of land implied purchase, sale and rent. As a consequence, the concepts of land as capital and rent appeared as well. Eventually, the nascent industry introduced capital, wages and profits as empirical realities. The way was paved for these empirical realities to enter the field of political economy and become the object of theoretical enquiries.

Since the classical theory of value was eventually part and parcel of the Russian synthesis, it is necessary to establish in this chapter *which* classical theory of value was used in these debates. Most of the answer to this question is to be found in Ziber's interpretation of Ricardo and Marx.[2] His interpretation of classical political economy was influential (see the epigraph above), both from a material and from a theoretical point of view. Let us first deal with that.[3]

From a material point of view, Ziber's influence was widespread. As far as Ricardo is concerned, Ziber offered the first comprehensive interpretation of his theory of value and capital in his dissertation (Ziber 1871). His translations of Ricardo's *Principles* (1873) and *Works* (1882) with his commentaries were often the only way for many Russians to get access to Ricardo's work. Almost all Russian economists quoted Ziber's translation explicitly, and Lenin is no exception to this rule. Even so, Ricardo's books remained relatively scarce, as evidenced by the following example. Having accused his student Klejnbort of reading Ricardo from secondary literature, Tugan-Baranovsky changed his mind when he learnt that no copy of Ricardo was available at the library, and he lent his own copy of Ziber's translation to his student (Klejnbort 2008, 191–192). The material impact is far greater where Marx is concerned. In his 1871 dissertation, Ziber analyses Marx's economic theory of value, money and the analysis of commodities for the first time in Russian literature. This reading of Marx's first volume of *Capital* appeared one year before the Russian translation of the original (Marx [1867] 1872). And when the original was temporarily banned through censorship, Ziber's digest of *Capital* was still available and played the role of a substitute (Zweynert 2002, 4.8.5). In addition to being physically more accessible, Ziber's exposition style was easier to read and understand than the original.[4] Moreover, Marx himself praised Ziber's 1871 dissertation in the 'Afterword to the Second German Edition' of *Capital*'s first volume (1873):

> An excellent Russian translation of 'Das Kapital' appeared in the spring of 1872. The edition of 3,000 copies is already nearly exhausted. As early as 1871, N. Sieber, Professor of Political Economy in the University of Kiev, in his work 'David Ricardo's Theory of Value and of Capital', referred to my theory of value, of money and of capital, as in its fundamentals a necessary sequel to the teaching of Smith and Ricardo. That which astonishes the Western European in the reading of this excellent work is the author's consistent and firm grasp of the purely theoretical position.
>
> (Marx [1873] 1906, 21)

Ziber's role in popularising Marx's work was important, especially for the first generation of Russian Marxists[5] and even further, since his work represented, and still represents, a 'valuable coda' to *Capital* (Smith 2001, 48) which surpasses Kautsky's popular volume on Marx (Guelfat 1970, 144). On this point, the Soviet historiography is consistent with contemporary views on Ziber as the first scientific interpreter of Marx and the first Marx propagandist in Russia. His doctoral dissertation on Ricardo's theory of value and capital (Ziber 1871) together with some papers on Marx's economic theory appeared together in his most famous work, *David Ricardo and Karl Marx in their Socio-Economic Researches* (1885). This was to become a bedside book for generations of Russian Marxists. The best illustration of this fact is perhaps contained in Lenin's following footnote, added to the 1908 edition of his 1897 *Characterisation of Economic Romanticism*:

The word 'realist' was used here instead of the word Marxist exclusively for censorship reasons. For the same reason, instead of referring to *Capital*, we referred to Sieber's book, which summarised Marx's *Capital*.

(Lenin [1908] 1972, 188)

But besides this role of popularising and disseminating the theories of Ricardo and Marx, Ziber was also conveying his own interpretation of the classical theory of value. This theoretical influence was not as widespread as the material influence that has just been reviewed but it had a deep impact on the understanding of the classical theory of value of several generations of Russian economists, foremost among them the Legal Marxists. Ziber may rightly be considered as a precursor of the Legal Marxists (see Zweynert 2002, 4.8.5).

Ziber's theoretical legacy may be summed up in three principles. First, the economy should be studied from a social point of view. Second, the economist must take average and universal facts into account if he pretends to offer general laws. Third, the economic development of societies takes a deterministic evolutionary road. This third point, albeit significant in understanding Ziber's posture towards Marx, will not be developed further, except for a few comments here (see White 2009). It follows from Ziber's deterministic evolutionary *Weltanschauung* that (i) he does not perceive the necessity of revolution, because of the unavoidable succession of socialism after capitalism; and (ii) he rejects Hegelian dialectics as being of any help in understanding Marx's economic theory.[6] Ziber considers that the latter instead followed the English deductive methodology:

This brief extract from the first chapter of Marx's work and the appendix to it at the end of the book contains, if I am not mistaken, the most essential features of the author's doctrine of value and the general properties of money. The peculiar language and the quite laconic manner of expression does little to facilitate the comprehension of his ideas, and in some cases has led to the accusation that he employs a metaphysical approach to the investigation of value. With the exception of a few places in the chapter where perhaps some statements are indeed made which do not really correspond to the truth, the accusation seems to me unjust. As far as the *theory* itself is concerned, Marx's method is the deductive method of the whole English school, and both its faults and its merits are those shared by the best of the theoretical economists.

(Ziber [1871] 2001, 30)

Ziber considers the Russian *obshchina* as a backward-looking institution doomed to failure, and those who defended it (the Populists) as performing counterproductively (in contradiction to Marx's later views on the issue, i.e. in his letter to Zasulich).

With this *Weltanschauung*, Ziber's reading of the classical economists reached the following conclusions. First, there is a striking continuity within the classical school, with Ricardo as the focal point: (i) past economists were imperfect Ricardians; (ii) Ricardo was mostly right, but used a style of exposition that prevented his successors from correctly understanding him; (iii) while Marx, bringing to light what was already but imperfectly developed in Ricardo, is his true follower.

This chapter analyses first Ziber's reading of the classical theory of value, with an emphasis on the Ricardo–Marx connection. Then, it examines Ziber's particular interpretation of the classical *labour* theory of value, in relation to the costs of production theory. Finally, it explains how Russian economists themselves depict the classical theory of value *after Ziber* or, in other words, how they read Ricardo *after* Marx.

Ziber on Ricardo and Marx

> The specific feature of his work [Ziber's] is that it emphasises the continuity of the theory of value from Smith to Marx through Ricardo.
>
> (Schütte 2002, 23)

In *David Ricardo and Karl Marx in their Socio-Economic Researches* (1885), Ziber presented a study of the general principles of Ricardo and his school on the issue of value and capital.[7] His book is organised in the following way:

1 On value in general and its elements
2 The doctrine of value of Ricardo, his predecessors and some of his successors
3 The theory of costs of production and of demand and supply
4 Marx's theory of value and money [the only translated chapter (see Ziber [1871] 2001)]
5 The notion of capital
6 On the origins and saving of capital
7 On the reason for the appearance of pure income from capital or the value of labour-power
8 Constant and variable capital. Simple and complex cooperation
9 The analysis of the theory of social cooperation
10 Machines and large-scale industry
11 The analysis of the theory of machine production
12 The theory of capital accumulation and the capitalist law of population
13 The analysis of the theory of capital accumulation and the refutation of Malthus's theory.

The above table of contents corresponds to the 1897 posthumous reprint of the 1885 first edition (the only change being the division of chapter 10 from 1885 into chapters 10 and 11 in 1897). The genesis of that work is older than 1885. In fact, his 1871 dissertation (*David Ricardo's Theory of Value and Capital in Relation to the Latest Contributions and Interpretations*) was based on the above chapters 1 to 7 being almost identical except for chapter 4, on Marx's theory of value. The 1871 version of the fourth chapter[8] is based on the first German edition of Marx's *Capital* (vol. I). In 1885 (and therefore 1897), chapter 4 appears doubled in size and enriched by a reading of the second German edition of Marx's *Capital* (vol. I). The additions to that chapter were already published in separate articles by Ziber between 1874 and 1877. Similarly, the new chapters 8 to 12 were published as separate articles during 1878. Only chapter 13 on Malthus appears in the 1880s as an extension of chapter 12.[9] It is therefore important to keep in mind that Ziber's thoughts on Ricardo were already established in 1871 and that his thoughts on Marx evolved between 1871 and 1878.

In his chapter 1, Ziber starts by describing some methodological principles or caveats that he considers important to follow in any investigation of the theory of value. According to these tenets, the economist must look at the economy from a social point of view; his attention should be directed towards average and permanent conditions, i.e. over a long period perspective,[10] and consider only typical economic acts (Ziber 1897, 16–27). The non-respecting of one of these principles is characteristic of the alternative theories (costs of production, supply and demand, subjective utility, scarcity, etc.) that Ziber systematically and successively dismantles in his third chapter.

These basic principles are already partly operating in Ricardo's predecessors. Thus, in an extensive review of the literature, Ziber looks for what was already Ricardian in the works of Boisguilbert, Hobbes, Petty, Locke, Steuart, Cantillon, Quesnay, Mercier de la Rivière, Le Trosne, Franklin and Smith (Ziber 1897, chap. 2, 50–74). When he came to consider Ricardo, Ziber found all the tenets operating.

For Ziber, Ricardo has a *labour* theory of value. The exchange value of two goods is therefore regulated by the comparative amounts of labour embodied in their production. Labour alone provides a general law of value. This does not mean that utility, or scarcity, or anything else have nothing to do with value. But these particular circumstances only play secondary roles in particular exchanges. As was recognised in the dominant – German – literature, Ricardo himself recognises the existence of these particular forces, either in the case of special products (rare statues and paintings, etc.) or in the local and temporal deviations of market prices around natural prices. These circumstances may produce only local and specific laws, while labour, as a social and objective force, as the living principle of every economic society, is the sole universal regulator of value, involved in every *typical* exchange.

In one of the numerous illustrations scattered throughout his book, Ziber replies to those objections that the labour costs of transportation are irrelevant for the determination of exchange value, based on the famous example of butter transported ten times between Paris and Marseille before being sold. Ziber answers that, while it is true that transportation costs will not be included ten times in the value of the butter, these are isolated and not typical costs. In a general, typical, normal situation, butter is not transported ten times, and diamonds are not found on the streets (Ziber 1897, 125–130).

The labour theory of value is valid in a social economy characterised by the division of labour and not only in the Smithian version of primitive societies. (Ziber does not believe in *societies* without capital goods, see 1897, 79). In that case, Ricardo also includes in the amount of labour that which is necessary for the production of the needed tools and machines. In short, Ricardo's theory of value considers labour as the internal quality of goods, because of its general, social and objective nature (Ziber 1897, 74–91). In Ziber's own words, Ricardo's achievement is a collective one:

> The labour theory, as the measure and regulator of exchange relations, least of all can be considered as the discovery of Ricardo, who only gave a sharp and clear formulation of the teachings of his predecessors [...]. To a certain extent this theory can be considered the domain of the whole mankind, because its consciousness, though more or less vague, is common in most peoples around the globe at various stages of development.
>
> (Ziber 1897, 86)

Ricardo's theory is, however, not free from faults. But these shortcomings, as Ziber explains, are mostly an issue of exposition, a question of *form*, and not of content (Ziber 1897, 91). For Ziber, many objections raised against this theory are easily overcome by using the appropriate terminology that Ricardo was lacking, but that Marx, as the genuine follower of Ricardo, eventually provided.

First of all, Ricardo and his school constantly studied the issue of the magnitude and the determinants of value, without ever examining the *form of value* (Ziber 1897, 186). This received a thorough treatment for the first time only in Marx's analysis.[11] And, as a consequence, Ricardo did not realise that labour had a dual form (abstract vs concrete), which impeded him from clearly distinguishing between the value of labour and the value of the product. Ricardo's apparent struggle to take into account in his theory of value the presence of profit is also a consequence of him not distinguishing labour from labour power. The law of value is not disrupted by the existence of profit. Profit is already *in* the product, but takes the form of profit only at the time of exchange (Ziber 1897, 111). Wage is not the value of labour, but the value of labour power. Here appears one of Marx's main improvements to the Ricardian labour theory of value: the notion of surplus value. Ziber then exposes, essentially in his chapters 7 and 8, Marx's other terminological improvements: surplus product, absolute and relative surplus value, the notion of exploitation as the source of profit, the rate of exploitation, etc. The overall tone of the discussion is best captured by the following sentence:

> all those who agree that the regulator of exchange relations and the creator of value is human labour must also, whether he likes it or not, agree with *its logical consequences, i.e. with Marx's theory of surplus product and surplus value.*
>
> (Ziber 1897, 332. Italics in original.)

With the introduction of the distinction between constant and variable capital (a further terminological improvement as compared to Ricardo), Ziber realised that two firms with various organic compositions of capital and the same rate of exploitation cannot achieve the same rate of profit. He foresees the transformation problem:

> We saw that not only the variable part of capital but also constant capital
> – production tools, auxiliary and raw materials – enters production. The
> proportion between those two parts of capital depends on technical con-
> ditions, and varies according to the branch of industry. But whatever may
> be the relation of constant to variable capital – 1:2, 1:10, 1:x – it does not
> change the validity of the law expressed above, which may be formulated
> as follows: with a given value for labour power and a uniform exploita-
> tion rate (i.e. with equal surplus labour time), the quantities of value and
> surplus value produced by way of various forms of capital remain in pro-
> portion to the quantities of the *variable part* of that capital, i.e. from
> those parts of capital which are living labour power. This becomes com-
> pletely clear when one remembers that surplus value is exclusively pro-
> duced by living labour power and, consequently, only by variable capital.
> The latter is so named because it grows during the process of production.
> And, in contrast, fixed capital, i.e. the product of previous – and there-
> fore dead – labour, only transfers its value to the final product by
> replication.
>   This law seems in contradiction to the factual evidence. It is well known
> that the textile manufacturer makes a relatively greater use of constant
> capital than, say, the baker. Yet the former does not consequently receive
> less profit than the latter. That should, however, be exactly the case if we
> hold that profit is obtained only through variable capital. Marx promised to
> explain this contradiction in the second volume of *Capital*.
>
> (Ziber 1897, 347–348)

Ziber does not go further on that issue than waiting for Marx's answer. Here, it can only be regretted that Ziber died at the early age of 44 and was thus unable to read volume II and, above all, volume III of *Capital*. It can be guessed that he would have positively welcomed Marx's transformation procedure since, based on the metamorphosis of surplus value into profit, it perfectly accords with Ziber's enthusiasm for Marx's study of *forms*.[12] On this, he was in line with Marx, ready to accept the antagonistic character of the contemporary mode of production:

> The introduction of the division of labour does not change the fundamental
> physiological principle that labour is followed by the consumption of the
> produced good. Thus, the exchange of the produced good follows the prin-
> ciple of the equivalence of labour. However, by introducing a distance
> between needs and their satisfaction, the division of labour introduced an

antagonistic process in the distribution of wealth, *foreign to the primitive social forms of production.*

(Ziber 1897, 86, emphasis added)

Ziber was fully conscious of the peculiarities of the capitalist mode of production, and most of the subsequent parts of his book are devoted to the exploration of what he calls *social cooperation*, which covers the issue of social coordination of human activities in the presence of a social division of labour, and in which the law of value occupies an important place.[13]

The following conclusions can be drawn from the above presentation of the theories of value of Ricardo and Marx. Ziber established a direct connection between their theories: they both had a labour theory of value. This Ricardo–Marx filiation survived for some time in Russian economic thought, thanks to Ziber's interpretation of Ricardo as a pure labour theorist of value.[14] It was relatively easy to maintain, at least until the publication of the third volume of *Capital* in 1894 (and in Russian translation in 1896). However, it would become more difficult with the third volume, in which Marx's theory of *value* confronts a Ricardian theory of *prices* of production. Here, Ziber would have been disappointed, for he did not see in Ricardo a prices of production theory, in the sense of a costs of production theory. For Ziber, the terms *costs of production* and *value* (understood as labour value) were often used awkwardly by Ricardo, but also synonymously to designate the same *labour theory of value*. The following section explains how he defended this claim.

Labour and costs of production

Nowhere does Ricardo consider surplus-value separately and independently from its particular forms – profit (interest) and rent. [...] When we speak of his theory of surplus-value, we are, therefore, speaking of his theory of profit, in so far as he confuses the latter with surplus-value, i.e., in so far as he only considers profit in relation to variable capital, the part of capital laid out in wages. We shall later deal with what he says of profit as distinct from surplus-value.

It is so much in the nature of the subject matter that surplus-value can only be considered in relation to variable capital, i.e., capital laid out directly in wages – and without an understanding of surplus-value no theory of profit is possible – that Ricardo treats the entire capital as variable capital and avoids constant capital, although he occasionally mentions it in the form of advances.

(Marx [1861–1863] 1971, 636)

In order to follow Ziber's claim that, for Ricardo, costs of production and labour value are synonymous, it is necessary to go back to the tenets of classical political economy according to Ziber. But first, in order to give an idea of how Ziber conducted his investigations, the latter justification, which is characteristic of his method of exposition, will be dwelt upon: first a few remarks, then a chronological examination of past authorities until the present one, and then his own remarks. Ziber studied the way in which economists ordered the 'various parts of science' (value, production, distribution, exchange), starting with old authors:

> With regard to some [...] economists, writing in the seventeenth and eighteenth centuries, then, if I am not mistaken, the position of the various parts of science was not ordered by them to a rigorously thought-out plan, but instead in a rather chaotic disorder, corresponding to the state of economic knowledge prevailing at that time.
>
> (Ziber 1897, 8)

He goes on: 'Physiocrats, with the notable exception of Le Trosne, introduced the notion of value only incidentally, while Smith first gives a theory of value before investigating the origin and the distribution of income.'[15] Ricardo, James Mill and McCulloch constitute, by following Smith on this point, a tradition which opposed John Stuart Mill, with his unfortunate and inconsistently followed inversion (Ziber 1897, 7–9). Besides, Ziber disregards those for whom '*l'échange, c'est l'économie politique (exchange is political economy)*' (Bastiat quoted by Ziber 1897, 7), since 'Exchange relations are inconceivable without value, but value is conceivable without exchange relations.' (Ziber 1897, 8). And he gives priority to value as 'the most essential domain of political economy' by emphasising the social role of value: what is isolated (the isolated economy) should be conceived as part of the 'social whole' (social economy) before it is ever possible to think about production and distribution of the social product (Ziber 1897, 8). This leads to Ziber's tenets – (1) the average and permanent conditions and (2) the preference for the social point of view – and their consequences.

(1) Average and permanent conditions. Although each economic phenomenon takes place at a given place and time, the 'method of average numbers' is a prerequisite for any scientific enquiry of the economic system. Ziber rejects the possibility of investigating *all* points in space and time, since it would require much more than just a life-long collection of data for a mass of statisticians. On the other hand, he rejects observation from only *one* point in space and time for his particularism.[16] He opts for the only relevant point of view according to him – the average location at the average moment – in order to distinguish the permanent effects from their accidental and temporary deviations and avoid confusing primary with secondary explanations. According to Ziber, who makes an extensive use of this argument, the average method is typical of the classical school.

Thus, while a woman may favour a fur coat in winter and a dress in summer, this preference is meaningless when observed at the average moment of the year (Ziber 1897, 31). Similarly, the time necessary to produce a given good should not be observed from the most skilful or from the worst representative of his profession, but from the average representative. Ziber invokes Quetelet's notion of the 'average man' to explain that the average worker is not a concrete isolated individual, but a social statistically constructed individual. This point is illustrated by Ziber from Edmund Burke's experimentation, according to which five farmers working together are more productive than the same five farmers each working in isolation (Ziber 1897, 18). The average man's production is not that of the isolated farmer, but a fifth of the social production of the group of farmers. This leads to the distinction between the individual and the social economy.

(2) *Individual and social economy.* Without defining it explicitly, Ziber frequently used the notion of 'individual economy'. (He used the terms 'individual economy', 'isolated economy' and 'private economy' synonymously.) The term was taken from the German literature to designate an economic entity of the smallest dimension (but not necessarily a single agent). In the examples used by Ziber, it alternatively represents a household, a firm, a Russian agrarian community or a landlord with his family, serfs and servants. On the other side, the social economy is the result of the interactions between the individual economies. Everything observed at the level of the individual economies is present in the social economy, but there are three fundamental differences between all individual economies and the social economy, and economists too often forget about them.

First, the social economy results from the cooperation of the productive powers of the individual economies, which are not observable when one looks at a unique individual economy. The simple or complex cooperation that results from the division of labour takes place only at the level of the social economy and depends on the society's level of development. The appropriate level of observation is therefore not the individual economy, but the *average* individual economy, which takes into account the complex relationships between individual economies – see the example of Burke above.

Second, each part of the social economy is in a situation of mutual dependence. If an individual firm produces more, it will certainly earn more; but if all individual firms produce more, this will hardly be the case. Therefore, the social economy cannot be considered from the point of view of the individual economy (Ziber 1897, 18–21).

Third, the individual economy is subordinated to the social economy: an individual economy cannot change the conditions of the social economy.[17] In short, the laws governing the individual economy cannot be applied to the social economy or vice-versa. Their domains of application should not be confused.[18]

Two major consequences for the theory of value are derivable from the two methodological principles that have just been described: (i) the notion of utility is considered as objective (Ziber 1897, 14–15, 29–41, 47); and (ii) the contradiction between costs of production and labour theory of value is only apparent.

(i) *Objective utility.* Ziber defines the notion of utility as the capacity of consumed goods to satisfy needs. He follows here an English tradition, opposed to the continental one according to which individual subjective judgement is the source of utility. For Ziber, 'utility is perfectly objective' (Ziber 1897, 29): human needs are classified according to well-known physiological requisites:

nourishment, clothing, housing.... In a social economy, at a given average moment, useful labour, which attributes utility to goods, is distributed to equally satisfy these needs. Of course, adds Ziber, one may prefer chocolate to a more nourishing plate, but this is only an individual 'caprice', and does not matter in average conditions in the average man. The same can be said of wood and bread. At a given moment, a man may first have need of bread, if he is hungry, or of wood, if he is cold. But on the average, bread and wood bring him an equal – qualitative – satisfaction.

Ziber refutes on this basis the idea that utility can be the source of exchange value, with a few counterexamples: utility of exchanged goods cannot be compared, since one is absolutely useless and the other absolutely useful for an exchanger. He goes further: two units of the same good are worth twice the value of one unit, not because they bring twice the utility, but because they cost twice as much to produce. Here the average method is central to the refutation of all subjectivist approaches: social production is directed towards the satisfaction of permanent needs; temporal variations around them, in which some see the true source of value, are nothing other than 'caprices'.

The consequence of this point of view should not be underestimated. The notion of objective utility is an important pattern of thought imposed on Russian economic thought by Ziber's theoretical agenda, as recognised by Dmitriev himself:

> Ziber's scientific authority consecrated this semi-conscious disregard for 'subjective' or 'psychological' theories of value, which established in our country from the very beginning the false idea that these theories contradict the positivist principles then prevailing in the minds of Russian society.
>
> (Dmitriev 1908, 16)

For Ziber, human needs being on average permanent, the activity of the social economy is directed towards the satisfaction of these needs. The underlying understanding of objective utility was opposed to the continental notion of subjective utility prevailing in Russia at that time, which had found its place beside costs of production in the theory of value. The idea that both labour and utility are objective factors can be invoked in explaining the delay in the reception of marginalism in Russia, which began tentatively in the early 1890s, starting from Tugan-Baranovsky's 'Study on the Marginal Utility of Economic Goods as the Cause of their Value' (Tugan-Baranovsky 1890, see next chapter.). But a still more fundamental pattern of thought follows.

(ii) Labour value and costs of production. For Ziber, most economists failed to understand correctly Ricardo's position concerning the source of value. Some support the idea that Ricardo had a labour theory of value, implying that quantities of labour embodied in goods are the only source of value. Others affirm that Ricardo supported a costs of production theory, implying thereby considerations other than labour. But while most saw a contradiction between the two incompatible positions,[19] Ziber has a simple solution: he looks at the economy from a social point of view, then from an individual point of view, and is then able to

make up his mind. From a social point of view, labour is the regulator of exchange value:

> From a bird's eye view of the social economy, by keeping in mind that the whole economy and its constituent parts are significantly different, and with regard to the diversity of the situations and forces of individual economies, there exists a neutral basis through which all economies have an equal right to change the form of their products by way of an exchange against other productions. In that case, we can be certain that the regulator of the exchange ratio can only be the labour contained in the product. There cannot be any other economic condition, common to all the economies [...]. Regardless of the existence of the division of labour, regardless of the form of output distribution in the society, in all cases the society spends a known quantity of effort with the aim of getting its means of subsistence.
>
> (Ziber 1897, 106–107)

From an individual point of view, however, costs of production seem to play the same role:

> But if one looks at things from the point of view of the individual economy in its most dominant form, i.e. the firm owner, then the issue presents itself in another form. [...] First, he pays wages to his workers. Second, he buys tools and materials for the production. Third, he pays interest on borrowed capital, in the case of course where the size of his firm does not enable him to limit himself to his own means. Prices of tools and materials also include the profit of those entrepreneurs in the other economic sectors involved. Finally, by selling the product of his own [individual] economy, the entrepreneur receives some surplus, exceeding all the mentioned expenses, which constitutes the profit of the firm. Thus, the quantity of product received in exchange must compensate for the cost of several components. One of them, wages, can be reduced in one way or another into labour and constitutes an expenditure. Another, interest, does not reduce to labour and constitutes another expenditure. Finally, a third component, the entrepreneur's profit, cannot be reduced to labour either, but constitutes an income. An immediate conclusion comes to mind: exchange ratios are not regulated by labour, which does not enter alone into the production of the good, but together with the other costs of production.
>
> (Ziber 1897, 107–108)

For Ziber, there is no doubt which point of view to favour:

> the costs theory is just a theory for the individual economy, transferred into the sphere of the social economy; and if the costs theory means something in the office and shop, it does not follow that it explains much of the relations in the socio-economic system.
>
> (Ziber 1897, 118)

Costs of production and labour value explain the same phenomena from two different points of view: the individual economy and the social economy.[20] Only the latter is pertinent to the study of classical political economy, defined by Ziber's tenets: social point of view, universal and average conditions. For Ziber, the fact that Ricardo did not strictly follow one of his methodological caveats (the individual economy should not be confused with the social economy) largely explains the misinterpretations of Ricardo's theory of value in the economic literature.[21] But often when he wrote about 'costs of production', he was rightly considering, for Ziber, the labour costs of producing.

Ziber's conception of Ricardo's theory of value as a pure *labour* theory of value is not unrelated to the success of the Ricardo–Marx filiation he established, for reasons that will now be set out. This filiation was to be the influential medium by which Ziber left a lasting legacy in Russian economic thought.[22]

Ricardo *after* Marx

Did Marx follow Ricardo, or did he introduce a departure from him? Marx's original intentions were without doubt to produce a critique of political economy, capable of rendering it obsolete. But at the same time, helped by Engels, he was the origin of the ambiguity that mars that issue, with his claim to follow classical political economy, even if distinct from vulgar political economy. That was only one step from what Dostaler called the 'transformation of the critique of political economy into Marxist political economy' (Dostaler 1978, 119, 125), and it was but a short step. It is nowadays readily admitted that there exists a possible (neo-) Ricardian reading of *Capital*. This reading sets itself the task of solving the transformation problem by way of putting Marxist political economy into systems of equations (the road opened up by Bortkiewicz). But there is also an acknowledgement that this reading narrows and departs from the extent of Marx's project, which followed the Ricardian path for reasons, such as external credibility, that were foreign to his original critical intentions. With the publication in 1905 by Kautsky of Marx's *Theories of Surplus Value* (1861–1863, the so-called volume IV of *Capital*), Marx appeared from that time onwards as a Ricardian economist.[23]

In Russia, the perception of the relationship between Marx and Ricardo progressed somewhat differently. Russian economists had long been kept away from Ricardo, considered as a representative of an 'abstract' branch of classical political economy – see the classification of economic schools in Vernadsky 1858. Therefore, and despite Ziber's efforts in the 1870s, Ricardo was little read, except by a very few non-conformists. His thinking arrived in Russia only through German mediation (not always sympathetic – see Knies) that presented Ricardo as a costs of production theorist who did not neglect subjective components, such as utility, or the interplay of supply and demand. This is, of course, far from Ziber's reading. But there is first of all another reason why the relationship between Marx and Ricardo was seen differently in Russia: Marx was no Ricardian economist; on the contrary, Ricardo was perceived as a 'pre-Marxist' economist. This can be explained in two steps.

First, Marx's theory invaded the whole Russian economic stage, and even the whole of public life, long before a real interest in Ricardo arose. Indeed, as early as 1860, Marx received a letter from a Russian journalist (Sazonov), informing him that a Professor (Babst) had conducted a public lecture on political economy in Moscow, whose first session was nothing but a paraphrase of Marx's *Critique of Political Economy* (Marx [1859] 1987; see also Rubel, in Marx 1965, cix–cx). Then, from 1877 until 1899, under the influence of A. I. Chuprov, Marx's theory, understood as a theory of historical materialism and a theory of value and exploitation, was approved and reproduced without reservation (Schütte 2002, 23). Thus, Marx's influence on Russian economists was considerable: 'Between 1870 and 1900, the works of almost all Russian economists were influenced by Marxism' (Schütte 2002, 22). Therefore, until the 1890s, all Russian economists were Marxists to some extent, no matter whether they were Populists, industrialists, socialists or even liberals. Marx meant something different for all of them, but it is difficult to find, apart from Bakunin or Chicherin, much opposition to him. In this great, yet undifferentiated, Marxist crowd there were many debates on the social significance and the domain of application of the theory, but the theory itself was not questioned. As a consequence, Marxism was taken as dogma:

> Thus, when Marx's ideas were disseminated in our country, the foundations for the recognition of the labour theory of value as an indisputable dogma – a uniquely true and definitive solution – were already completely prepared. The fascination for Marx and the erroneous representation of the continuous link between his theory of value and the theory of labour exploitation strengthened the 'faith' in the labour theory into a more fanatical and intolerant attitude towards other points of view and criticisms.
>
> (Dmitriev 1908, 16)

This was particularly true of the more orthodox Marxists:

> The attitude of the orthodox Marxists was the most clear-cut: whatever truths there were in classical analysis were preserved in Marxism. In consequence, they never developed classical economic theory directly. Nor were they interested in doing so indirectly, by elaboration on Marx's technical economic analysis.
>
> (Howard and King 1998, 150)

It was the social, critical and prophetic parts of Marx's work that were fascinating. In his theory of the value of the commodity, the prominence of human labour was highly esteemed by Russians, and it was sufficient. There was no need to read Ricardo, since the latter was perceived as a predecessor of Marx, but without the social, critical and more applied dimension. Moreover, Ziber's Ricardo was in full conformity with that picture. Marx's law of value, which was that of Ricardo, was thus not further questioned.

Only as a second step was Ricardo eventually read. It began with the publication of the third volume of Marx's *Capital* in 1894 (1896 in Russian). With this publication, some of these Russian Marxists came to realise that Marx was entangled in a serious contradiction that he had failed to solve: the incompatibility, or difficulty of conciliating his law of value with a theory of prices that, as if it was not enough, was called *Ricardian* in the Western literature. It was soon realised, in those circles that dared to criticise Marx (the Legal Marxists), that the whole of Marx's construction was in danger, since it was based on his law of value and the invalidity of the latter might endanger the former. As a consequence, Marx's law of value was, for the first time in the Russian Marxist literature, no longer considered untouchable.[24] The participants in these new debates started to read Ricardo's work. Ricardo was read either to criticise Marx, or to defend him. Ricardo was read *after* Marx.

What emerges from this Ricardo *after* Marx and what remains of Marx after these readings of Ricardo? Does the classical theory of value divide into two – a Ricardian and a Marxian branch? It is clear that, in these matters, Ziber's influence is quite strongly felt on those Russian Marxists who dared to study Marx critically after the publication of the third volume of *Capital*. It is shown in Chapters 4 and 5 how, in his attempt to rescue Marx, Tugan-Baranovsky replaced Marx's theory of value with his own. He achieved this with an articulation between labour value and costs of production that is strongly reminiscent of Ziber's own approach. As for Shaposhnikov (Chapter 6), who entered the stage after these debates, following Dmitriev's analytical tools but without his intentions, he nevertheless attempts to reconcile Marx with Ricardo.

The reception of classical political economy and the formation of a consistent idea of what the classical theory of value looks like owes much, in Russia, to the pioneering work of Ziber in the 1870s. His first and foremost legacy on Russian economic thought is to have been the first to give people the taste for abstract research in political economy in a country where that science had only been invoked in relation to policy issues. With this path opened, Ziber paved the way for the next generations of Russian economists working on the theory of value and prices (Bilimovic, Bukharin, Dmitriev, Orzhencky, Rubin, Shaposhnikov, Slutsky, Struve, Tugan-Baranovsky, Woytinsky and Yurovsky). The second legacy left by Ziber consists of his consistent methodological insights in the form of an attitude favouring the study of social (vs individual) and objective (vs subjective) relations, which offered the possibility of delaying for some time the introduction of the new marginalist theories. The third, and potentially most interesting, legacy that Ziber offered to his successors is his reconstruction of the classical paradigm, based on two points: (i) the rejection of the costs of production theory in favour of a labour theory of value, which was far from the ' "modernised" form of classicism then prevailing in Britain' (Scazzieri, see epigraph at the beginning of the chapter); and (ii) a strong continuity hypothesis between Ricardo and Marx. The latter was consistent, in Russia, with the discovery of Ricardo after Marx. But when the transformation problem first reached Russia, in the mid-1890s, the continuity hypothesis was seriously challenged. This gave birth to a handful of replies, which are examined in the following chapters of this book. But Ziber's influential reading had already given a sound idea of what a classical theory of value was, and the replies to that challenge were shaped by it.

Of course, this is a *ceteris paribus* story, which does not yet take into account another threat to that classical theory of value: the simultaneous introduction of marginalism in Russia in the 1890s.

Notes

1 For Zweynert, this transformation is the result of a struggle between 'historicity' and 'reason' (Zweynert 2008).
2 This only means that, albeit there were alternative classical interpretations at hand (see Chapter 1), they are not relevant for they did not significantly influence the Russian synthesis.
3 In the most comprehensive bibliographical resource on Ziber to date, Rezul gives the following rather hagiographic statement on Ziber's achievements:

> 1. Ziber was the first to popularise and comment on the doctrines of Marx in Russia and in the Ukraine. 2. Ziber was the author of the first Marxist work on the history of primitive economic culture ... 3. Ziber was the first to translate Ricardo into Russian and therefore to give access to this great pre-Marxist economist ...
> (Rezul 1931, 142–143).

The list goes on and credits Ziber with the first Marxist evaluations of Rodbertus and of Henry George's works, and with the first sceptical Marx-based approach towards the *obshchina*, etc.
4 Zweynert (2002, 4.8.2) aptly remarks that this is not done without contortions. Much more kind to Ziber, D. Smith remarks: 'Several aspects of Marx's theory which remain obscure to many critics can be better understood in the light of Sieber's exposition'. (Smith 2001, 48).
5 Such as Plekhanov, Axelrod, Skvorcov. For a survey, see Smith (2001, 51–53).
6 It is important to consider that 'another' Marx, probably closest to the 'true' Marx, was possible: the Hegelian Marx, genuinely interested in Russia, that Engels disregarded while preparing volumes II and III of *Capital*. This Marx is convincingly characterised in White's *Karl Marx and the Intellectual Origins of Dialectical Materialism* (1996). Here, however, it is the non-Hegelian Ziber's Marx that has been (historically) conveyed until the Russian synthesis.
7 Nikolay Ivanovich Ziber (1844–1888) was educated in an intellectual environment, the Kiev school of political economy, in which the theories of Smith and Ricardo were well disseminated. He learnt their theories with his teachers – the future Russian Minister Bunge and Cekhanovecky – and was certainly introduced to Marx's work by the latter. He completed his training with a state-sponsored journey to Europe, where he had the opportunity, among others, to attend the lectures of Knies and Roscher.
8 It appears that the 1871 edition of that chapter is the only work of Ziber that has been translated into English so far. See Ziber ([1871] 2001).
9 White's careful comparison of the 1871 and the 1885 editions is greatly acknowledged (White 2001, 15–16). Further, the 1897 edition of Ziber is quoted, except for some passages from the English edition of the 1871 edition's fourth chapter.
10 The exact expression is '*v tečenie prodolžitel'nogo vremeni*', i.e. in the course of a long period (Ziber 1897, 85).
11 Most of Ziber's chapter on Marx's theory of value (in both the 1871 and the 1885 editions) concentrates on that issue, starting from the natural (value in use) vs the social

(value in exchange) form of commodities, and extending to the single, universal and money equivalent forms of value.

12 Moreover, he would certainly have been a better advocate of Marx in the debates on the transformation problem. Indeed, Ziber was a skilful defender of Marx's theory since he had already defended him against his Russian detractors, from the liberal to the Populist poles. On Ziber's defences of Marx, and on Marx's strong appreciation of those defences, see Smith (2001, 53–57) and White (2009, 8–11).

13 There is here a connection that may have been overlooked between Ziber and Rubin (from the 1870s to the 1920s) on the link between Marx's law of value and the coordination of social activities. See Rubin ([1928] 1972) and Faccarello (1983).

14 For alternative Russian interpretations of Ricardo, see Melnik (2014).

15 Ziber considered that, in the *Wealth of Nations*, Smith studied the origin and distribution of income, *after* having preliminarily given a theory of value (Ziber 1897, 7). This makes sense as far as the order of chapters in the *Wealth of Nations* is concerned. As for the logical order between value and distribution in Smith's work, this point remains controversial in the literature. An interesting insight is supplied by Sinha, who claims that this issue is meaningless for Smith, because the latter thought in terms of representation, and not in terms of cause and effect (Sinha 2010, 47–48).

16 In these debates, Ziber, who personally attended in the early 1870s the lectures of Roscher in Leipzig and of Knies in Heidelberg, seems to favour the latter's point of view over the former's in the debate that was later recounted by Max Weber (see Gioia 2000, 49–50).

17 'The market has not the slightest need to know if an individual economy needs to expend more or less labour than required in the manufacture of a given good' (Ziber 1897, 21).

18 According to Ziber, the most fundamental mistakes in the history of economic thought come from this confusion. The mercantilists' main fallacy, for example, has been to confuse the role of money in the individual economy, where it represents wealth, and in the social economy, where it does not (Ziber 1897, 17).

19 The question is still open today, and Stigler's 93 per cent conciliatory (or realist) position satisfies neither camp. See Stigler (1958).

20 This is quite similar to the modern micro vs macro division in economics.

21 Ricardo did follow, on the contrary, another methodological caveat, i.e. the average method.

22 This will become particularly clear in Chapters 5 and 6, where Ziber's influence on Tugan-Baranovsky and on Shaposhnikov will be recognised.

23 The only exception at that time was Diehl, trying to do his utmost to distinguish Ricardo from Marx. See Jorland (1995, 246–262).

24 Russian reactions to the third volume of Marx's *Capital* (on the transformation problem, the falling rate of profit, the concept of exploitation, etc.) were in some ways identical to those encountered in Western countries, although, in some cases, they anticipated or were anticipated by them. The overall tone within the revisionist (vs orthodox) branch was to leave the theory of value to retain an empirical notion of exploitation, and save what could be saved from the remainder of Marx's *grand œuvre*. See Howard and King (1995, 31–32 and 43–51). For Tugan-Baranovsky's reactions, see Chapter 4.

References

Dmitriev, Vladimir Karpovich. 1908. 'Teoriâ cennosti. Obzor literatury na russkom âzyke (Value Theory. Review of the Literature in the Russian Language)'. *Kritičeskoe Obozrenie*, VII: 12–26.

Dostaler, Gilles. 1978. *Valeur et prix. Histoire d'un débat.* Montréal: François Maspero, Presses Universitaires de Grenoble, Les presses de l'Université du Québec.

Faccarello, Gilbert. 1983. 'La loi de la valeur et le problème de la coordination des activités économiques'. *L'homme et la société*, 67–68: 153–177.

Gioia, Vitantonio. 2000. 'L'école historique allemande d'économie'. In Alain Béraud and Gilbert Faccarello, eds, *Nouvelle histoire de la pensée économique*, vol. 3, chap. XXIX, 30–73, Paris: La Découverte.

Guelfat, Isaac. 1970. 'Aux sources de la marxologie authentique: N. I. Ziber'. *L'homme et la société*, 17(1): 141–148.

Howard, Michael C. and John E. King. 1995. ' "A Past and a Present, but No Abiding Future": The Critical Reception of Volume III of Capital, 1894–1900'. *History of Economic Ideas*, III(1): 27–69.

Howard, Michael C. and John E. King. 1998. 'Classical Economics in Russia'. In Heinz D. Kurz and Neri Salvadori, eds, *The Elgar Companion to Classical Economics*, vol. 1, 149–154. Cheltenham and Northampton: Edward Elgar.

Jorland, Gérard. 1995. *Les paradoxes du capital.* Paris: Odile Jacob.

Klejnbort, L. M. 2008. 'Vstreči. M. I. Tugan-Baranovskij (Meetings with Tugan-Baranovsky)'. In Leonid Dmitrievich Shirokorad and Anton Leonidovich Dmitriev, eds, *Neizvestnyj M. I. Tugan-Baranovskij (Unknown M. I. Tugan-Baranovsky)*, 181–237, text prepared by Chris Monday and Anton Leonidovich Dmitriev. St Petersburg: Nestor-Istoriâ.

Lenin, Vladimir Ilich. [1908] 1972. 'Characterisation of Economic Romanticism', second edition. In *Collected Works*, vol. 2, 129–266. Moscow: Progress Publishers.

Marx, Karl. [1859] 1987. 'A Contribution to the Critique of Political Economy'. In Karl Marx and Friedrich Engels, *Collected Works*, vol. 29. Moscow: Progress Publishers.

Marx, Karl. [1861–1863] 1971. *Theories of Surplus Value.* Moscow: Progress Publishers.

Marx, Karl. [1867] 1872. *Kapital, Tom 1.* First Russian edition, translated by G. Lopatin and Nikolay Francevich Danielson. St Petersburg: Polâkov.

Marx, Karl. [1873] 1906. 'Afterword to the Second German Edition'. In *Capital: A Critique of Political Economy. Volume I: The Process of Capitalist Production*, 16–26. New York: The Modern Library.

Marx, Karl. [1894] 1896. *Kapital, Tom 3.* First Russian edition, translated by Nikolay Francevich Danielson. St Petersburg: Polâkov.

Marx, Karl. 1965. *Oeuvres Économie*, vol. I of Bibliothèque de la Pléiade. Paris: Gallimard.

Melnik, Denis. 2014. 'The Diffusion of Ricardo's Theory in Russia'. In Gilbert Faccarello and Masashi Izumo, eds, *The Reception of David Ricardo in Continental Europe and Japan*, chap. 6, 195–211. London: Routledge.

Rezul', Â. G. 1931. 'N. I. Ziber (Bibliografija)'. *Katorga i Ssylka*, 7: 142–174.

Ricardo, David. 1873. *Sočineniâ Davida Rikardo Vyp. 1 (Works of David Ricardo Vol. 1).* Translated by Nikolay Ivanovich Ziber. Kiev: Univ. Typ.

Ricardo, David. 1882. *Sočineniâ Davida Rikardo (Works of David Ricardo).* Translated by Nikolay Ivanovich Ziber. St Petersburg: Panteleev.

Rubin, Isaak Ilich. [1928] 1972. *Essays on Marx's Theory of Value.* Translated by Miloš Samardźija and Fredy Perlman from the third edition. Detroit, MI: Black and Red.

Scazzieri, Roberto. 1987. 'Ziber on Ricardo'. *Contributions to Political Economy*, 6: 25–44.

Schütte, Frank. 2002. *Die ökonomischen Studien V. K. Dmitrievs.* Ph.D. diss., Technische Universität Chemnitz. Available at: http://monarch.qucosa.de/fileadmin/data/qucosa/documents/5136/data/start.html (accessed on 5 August 2014).

Sinha, Ajit. 2010. *Theories of Value from Adam Smith to Piero Sraffa*. New Delhi: Routledge.

Smith, David Norman. 2001. 'The Spectral Reality of Value: Sieber, Marx, and Commodity Fetishism'. *Research in Political Economy*, 19: 47–66.

Stigler, George J. 1958. 'Ricardo and the 93% Labor Theory of Value'. *American Economic Review*, 48(3): 357–367.

Tugan-Baranovsky, Mikhail Ivanovich. 1890. 'Učenie o predel'noj poleznosti hozâjstvennyh blag kak pričina ih cennosti (Study on the Marginal Utility of Economic Goods as the Cause of their Value)'. *Ûridičeskij Vestnik*, XXII(10/2): 192–230.

Vernadsky, Ivan Vasilevich. 1858. *Očerk istorii političeskoj èkonomii (Essay on the History of Political Economy)*. St Petersburg: Èkonomičeskij Ukazatel'.

White, James D. 1996. *Karl Marx and the Intellectual Origins of Dialectical Materialism*. London: Macmillan.

White, James D. 2001. 'Nikolai Sieber and Karl Marx'. *Research in Political Economy*, 19: 3–16.

White, James D. 2009. 'Nikolai Sieber: The First Russian Marxist'. *Revolutionary Russia*, 22(1): 1–20.

Ziber, Nikolay Ivanovich. 1871. *Teoriâ cennosti i kapitala Rikardo s nekotorymi iz pozdnejših dopolnenij i raz'âsnenij (David Ricardo's Theory of Value and Capital in Relation to the Latest Contributions and Interpretations)*. Kiev: Univ. Izv.

Ziber, Nikolay Ivanovich. [1871] 2001. 'Marx's Theory of Value and Money'. *Research in Political Economy*, 19: 17–45.

Ziber, Nikolay Ivanovich. 1885. *David Rikardo i Karl Marks v ih obŝestvenno-èkonomičeskih issledovaniâh (David Ricardo and Karl Marx in their Socio-Economic Researches)*. First edition. St Petersburg: Stasiulevich.

Ziber, Nikolay Ivanovich. 1897. *David Rikardo i Karl Marks v ih obŝestvenno-èkonomičeskih issledovaniâh (David Ricardo and Karl Marx in their Socio-Economic Researches)*. Reprint of the first edition. St Petersburg: I. D. Sytin.

Zweynert, Joachim. 2002. *Eine Geschichte des ökonomischen Denkens in Russland. 1805–1905*. Marburg, Germany: Metropolis Verlag.

Zweynert, Joachim. 2008. 'Between Reason and Historicity: Russian Academic Economics, 1800–1861'. In Vincent Barnett and Joachim Zweynert, eds, *Economics in Russia: Studies in Intellectual History*, chap. 5, 57–73. Aldershot, UK: Ashgate.

3   Marginalism in Russia

> And this abnormal situation [the Russian faith in Marx] lasted more than 20 years. During this very time, an unprecedented fact happened in the annals of science: during a whole quarter of a century, Russian economic science 'did not notice' the biggest current, by magnitude and consequence, of European economic science. This current reached all civilised countries in Europe, crossed the ocean to the New World, and found followers there, as well as in the Old World, among the most outstanding theoretical economists.
>
> We are speaking, of course, of the psychological trend, better known under the name of the 'marginal utility' school.
>
> (Dmitriev 1908, 16–17)

The classical school of political economy settled slowly in Russia; its tenets were discussed, modified and adopted. Things went differently with marginalism. This was introduced more abruptly in Russia in the 1890s, after a 20 year delay – this is not exceptional, if one compares this case with the reception of Walras in France. This delay has been explained by the rejection of subjectivism in political economy, in large part due to Ziber's interpretation of the classics (see Chapter 2). Once in Russia, marginalism was not widely discussed. It was either rejected or adopted. But those who did adopt it perceived it as a potential *complement* to former theories, certainly not as a replacement: 'Virtually no one considered marginalism as the basis of a new, independent and consistent paradigm' (Makasheva 2009, 29). Classical political economy focused on the objective conditions of production. For many, this was sufficient. For some, it was a scientific improvement to consider *also* exchange and subjective evaluations: the latter introduced the 'missing demand' within political economy.

The history of the reception of marginalism in Russia has only very recently been discussed in the literature. In this respect, Pokidchenko (2005, 104–113) provides a useful bibliographical guideline. For her part, Makasheva (2009) provides a general overview in which the reception of marginalism is considered on a very large scale: a first discovery at the end of the nineteenth century and a second at the end of the twentieth. Her story is paralleled with the contrasting history of mathematical economics in Russia. In fact, mathematical political economy emerged in Russia slightly before the 1890s and did not disappear during the twentieth century when marginalism was banned.[1] Finally, the neglected history of the reception of Walras's ideas is examined here (first published in Allisson 2009), for the influence they had on the Russian mathematical economists.[2]

Chronologically, there were two main marginalist influences in Russia: first an Austrian one (in the 1890s), and then a mathematical one. While the second influence was clearly Walrasian (from the end of the 1890s to the beginning of the 1910s), English marginalists started to gain influence in Russia at the end of the 1910s. Therefore, as far as the Russian synthesis is concerned, marginalism is essentially an Austrian, and then a Walrasian affair. It is even possible to say that the reception of the latter was conditioned by the former. The Austrian masters – Menger, Böhm-Bawerk and Wieser – were favoured for linguistic reasons, but also for their clarity of thought. Thus, the new economic terms introduced to the Russian language through German were reused when mathematical marginalist economics was eventually considered.

This Austrian domination contributed to the neglect of the marginalist theories of production, for early Austrians were concerned with exchange and not yet with production (but for reasons that were unclear to the Russians, though, Austrians were also interested in distribution issues (see Chapter 6)). And even if Walras had a theory of production, it was ignored by Russians.

In order to understand better what Russians, and above all those who were engaged in the Russian synthesis, understood by *marginalism*, the history of the reception of marginalism in Russia follows. In this story, Jevonsian marginalism is put aside on purpose, as it played, culturally and theoretically, the least important part. It had to wait for Marshall to make Jevons more appealing, most often through German mediation. Brentano, influential in Russia, incidentally prefaced the first German translation of Marshall's *Principles of Political Economy* in 1905. English marginalism therefore had to wait. This is not particular to Russia. At the same period in many European countries, marginalism was also a Continental affair.

In what follows, an overview of the spread in Russia of Austrian marginalism and of Walras is first given. Then the Russian reading of Walras's theory of exchange is offered in order to explain why and how his theory of production was in the end disregarded.

Reading Menger's scheme in Russia

When marginalism entered Russia in 1890,[3] it was already what Jaffé called a 'homogenised' version. It was the textbook version of the 'marginalist revolution' as the contemporary discovery of Menger, Jevons and Walras that was imported to Russia. Wieser had already provided such a story in the foreword to his *Natural Value* (1889), and here is how that story reappears in the *Brockhaus-Efron* encyclopedia, under the pen of Manuilov:

> Carl Menger, simultaneously with Jevons and Gossen, but quite independently from them, provided an explanation of the fluctuations of use–value in

relation to the amount of evaluated goods. At the basis of his theory lies the so-called idea of marginal utility.

(Manuilov 1903)

In Wieser's opinion, it was clear that Menger, Jevons, Walras *and* Gossen arrived at the same conclusions *independently*. But only Menger, Jevons and Walras did it *simultaneously*. In the above quotation, Manuilov's erroneous replacement of Walras by Gossen captures the spirit of the times: Walras is known from secondary sources only; and marginalism is an all-Austrian affair. A brief overview of the reception of Austrian and Walrasian marginalism follows.

Tugan-Baranovsky's very first paper, entitled 'Study on the Marginal Utility of Economic Goods as the Cause of their Value' was published in the Muscovite *Ûridičeskij Vestnik* (Legal Herald) in 1890. This first printed exposition of the theory of marginal utility in the Austrian spirit was followed by a few others in the 1890s: Zalesky (1893) and Orzhencky (1895). Many more appeared in the early twentieth century.

Tugan-Baranovsky's inaugural presentation well captures the overall tone of these works. According to him, the founding fathers of the theory of marginal utility are Gossen, Jevons, Menger and Walras (Tugan-Baranovsky 1890, 193). But after this mention, attention is focused on Menger, the 'most intelligible' of them, and his followers. Therefore, Tugan-Baranovsky's marginalism is unmistakably Austrian. He held their writings in high esteem. Menger is presented mainly through his most distinguished disciples, Wieser and Böhm-Bawerk, whose works form the main source of Tugan-Baranovsky's 1890 paper. An authorised translation of Böhm-Bawerk's *Kapital und Kapitalzins* was even supervised and prefaced by Tugan-Baranovsky in 1909.

According to Tugan-Baranovsky's presentation, subjective value is determined by human will, through the evaluation of the ability of a good to satisfy one's needs:

Only the theory of marginal utility explains the dependence between the value of goods and their ability to satisfy our needs in different degrees, in full agreement with facts.

(Tugan-Baranovsky 1890, 221)

These different degrees and scales were invariably represented by Tugan-Baranovsky as so-called 'Menger's schemes'. These played an important role in Russian literature. Within the Russian synthesis they were still important for Shaposhnikov, but their usage declined for the other mathematical economists.

Menger's schemes depict 'abstract' and 'concrete' utilities, often supplied with numerous examples to prove that the law of decreasing marginal utility is a representation of the general process of evaluation. Tugan-Baranovsky would have added in 1909 that this process of evaluation is the general case in which Weber and Fechner's psycho-physical law fits (Tugan-Baranovsky 1909, 60–68).

Table 3.1 Menger's schemes in Tugan-Baranovsky

I.	II.	III.	IV.	V.	VI.	VII.	VIII.	IX.	X.
10	.	.	.	.	.	.	.	.	.
9	9	.	.	.	.	.	.	.	.
8	8	8	.	.	.	.	.	.	.
7	7	7	7	.	.	.	.	.	.
6	6	6	6	6	.	.	.	.	.
5	5	5	5	5	5	.	.	.	.
4	4	4	4	4	4	4	.	.	.
3	3	3	3	3	3	3	3	.	.
2	2	2	2	2	2	2	2	2	.
1	1	1	1	1	1	1	1	1	1
0	0	0	0	0	0	0	0	0	0

Source: Tugan-Baranovsky (1890, 197).

His enthusiasm for Weber–Fechner seems to come from Brentano's *Die Entwicklung der Werthlehre* (1908).

Menger schemes appeared several times throughout Tugan-Baranovsky's writings. Table 3.1 is the first of them. It is strangely aligned in the bottom-line of the table. It shows, for good *I*, the 'concrete', i.e. cardinal, utilities (10, 9, 8, 7, ...) satisfied by the consumption of (1, 2, 3, 4, ...) units of it. The same applies for good *II* (9, 8, 7, 6 ...) etc. Then, following Gossen, one of Tugan-Baranovsky's heroes, the marginal utilities of two goods (say *I* and *V*) should be equal at equilibrium, implying for given prices and budget, that five units of *I* are consumed together with one unit of *V*. The concrete utility of the last unit of each of these consumed goods, i.e. their marginal utility, is equal to 6, whereas the total utility is equal to 46: the five units of good *I* ($10+9+8+7+6=40$) and the first unit of good *V* (6). Tugan-Baranovsky's exposition is developed at length using an Austrian vocabulary. It should be noted that the reference to Gossen was mediated through Wieser's *Natural Value* (1889).

It is further important to understand that, in a sense, Austrian marginalism was perceived as a development of the theoretical branch of political economy, in the same abstract direction towards which Ricardo conducted political economy in his time. Menger and Böhm-Bawerk were thus adopted for they improved *theoretical* political economy, leaving untouched other more applied branches, and Walras was later appreciated for exactly the same reason.

First Russian readers of Walras (1890–1919)

During the period 1890–1919, Léon Walras was not widely read in Russia. As already seen (Chapter 1 above; Zweynert 2002; Barnett 2004a, 2004b), the heavy influence of various strands of Historicism in the period under consideration is a major analytical element for the a priori rejection of the method used by Walras. Most economists were attracted by industrial and agrarian debates and by the fate of capitalism in Russia. The inductive method was perceived as more useful than pure abstractions to answer these important questions; in particular, the use of statistics within political economy was much more widespread than the application of mathematics to theoretical economics. Moreover, unlike statistics, but as in Western Europe, mathematics was not part of the syllabi of the Law Faculties where economics was taught (Karataev 1956, 209–210). For Shaposhnikov, the fact that 'Walras's works are similar in every respect, in form and in content, to mathematical treatises explains to a large extent why they are not yet estimated at their true value' (Shaposhnikov 1912b). The mathematical symbols played against Walras as they played against V. K. Dmitriev, who looked for a publisher for years. Lastly, Walras wrote in French, a language with which the Russian intelligentsia was no longer conversant at the end of the nineteenth century: German universities and academic literature were definitely favoured for stays abroad and serious analytical reading.

Yet despite this unfavourable context, Walras was read by some Russian economists. His name first appeared in 1890 in Tugan-Baranovsky's above-mentioned paper which introduced marginalism in Russia in its Austrian version (Tugan-Baranovsky 1890). It has to be noted that this is only the first time that the name of Walras appears for his works related to marginalism – his earlier 1860s works (especially on taxation) were already referred to in the Russian literature. This brief appearance was nothing but a passing reference, and it obviously originated from secondary literature, from Wieser's *Natural Value* (1889).

One year later, the journal *Russian Thought* published an anonymous review of the second edition of Walras's *Éléments* ([1889] 1988; see Anonymous 1891). Its tone is harsh since the author, obviously under a Marxist influence, rejects the marginal utility theory, the use of mathematics in economics and Walras's broad definition of capital (which also includes people). Nevertheless, this review is the first instance of Walras's magnum opus being mentioned and analysed in the Russian language.

In 1897, L. Winiarski published a panegyric of the use of mathematics in economics in the newly founded *Naučnoe Obozrenie* (Scientific Review) of St Petersburg. Winiarski provides a non-technical and worthwhile exposition of Walras's *Elements of Pure Economics* (Winiarski 1897). The paper is very much in favour of Walras's method and, for this reason, the editors of the journal added a warning at the beginning of the paper indicating that their viewpoint is different from their contributor's. The paper provides a mere description of the successive steps leading to the general equilibrium theory (exchange, production, capital formation). Winiarski published numerous papers on Walras, but his 1897 'Mathematical Method in Political Economy' is the only one to be published in Russian. Winiarski is probably Walras's most faithful proponent within Russian publications, but his paper seems to have gone unnoticed.[4]

V. K. Dmitriev's well known *Economic Essays* ([1904] 1974) also contain many references to Walras's *Elements* (first edition). In his first essay on Ricardo's theory of value, Dmitriev introduces in Russia Walras's unfortunate criticism of Ricardo (Dmitriev [1904] 1974, 51–52), with the aim of overcoming it (see below). In contrast, Dmitriev's third essay – on marginal utility – is more in favour of Walras, and credits Walras as being 'the creator of marginal utility theory' at least 'in its developed form' (Dmitriev [1904] 1974, 182). Walras's exchange equations and maximum conditions are commented on by Dmitriev in a spirit presenting Walras as a good economist, but certainly not the greatest of mathematicians.

E. E. Slutsky refers to Walras's *Elements* (1900, fourth edition) only in his 1910 master thesis. This work, entitled *The Theory of Marginal Utility*, includes many discussions on subjects such as hedonism, psychical phenomena, decision theory, Austrian theory of value, budget constraint and the theory of markets.[5] Slutsky analyses among other things the law of supply and demand and the theory of marginal utility on the basis of Walras's equations of exchange. In subsequent publications, Slutsky never came back to Walras. In 1910, as far as mathematical economics is concerned, Slutsky drew on Pareto's *Manuel*, Cassel and Wicksell more than on Walras. In his famous 1915 Paretian paper 'On the Theory of the Budget of the Consumer', Walras is not even mentioned. By the end of the 1920s, Slutsky was in correspondence with Frisch, and more inclined towards the econometric society and had moved away from Walras's already dated contributions.

Thanks to N. N. Shaposhnikov, Walras's theory finally entered into Russian encyclopaedias in 1912, more than twenty years after its first appearance in Russia (and long after Jevons and Menger). Shaposhnikov wrote an entry on Walras in the *Brockhaus-Efron Encyclopaedia* (Shaposhnikov 1912b), and a shorter one in *Granat Encyclopaedia* (Shaposhnikov 1912c). Both present Walras favourably as the modern representative of the mathematical school in political economy and the creator of a complete, almost definitive, subjective theory of value. Shaposhnikov is Walras's best promoter in Russia, and he is also much interested in Walras's *Elements* (fourth edition), to which he devotes the first chapter of his book *Theory of Value and Distribution* (Shaposhnikov 1912a).

In his first writings, the Bolshevist N. I. Bukharin demonstrates a thorough knowledge of his main opponent, i.e. bourgeois economic theory. It is common knowledge that Bukharin concentrated his efforts against Austrian subjectivism, but he did not do so exclusively. His *Economic Theory of the Leisure Class* (Bukharin [1919] 1927) mentions various writings of Walras.[6] He first became acquainted with Walras's works at the University of Moscow in the early 1910s at a seminar on value and distribution theories given by Shaposhnikov. He deepened his knowledge of Walras during his exile in Switzerland at Lausanne University Library (Bukharin [1919] 1927, 1).

The last commentator on Walras before the 1920s is L. N. Yurovsky, who wrote the *Essays on Price Theory* (1919) in which Walras's *Elements* (fourth edition) plays a significant role. His *Essays* described the most modern discoveries in the theory of prices and recounted its evolution from Ricardo to Walras.

A great Walras expert is missing from this account, mainly because his part in it is rather indirect. Nevertheless, Bortkiewicz contributed to some extent to the spread of Walras's works in Russia. Although he never published any of his works on Walras (or on economics) in Russian, he may have been a bridge between Walras and Russia through his personal contacts. His lengthy correspondence with A. A. Chuprov, a Russian colleague living, like Bortkiewicz, in Germany, tells us that Bortkiewicz's home was always open to Russian statisticians and economists passing through Berlin. Chuprov himself indicates that he read Walras and Pareto on Bortkiewicz's advice.[7] Bortkiewicz's correspondences with Slutsky, Chetverikov and Ptukha are replete with statistical discussions. More encouragingly, the letters from Shaposhnikov – the author of the entries on Walras – show that he met Bortkiewicz almost on a yearly basis in Germany in the early 1910s, and that they frequently spoke about Walras.[8] Hence, Bortkiewicz was perceived in Russia not only as a Ricardian proofreader of Marx, but also as a first class connoisseur of Walras. It should be remembered that, in the late 1880s, while still a student, Bortkiewicz was actively corresponding with Walras, and that the latter engaged him to support general equilibrium against Edgeworth's attacks.

Walras's exchange theory

To sum up, there were a handful of first-class economists who read Walras's *Elements* in Russia: Dmitriev, Slutsky, Shaposhnikov, Bukharin, Yurovsky, Winiarski, Bortkiewicz.[9] In what follows, their writings on Walras's theory of exchange are analysed around the following three thematic elements: pure economics and mathematics, *rareté* and exchange, and equilibrium and *tâtonnement*.

Pure economics and mathematics

The theory of exchange is the stepping-stone to Walras's pure economics, itself a component of his tripartite vision of political economy. In Part I of his *Elements of Pure Economics* (henceforth, all quotations to Walras *Elements* are taken from Jaffé's translation (Walras 1954), with references to Parts, lessons – L, and paragraphs – §) Walras outlines the distinction between pure, applied and social economics as the threefold consequence of the scarcity of social wealth: exchangeability, reproducibility and appropriability. Pure economics is concerned with the theory of value in exchange, applied economics with the theory of industry and social economics with the theory of property and distribution (L. 3).[10] As far as pure economics is concerned, the method is mathematical, since the value in exchange is a measurable magnitude (§30). For Walras, 'the mathematical method is not an *experimental* method; it is a *rational* method', drawing ideal types from real types, constructing a pure science without frictions 'which resembles the physico-mathematical sciences' (§30). The mathematical method is even, as Walras once wrote to Bortkiewicz, 'the rigorous and definite form of the deductive method in pure economics' (Letter from Walras to Bortkiewicz, 6 December 1887, in Jaffé 1965, letter 821).

Few Russians were concerned with Walras's original tripartite vision. Even if he focused mostly on pure economics, Bortkiewicz shared by the end of the 1880s the spirit of the Walrasian system: '[your] system is inherent to my way of conceiving the economic world' (Letter from Bortkiewicz to Walras, 13 September 1891, in Jaffé 1965, letter 1024). He equally shared his social programme (ibid., 12/24 April 1888, letter 829) – namely the collective ownership of land and rent – which explains, for example, his sympathetic understanding of the Walrasian trilogy in his review of the *Études d'économie sociale* (Bortkiewicz 1898).

Winiarski read Walras's pure, applied and social economics, but hardly commented on the links between them. Winiarski relies, for his own developments, on Walras's pure economics, but with the intention of reaching wider conclusions in the field of social economics. More succinctly, the author of the anonymous review asserts that Walras limited his investigations to the scientific part of political economy (Anonymous 1891, 22, quoting L. 2 of the *Elements*, on science vs art). For his part, complaining that bourgeois economic theory 'relegates production to the background', Bukharin erroneously confines Walras's treatment of production to applied economics only (Bukharin [1919] 1927, 55n). Yurovsky defines the role of pure theory within economic science: pure economics (which is not a natural science) is only useful as an auxiliary science helping to understand the logical structure of the working of a 'real-world' economy.

Besides these short comments (or, for Dmitriev, Slutsky and Shaposhnikov, the absence of comments), the status of pure economics within the Walrasian system was not debated in Russia. The *Elements of Pure Economics* were extracted from this system, separated from its applied and social counterparts, to become an independent system of *pure* economics (*theoretical* was the term used in Russia). This extraction of Walras's *Elements* is of course not specifically Russian.

Conversely, much ink has been spilled over the mathematical method used by Walras. Apart from the author of the anonymous review, for whom 'the diligent use of mathematical formulas doesn't spare Walras from a host of inconsistencies' (1891, 23), and Bukharin, for whom mathematics does not seem to be a major methodological issue,[11] the mathematical method was what attracted the Russians to Walras.

In 1887, Bortkiewicz complained that Russia remained 'totally foreign to recent advances in the theory of [the economic] science'. This science was 'dominated by the preponderant influence of German economic science' but Bortkiewicz remained confident in an upcoming reaction against historicism in Russia, which would introduce the mathematical method (Letter from Bortkiewicz to Walras, 10/5 November 1887, in Jaffé 1965, letter 818). Bortkiewicz was a supporter of this method, and he was eventually followed by a generation of Russian mathematical economists: Dmitriev, Slutsky and Shaposhnikov.

Winiarski completely embraces the mathematical method which was, according to him, initiated by Cournot and developed by Walras. His Russian paper begins with a very pedagogical, step-by-step apology for the use of this method in economics. In a very optimistic tone, he describes a three-stage theory of the evolution of knowledge:

> The first stage is purely qualitative, the second is already quantitative, i.e. mathematical, but not yet precise, and it is only at the third stage that

knowledge becomes exact. Astronomy has already reached the third stage [...]. Social sciences are still in the first stage, of which only political economy has started entering into the second.

(Winiarski 1897, 3)

Walras fully contributed to the transition to the second stage, and Winiarski without doubt hoped to push forward into it.

Throughout his *Economics Essays*, Dmitriev uses the mathematical method – sometimes even Walras's very notation – without exposing his reasons. Instead, he quotes some authorities inclined towards mathematics in the epigraphs to his first essay: Leonardo da Vinci, Kant, Carey, Wundt, Slonimsky, von Thünen and Cournot (Dmitriev [1904] 1974, 37). His only explicit statement about the mathematical method, directed towards a better distinction of genuine mathematical works from fake sophistic versions, is found in a footnote to a review article entitled 'Value Theory' published in 1908:

Under the mathematical method, the use of mathematical tools *in order to prove* a proposition of economic theory should be understood: the use of algebraic *notation* and even of a full set of formulas for the expression of *conclusions, that are not obtained by the mathematical method*, but by the usual logical and literal methods, doesn't make a mathematical theory and is not a sufficient reason to include such works (quite numerous in Russia) in the works of the 'mathematical school' in the established sense of the term.

(Dmitriev 1908, 25)

Slutsky studied mathematics, and for him, its usefulness within political economy seemed evident. Shaposhnikov claims to be part of the mathematical school (Shaposhnikov 1912a, ii), even if he uses symbols parsimoniously. Eventually, Yurovsky's position contrasts with Winiarski's optimism:

Political economy deals with magnitudes and in this meaning is a mathematical science. Approving this statement does not yet mean subscribing to the following words of Walras, according to which in the nineteenth century 'mathematical economics will rank with the mathematical sciences of astronomy and mechanics'.

(Yurovsky 1919, 71)

From this general outlook, it appears that most Russians read Walras's *Elements* because of its mathematical content, and not in spite of it.

Rareté *and the theory of exchange*

The cornerstone of Walras's theory of exchange is his notion of *rareté* (scarcity), which Bukharin expertly tracked down to the writings of Auguste Walras, the father of Léon. *Rareté* should not be understood in its common sense, namely the status of what exists in a small amount of quantity, but in the specific, scientific, sense as stated by Walras: 'In political economy, however abundant a thing may be, it is scarce whenever it is useful and limited in quantity' (Walras 1954, §22). This dual acceptation of the word was understood by Russians. They associated Walras's *rareté* with their *predel'naâ poleznost'* (which denotes marginal utility, and was introduced in the Russian language through the German *Grenznutzen*). The only exception to this rule was the author of the anonymous review, who rejects Walras's theory of value on the basis of an empirical example, wherein the prices of specific goods (gold, silver, platinum) were not proportional to their worldwide available quantities (Anonymous 1891, 22). Obviously, *rareté* was taken here as only 'limited in quantity', and not as something that is 'useful', in some intensity.

One of the most specific features of Walras's theory of exchange, as compared to other marginalist theories, is his construction from the value in exchange to *rareté* and from the effect to the cause (and not vice versa): Walras starts from the (ideal) fact of exchange, then constructs the effective demand and supply curves, from which he derives the utility (or want) curves, in order to prove that the satisfaction of wants is maximum when exchange prices are proportionate to the *raretés*. In other words, the cause of value (marginal utility) is scientifically derived, and not postulated, from Walras's ideal types of value in exchange (see especially §§40 and 101 of the *Elements*). If this fact is evident for Bortkiewicz – who even suggested to Walras some corrections to the *Elements* with regard to the utility curves and the conditions of the theorem of maximum utility of commodities – Winiarski and Dmitriev, it is not quite clear if this was always the case for Shaposhnikov, Yurovsky or even Slutsky.

Taken separately, these steps were understood by Russian readers. For example, Yurovsky fully agreed with Walras that even if 'intensive utility, considered absolutely, is so elusive, since it has no direct or measurable relationship to space or time', one just needs to 'assume that such a direct and measurable relationship does exist' (§74, quoted by Yurovsky 1919, 53). Yurovsky then supports the theorem of maximum utility (1919, 59), before presenting Walras's exchange equations and treatment of the law of supply and demand (1919, 80–86). His exposition follows a different order from Walras's. Slutsky (1910, 363–371 and 385–388) and Shaposhnikov (1912a, chap. 1) present the same interpretation.

Nevertheless, Russians retained the idea that 'values in exchange are proportional to the *raretés*', which they correctly associated with the 'last intensity of the last want satisfied' (Walras 1954, §100). This good level of understanding was facilitated by Walras's adequate use of well-defined terms, understandable to all: Bortkiewicz praises Walras's 'good choice of definition and economic concepts' (Bortkiewicz 1890, 80) while Yurovsky congratulates him for stressing the 'need for a definition of Political Economy' (title of §1 of *Elements*, quoted by Yurovsky, 1919, 3). The proofs of the theorem of the maximum utility, for example, are tackled without problem by Dmitriev, Slutsky and Winiarski, whereas Bortkiewicz himself contributed to its formalisation. Not all the technical details of Walras's demonstrations were understandable to all. Nevertheless, all understood that there exists a solution to a system of equations as long as the number of equations is equal to the numbers of unknowns.

These values in exchange possess a particularity: they are *equilibrium* values. In order to complete the discussion on exchange, and since the definitions of equilibrium are quite numerous, the next paragraphs detail some of the Russian interpretations of Walrasian economic equilibrium.

General equilibrium and tâtonnement

The notion of equilibrium – with general interdependence as a key feature – is inherent to Walras's conception of pure economics. The nature of his general economic equilibrium has been and is still subject to much speculation. Walras's own *Elements* underwent some substantial modifications on this theme between the first (1874–1877) and the fourth edition (1900).[12] Many significant issues gave rise to controversial interpretations, which involve the inseparable notions of equilibrium and *tâtonnement*: Is equilibrium reached, if at all, by *tâtonnement*? Does *tâtonnement* introduce dynamics into a static system, and so on. These questions are still debated today (see Baranzini 2011), and were already tackled by Walras and his contemporaries.

For Bortkiewicz, the question of exchange is addressed by Walras in purely static terms (Bortkiewicz 1890, 86). The role he assigned to *tâtonnement* is more ambiguous: on the one hand, it is 'the way of resolution of the equations', namely a technical problem coping with pure static economics; on the other, it is 'not a problem of algebra', but a 'real process, actually used in the market', depicting a necessary conceptual link between the real market and the theory.

For Winiarski, Walras's greatest merit was in producing the static equations of economic equilibrium. He hastened to add that 'it remains to constitute dynamic economics', and that he was about to accomplish this task with his *Mécanique sociale* (Winiarski 1900, 239). Walras's static equilibrium 'is an ideal state towards which the forces acting on the market are constantly moving closer, without ever perfectly reaching it' (Winiarski 1897, 12). Winiarski describes *tâtonnement* as a practical method used in the markets to solve a system of equations. It works as a 'mechanism consisting of the fall and rise of prices [...] until a single price is obtained for each good', and is 'superior in precision to what the most ingenious mathematician could do in his cabinet' (1897, 12).

For Yurovsky, Walras's greatest achievement was in embodying in a single theory the general interdependence of economic variables. The notion of equilibrium is central in Yurovsky's *Essays on Price Theory*; he tries to develop a typology of economic systems, starting from static equilibrium to dynamic equilibrium and cycle theory. Walras's exchange equilibrium belongs to static equilibrium, while cycle theory belongs to the notion of disequilibrium. There is therefore room for a pure dynamic theory in Yurovsky's typology. Static equilibrium studies the relation between supply and demand, while dynamic equilibrium incorporates the processes of production, distribution and accumulation of income. From this point of view, Yurovsky praises Walras's (unfortunately unsuccessful) efforts to build a pure dynamic theory in his lessons 35 and 36 (on the continuous market and the progressive economy). In this context, *tâtonnement* has nothing to do with theory, but with actual markets:

> In a real world market, the demand and the supply of participants are not precisely known; therefore, the approximation towards the equilibrium price happens by *tâtonnement*.
>
> (Yurovsky 1919, 145)

Yurovsky's understanding of *tâtonnement* is far from original, but apart from Bortkiewicz and Winiarski, this notion was completely neglected by the Russians.

For Shaposhnikov, Walras's greatest achievement is in solving the problem of value in its entirety: 'any theory which does not consider the relationship of dependency between the prices of goods can not claim a scientific completeness' (Shaposhnikov 1912a, 12). For Bukharin, 'Léon Walras's exchange equations […] are static', which is a fallacy, since they are unable to cope with social dynamics which are 'the most important problems of political economy' (Bukharin [1919] 1927, 60n). Dmitriev separates the real 'fluctuations' (the rise and fall of prices) from the theoretical 'equilibrium prices' (Dmitriev [1904] 1974, 145). Slutsky is only interested in the mathematical meaning of the equilibrium (Slutsky 1910, 369–371). The anonymous author does not even mention the word equilibrium.

From an overall point of view, Walras's theory of exchange was globally well received and understood by Russian economists. Its mathematical exposition did not put off its readers, and its status of pure economics fitted smoothly within their own various conceptions of economic science. The notion of *rareté* was correctly identified as the source of value in exchange. The general equilibrium was generally perceived as a static theory, and *tâtonnement*, if discussed at all, was relegated to a realistic market process.

Exchange without production

That reading of Walras's exchange theory is not specific to Russian economists. On the contrary, Walras's theory of production stimulated a peculiar reading, more precisely a non-reading. It is possible to split these Walrasian readers into two groups: those living in Western Europe (Bortkiewicz and Winiarski, the 'Continental Russians'), and those living in Russia. The second group shares a common non-reading of Walras's theory of production. Such an 'insular' reading is easily explained by the strong classical imprint prevailing in Russia (see Chapter 2). It is explained below that Walras himself was not completely foreign to the fact that his theory of exchange was adopted without his theory of production.

An insular reading: continental Russians v. Russians in Russia

Bortkiewicz's position on the matter may be summed up in one statement: 'we believe that the mathematical theory of production is feasible, as the theory of exchange' (Bortkiewicz 1890, 83). Bortkiewicz correctly felt the imbrications of Walras's theories, as 'a fortunate mathematical division of the problem, which consists in seeking successively the equilibrium of exchange, the equilibrium of production and the equilibrium of capital formation' (1890, 80). Even if he had many doubts about the theorem of maximum utility of new capital goods (see Bridel 2008, 725–729), he agreed with Walras's static theory of production and understood, in particular, the secondary – and not causal – role played in it by the costs of production.

Winiarski equally understood the overlapping nature of Walras's exchange, production and capital formation theories – the exchange theory considers the number of goods as given, while the theory of production determines that while considering the amount of capital goods as given, that being determined in the theory of capital formation (Winiarski 1897, 13–17). Despite his reservations concerning the applied significance of the general equilibrium because of historical monopolies, Winiarski noticed that all contradictions encountered in Marx's theory disappear with Walras's general equilibrium theory: 'there are no differences between value, prices and costs of production: they are the same!' (Winiarski 1896, 95).

For the Continental Russians, Bortkiewicz and Winiarski, Walras's theories of exchange and production are logically connected. For the other Russians, there is no theory of production at all. The author of the anonymous review rejects Walras's definition of capital and consequently does not even touch upon the theory of production. Bukharin notes that Walras treats the quantities of goods as given in his theory of exchange, and remarks that 'here again there is no thought of production' (Bukharin [1919] 1927, 56n). However, he seems to have forgotten to read Walras's theory of production. Slutsky mentions Lesson 20 of the *Elements* (Production equations) in a footnote as a curiosity (Slutsky 1910, 339). Dmitriev does not even mention Walras's theory of production in his *Economic Essays*.[13] Shaposhnikov, evoking the theory of exchange, comments: 'The possibility of modifying, through production, the quantity of goods entering into the market does not bring a tangible change. The condition of proportionality between prices and *rareté* of goods remains' (Shaposhnikov 1912b). Therefore, for Shaposhnikov, the production can be conceptualized in Walras's theory of exchange only as a non-disturbing external device modifying a mathematical constant, but not as a theory of production. Yurovsky makes no mention of Walras's theory of production, apart from a description of the types of capital and income (Yurovsky 1919, 205).

While Bortkiewicz and Winiarski accepted Walras's theory of production, the Russian readers totally ignored it. The reasons for such 'insular reading' are in the main found in the cultural environment in which these Russian economists read Walras. The association of production theories with the classical paradigm owes much to Ziber's objective reading of Ricardo and of Marx.[14] Furthermore, marginalism was already associated principally with exchange and not production, since the first Austrian texts, which were read *before* Walras in Russia, were associated with a 'catallactic' revolution, i.e. with a new theory of exchange. The spheres of exchange and production were largely separated: the first deals with a subjective theory of demand of which production was ruled out a priori, while the second was handled by the objective classical theory of value. There was therefore no oddity in seeing in Walras's work only a theory of exchange dealing exclusively with subjective demand. But there is yet another reason why the Russians favoured a *classical* theory of production, after having accepted Walras's theory of exchange, and this reason is to be found in Walras's own writings.

Walras's unfortunate criticism of Ricardo

There is a portion of Walras's *Elements* which immediately and almost systematically attracted the attention of Russian economists: lessons 38–40 (Walras's *Elements*, Part VII, Critique of Systems of Pure Economics) contain the expositions and refutations of the English theories of the prices of products, rent, wages and interest. Walras's circularity argument against the English school particularly attracted the attention of his Russian readers:

Let P be the aggregate price received for the products of an enterprise; let S, I and F be respectively the wages, interest charges and rent laid out by the entrepreneurs, in the course of production, to pay for the services of personal faculties, capital and land. Let us recall now that, according to the English School, the selling price of products is determined by their costs of production, that is to say, it is equal to the cost of productive services employed. Thus, we have the equation

$$P = S + I + F$$

and P is determined for us. It remains only to determine S, I and F. Surely, if it is not the price of the products that determines the price of productive services, but the price of productive services that determines the price of products, we must be told what determines the price of the services. That is precisely what the English economists try to do. To this end, they construct a theory of rent according to which rent is not included in the expenses of production, thus changing the above equation to

$$P = S + I$$

Having done this, they determine S directly by the theory of wages. Then, finally, they tell us that 'the amount of interest or profit is the excess of the aggregate price received for the products over the wages expended on their production'; in other words, that it is determined by the equation

$$I = P - S$$

It is clear now that the English economists are completely baffled by the problem of price determination; for it is impossible for *I* to determine *P* at the same time that *P* determines *I*. In the language of mathematics, one equation cannot be used to determine two unknowns. This objection is raised without any reference to our position on the manner in which the English School eliminates rent before setting out to determine wages.

(Walras 1954, §368)

Dmitriev himself quotes this entire passage (in Dmitriev [1904] 1974, 51–52) with the aim of proving that this argument is not imputable to Ricardo (see Kurz and Salvadori 2002). Under some assumptions, he succeeded in determining prices of production (*P*) that bypass Walras's criticism (Dmitriev [1904] 1974, 50–80). Dmitriev's equations were restated by Slutsky (1910, 376), Shaposhnikov (1912a, 41–46), and Yurovsky (1919, 100), ruining Walras's criticism of Ricardo. Moreover, Shaposhnikov rejected the criticism of circularity with the idea that costs of production and the prices of goods mutually influence each other, as in Walras's general equilibrium (Shaposhnikov, 1912a, 37–39). Yurovsky, for his part, was very interested in Walras's mathematical formulation of Ricardo's theory of rent (L. 39, quoted by Yurovsky 1919, 103–105): far from seeing it as a critique of Ricardo, Yurovsky, on the contrary, sees here a link between the English school and the 'school of Walras'.

Far from acting as a scarecrow, Walras's criticism of the English school had the opposite effect on Russians. They remained convinced, against Walras, that the analysis of the sphere of production, in the Marx–Ricardo line, had a solid future next to the analysis of the sphere of exchange, in the newer line of Walras.

Summing-up the two ingredients of the Russian synthesis

Marginalism appeared late in Russia in the 1890s. It was first the Austrian version of marginalism that attracted the attention of Russian economists in general, and of Tugan-Baranovsky in particular, who, as far as could be ascertained, never read Walras. But, from the beginning of the twentieth century, Russia provided Walras's *Elements of Pure Economics* with a fair number of readers until 1920, and in this regard, has nothing to envy from other European countries. These readers can be classified according to the environment in which they evolved. Bortkiewicz and Winiarski found no contradictions in Walras's pure system as a whole, and in particular between his theory of exchange and theory of production. The anonymous author was from the beginning against Walras, and Bukharin was only marginally interested in Walras, his true nemeses being the Austrians.

But a small group of economists, Dmitriev, Slutsky, Shaposhnikov and Yurovsky, offered a peculiar Russian reading of Walras's *Elements*. They completely adopted his theory of exchange, and at the same time completely neglected or even rejected his theory of production. These Russians were not willing to accept Walras's pure theory in its entirety: his theory of exchange was revolutionary, but perfectly fitted into their vision of pure economics. His theory of production was inconsistent with that vision. Hence, Russians gathered from Walras a general theory of exchange but not a theory of production. Furthermore, they adopted his idea of equilibrium and generalised interdependence. Eventually, most of them, Tugan-Baranovsky excepted, adopted his mathematical method. The integration of this subjective and mathematically-formulated theory of exchange into their objective theory of production is at the heart of their synthesis.

Protagonists of the Russian synthesis were keen to address theoretical issues, emancipating themselves from the heavy influence of the German historical school. They were confronted with the necessity of studying theoretical issues with the Marxian transformation debate. This led them to turn to the more abstract branch of classical political economy. This is why they read Ricardo *after* Marx.

They were convinced, within the classical theory of value, that labour value and costs of production were not competing theories but have two different domains of application. Ziber's influence on Russian economic thought is particularly strong on the protagonists of the synthesis.

Moreover, during these busy 1890s, at a time when faith in Marx was vacillating, marginalism entered the stage: the Austrians first, Walras followed (while English marginalists brought up the rear). Marginalism was welcomed by the critics of Marx as a useful complement. As a consequence, they retained from marginalism only a theory of exchange, and discarded the theory of production. Once again, each theory had its domain of application: the marginalist theory of exchange applied to the subjective side of their study; the classical theory of production to the objective side of their study of economic phenomena.

Difficulties arose when they tried to articulate both sides. They had to find a common language to render a dialogue possible between them. This is the research programme of the Russian synthesis, and the object of the second part of this book, starting with Tugan-Baranovsky and following with the mathematicians.

Notes

1 The history of mathematical political economy in Russia is better known. See Shukov (1988), Kljukin (2003), and Belykh (2007).
2 As for 'Soviet marginalism', or the rediscovery during the Soviet period of mathematical techniques at the margin in the context of planning and optimisation (Novozhilov, Nemchinov and Kantorovich), see Zauberman (1975) and Belykh (2007, chap. 3–4).
3 This is of course a useful fiction. The earlier reference to Gossen, the too slight interest in Cournot (Slonimsky 1878), and the fashion for von Thünen (Raskov 2008) have already been evoked in this sense. But this is a non-harmful fiction.
4 Léon Winiarski was a Polish sociologist teaching at that time mathematical political economy at the University of Geneva. He was in the early 1890s a student of Walras and Pareto, and one of Walras's rare disciples.
5 Slutsky (1910). This master thesis was awarded a gold medal. The manuscript is

deposited at the National Library Vernadsky, in Kiev, Ukraine. It was first published in a Ukrainian translation in 2006, then in Russian in 2010.

6 Bukharin never quotes Walras's *Elements of Pure Economics*, but instead the *Études d'économie sociale* (1896), the *Théorie mathématique de la richesse sociale* (1883) and the 'Principes d'une théorie mathématique de l'échange' (in *Journal des économistes*, 1874).

7 Letter dated 10 March 1898. The correspondence between Bortkiewicz and A. A. Chuprov (211 letters between 1895 and 1926) was published in Sheynin (2005).

8 Letter dated 12 July 1913. The letters sent to Bortkiewicz are kept in the Bortkiewicz Archives (Universitätsbibliothek Manuskript und Musikabteilung Kapsel 7) in Uppsala, Sweden. Sheynin published the letters from Chuprov and from Slutsky. Shaposhnikov's letters are still unpublished, but at the time of printing this book there is a project for publication by Petr N. Kljukin.

9 The fourth edition was the most widely read in Russia. Only Bortkiewicz and Winiarski, who knew Walras personally, as well as Bukharin, who came to Lausanne after Walras's death, read a larger corpus than the *Elements*.

10 For a more elaborate conception of the division of sciences in Walras's work, see Potier (1994).

11 Bukharin was trained in mathematics and was able to read easily the works of the members of the mathematical school and sometimes even used algebra himself when dealing with Marxian schemes of reproduction. He did not use the mathematical method as an argument for/against his opponents.

12 It is sufficient to read Jaffé's translator's notes (in Walras 1954) or Mouchot's 'Histoire des différentes éditions des Éléments d'économie politique pure' (in Walras 1988) to be convinced of this evolution.

13 To be precise, Dmitriev quotes a passage from lesson 22 (The principle of free competition), which is part of Walras's production theory, but only out of context, and in comparison with Cournot's and his own theory of competition (Dmitriev [1904] 1974, 149).

14 'Finally, the main argument against marginalism was that it did not fit with the tasks of political economy, understood as the identification of *objective* laws in the socio-economical field' (Makasheva 2009, 29).

References

Allisson, François. 2009. 'Reception of Walras's Theory of Exchange and Theory of Production in Russia'. *The History of Economic Thought*, 51(1): 19–35.

Anonymous. 1891. 'Review of *Éléments d'économie politique pure*, by Walras. 2nd edition, 1889'. *Russkaâ Mysl'*, 1: 22–24. Original and French translation available at http://francois.allisson.co.

Baranzini, Roberto. 2011. 'La concurrence et le tâtonnement à la lumière du réalisme walrassien. Une note sur les six premières sections des Éléments'. In Roberto Baranzini, André Legris and Ludovic Ragni, eds, *Léon Walras et l'équilibre économique général. Recherche récentes*, 153–167. Paris: Economica.

Barnett, Vincent. 2004a. 'Historical Political Economy in Russia, 1870–1913'. *European Journal for the History of Economic Thought*, 11(2): 231–253.

Barnett, Vincent. 2004b. 'Tugan-Baranovsky, the Methodology of Political Economy, and the "Russian Historical School"'. *History of Political Economy*, 36: 79–101.

Belykh, Andrej Akatovich. 2007. *Istoriâ Rossijskih èkonomiko-matematičeskih issledovanij (History of Russian Mathematical-Economic Investigations)*. Second edition. Moscow: LKI.

70   *The origins of the Russian synthesis*

Böhm-Bawerk, Eugen von. 1909. *Kapital i pribyl' (Capital and Interest)*. Authorised translation from the second German edition by L. I. Forbert, under the supervision and with a preface by Mikhail Ivanovich Tugan-Baranovsky. St Petersburg: Rozen.

Bortkiewicz, Ladislaus von. 1890. 'Review of Léon Walras, *Éléments d'économie politique pure, ou Théorie de la richesse sociale*, 2e édition, Guillaumin et Cie, Paris'. *Revue d'économie politique*, 4(1): 80–86.

Bortkiewicz, Ladislaus von. 1898. 'Review of Walras L. *Études d'économie sociale*. Lausanne–Paris, 1896'. *Jahrbuch für Gesetzgebung, Verwaltung und Volkswirtschaft im Deutschen Reich*, 22: 1075–1078.

Brentano, Lujo. 1908. *Die Entwicklung der Werthlehre*. Munich: Verlag der Akademie.

Bridel, Pascal. 2008. 'Bortkiewicz et Walras. Notes sur une collaboration intellectuelle avortée'. *Revue d'économie politique*, 118(5): 711–742.

Bukharin, Nikolay Ivanovich. [1919] 1927. *Političeskaâ èkonomiâ rant'e (Economic Theory of the Leisure Class)*. London: Martin Lawrence.

Dmitriev, Vladimir Karpovich. [1904] 1974. *Èkonomičeskie očerki (Economic Essays)*. Moscow: Rikhter. First essay published in 1898. Moscow: Moscow University. Second and third essays published in 1902. Moscow: Rikhter. English edition, Domenico Mario Nuti, ed., 1974. London: Cambridge University Press.

Dmitriev, Vladimir Karpovich. 1908. 'Teoriâ cennosti. Obzor literatury na russkom âzyke (Value Theory. Review of the Literature in the Russian Language)'. *Kritičeskoe Obozrenie*, VII: 12–26.

Jaffé, William. 1965. *Correspondence of Léon Walras and Related Papers*. Amsterdam: North Holland.

Karataev, Nikolay Konstantinovich. 1956. *Èkonomičeskie nauki v Moskovskom universitete. 1755–1955 (Economic Science at the University of Moscow. 1755–1955)*. Moscow: Izd. Moskovskogo Universiteta.

Kljukin, Petr Nikolaevich. 2003. 'Razvitie rossijskoj èkonomiko-matematičeskoj školy v pervoj treti 20 veka (Development of the Russian Economic-Mathematical School in the First Third of the Twentieth Century)'. In Y. V. Yakovec, ed., *Rossijskie èkonomičeskie školy (Russian Economic Schools)*, chap. 14, 256–307. Moscow: IFK-MFK.

Kurz, Heinz D. and Neri Salvadori. 2002. 'One Theory or Two? Walras's Critique of Ricardo'. *History of Political Economy*, 34(2): 365–398.

Makasheva, Natalia A. 2009. 'Kak maržinalizm prohodil v Rossiû? Dva èpizoda iz istorii (How Marginalism Settled in Russia? Two Episodes from History)'. *Terra economicus*, 7(3): 29–41.

Manuilov, Aleksandr Apollonovich. 1903. 'Cennost' (Value)'. In *Ènciklopedičeskìj slovar' (Encyclopaedic Dictionary)*, vol. 38, 326–330. St Petersburg: Brockhaus and Efron.

Marshall, Alfred (1905). *Handbuch der Volkswirtschaftslehre*. German translation of the fourth English edition by Hugo Ephraim and Arthur Salz, with a preface by Lujo Brentano. Stuttgart: J. G. Cotta.

Orzhencky, Roman Mikhajlovich. 1895. *Poleznost' i cena (Utility and Price)*. Odessa: Hakalovskij.

Pokidchenko, M. G. 2005. 'Social'no-èkonomičeskaâ mysl' Rossii serediny XVIII–načala XX v. (Social and Economic Thought in End of Nineteenth–Beginning of Twentieth Century Russia)'. In M. G. Pokidchenko, L. N. Speranskaja and T. A. Drobyshevskaja, eds, *Puti Razvitiâ èkonomiki Rossii: teorija i praktika (Path of Development of the Russian Economy: Theory and Practice)*, 11–128. Moscow: INFRA.

Potier, Jean-Pierre. 1994. 'Classification des sciences et divisions de "l'économie politique et sociale" dans l'oeuvre de Léon Walras: une tentative de reconstruction'. *Economies et sociétés, série PE (Œconomia)*. 20–21: 223–277.

Raskov, Danila E. 2008. 'Thünen's Economic Ideas in Russia'. In *Das Thünensche Erbe im Spannungsfeld zwischen Globalisierung und Regionalisierung*, vol. 9 of Tellower Thünen-Schriften, 35–57. Tellow, Germany: Thünen-Museum and Thünengesellschaft.

Shaposhnikov, Nikolay Nikolaevich. 1912a. *Teoriâ cennosti i raspredeleniâ (Theory of Value and Distribution)*. Moscow: Mysl'.

Shaposhnikov, Nikolay Nikolaevich. 1912b. 'Walras'. In *Novyj Ènciklopedičeskij Slovar' (New Encyclopaedia)*, vol. 9, 460–461. St Petersburg: Brockhaus and Efron. Original and French translation available at http://francois.allisson.co.

Shaposhnikov, Nikolay Nikolaevich. 1912c. 'Walras'. In *Ènciklopedičeskij Slovar' (Encyclopedia)*, vol. 7. Moscow: Granat.

Sheynin, Oscar B. 2005. *V. I. Bortkiewicz, A. A. Chuprov. Perepiska. 1895–1926 (Correspondence between Bortkiewicz and Chuprov, 1895–1926)*. Available at www.sheynin. de/download/9_Perepiska.pdf.

Shukov, N. S. 1988. 'Mathematical Economics in Russia (1867–1917)'. *Matekon*, 24: 3–31.

Slonimsky, Lûdvig Zinovevich. 1878. 'Zabytie èkonomisty. Tjunen i Kurno (Thünen and Cournot: Forgotten Economists)'. *Vestnik Evropy*, 9: 5–27.

Slutsky, Evgeny Evgenevich. 1910. *Teoriâ predel'noj poleznosti (Theory of Marginal Utility)*. Master's thesis, University of Kiev, Manuscripts section, National Library Vernadsky, Kiev, F. I, No 44850. Ukrainian published edition, 2006. Kiev: KNEU. Russian first publication, 2010. Moscow: Eksmo.

Slutsky, Evgeny Evgenevich. 1915. 'Sulla teoria del bilancio del consumatore'. *Giornale degli economisti*, 51: 1–26. English translation by Olga Ragusa, 1952. 'On the Theory of the Budget of the Consumer'. In George S. Stigler and Kenneth T. Boulding, eds, *Reading in Price Theory*, 27–56. Homewood, IL: Irwin.

Tugan-Baranovsky, Mikhail Ivanovich. 1890. 'Učenie o predel'noj poleznosti hozâjstven-nyh blag kak pričina ih cennosti (Study on the Marginal Utility of Economic Goods as the Cause of their Value)'. *Ûridičeskij Vestnik*, XXII(10/2): 192–230.

Tugan-Baranovsky, Mikhail Ivanovich. 1909. *Osnovy političeskoj èkonomii (Principles of Political Economy)*. St Petersburg: Slovo. Reprint of the fourth edition, 1998. Moscow: Rosspèn.

Walras, Léon. 1954. *Elements of Pure Economics or the Theory of Social Wealth*, translated by William Jaffé. London: Allen & Unwin.

Walras, Léon. 1988. *Éléments d'économie politique pure*, vol. VIII of *Auguste et Léon Walras oeuvres économiques complètes*. Variorum edition by Claude Mouchot. Paris: Economica.

Wieser, Friedrich von. 1889. *Der natürliche Werth*. Vienna: Hölder.

Winiarski, Léon 1896. '*Éléments d'économie politique pure*, par Léon Walras, 3 édit. 1896. Paris–Lausanne, Rouge, éditeur'. *Revue socialiste*, 24(139): 113–116.

Winiarski, Léon. 1897. 'Matematičeskij metod v političeskoj èkonomii (The Mathematical Method in Political Economy)'. *Naučnoe Obozrenie*, 4(XII): 1–24.

Winiarski, Léon. 1900. 'Essai sur la mécanique sociale. IV. L'énergie sociale et ses mensurations'. *Revue philosophique*. Republished in Giovanni Busino, ed., 'Léon Winiarski et la Mécanique Sociale', *Revue européenne des sciences sociales*, 14: 244–290. Geneva: Droz.

Yurovsky, Leonid Naumovich. 1919. *Očerki po teorii ceny (Essays on Price Theory)*. Saratov, Russia: Saratov University.

Zalesky, V. F. 1893. *Uchenie o proiskhozhdenii pribyli na kapital. Otd. I. Uchenie o cennosti (Study on the Origin of Profit on Capital. First Part: Study on Value)*. Kazan, Russia: Univ. Tip.

Zauberman, Alfred. 1975. *The Mathematical Revolution in Soviet Planning*. London: Oxford University Press.

Zweynert, Joachim. 2002. *Eine Geschichte des ökonomischen Denkens in Russland. 1805–1905*. Marburg, Germany: Metropolis Verlag.

Part II
The Russian synthesis

4 Tugan-Baranovsky on capitalism and socialism

> Is there really anything uglier than a modern city? One must have been in London and breathed its air, loaded with coal dust smoke that blackens the walls of homes and descends on the streets at times of fog. It is necessary to have breathed this air, to have seen this dirty gray liquid that flows into the River Thames ... to get an idea of what capitalism can do to a city. The countryside is no less spoiled by capitalism: it destroys forests, dirties rivers and obliterates the local flavours, destroys manners and removes national customs. Capitalism levels all things to the same uniform, drab and tasteless pattern.
>
> There is therefore no reason to be surprised that among the contemporary artists who think, among those who understand the close correlation between arts and the general order of social life, a particular trend came to light, which can be called aesthetic socialism, and is a protest against the capitalist order.
>
> (Tugan-Baranovsky 1913b, 33)

Mikhail Ivanovich Tugan-Baranovsky was a socialist and, as such, was convinced that the construction of a better world was possible.[1] Although he believed that future society would be concerned with the highest artistic, philosophical and spiritual issues, he thought that economic questions were more urgent and were a necessary prerequisite. He devoted most of his time and energy to the economic design of this future society.

Born in Kharkov province in 1865, Tugan-Baranovsky came to the capital, St Petersburg, in the 1880s to study natural sciences. He was involved in revolutionary circles and was even considered by the tsarist police to be the second-in-command of a secret group of students who intended to assassinate the Tsar. Tugan-Baranovsky was banished from the capitals (Moscow and St Petersburg) for several years and sent back to his province, while the group leader, Aleksandr Ulyanov (Lenin's elder brother), was sentenced to death and executed in 1887. This event affected Tugan-Baranovsky, who adopted a less clandestine attitude in his future actions. He continued his studies in natural sciences at Kharkov University and, in parallel, studied economics at the law faculty. His two Moscow dissertations – his 1894 master's thesis on the study of industrial crises and his 1898 doctoral thesis on Russian industrial history – gave him a solid reputation in academic circles.

Tugan-Baranovsky's academic career was both hindered and boosted by his socialist ideas. Institutionally, it was clearly hindered. He deserved a position as professor at the St Petersburg Imperial University, but some of his colleagues denounced him as too 'socialist'.[2] Therefore, he remained a *privat docent* (unremunerated lecturer) for years, desperately waiting for the confirmation of his professorship from the Ministry of Education. He was even sent back to his province again at the beginning of the twentieth century until after the 1905 revolution for political unreliability. But all these administrative annoyances only increased his popularity among his students. He was famous for the clarity and freshness of his lectures and seminars. One of his students, Klejnbort, recalls:

> Even while still a natural science student, I was addicted to his course. And not just because he could speak so vividly – economic categories accurately came alive through his clear and vivid description – or because the timbre of his voice was so sonorous and compelling, but, mainly because he taught us to think, he led us to the creative part of our minds.
>
> (Klejnbort 2008, 189)

He taught at the same time at various more liberal educational institutions, where he had greater freedom to organise his seminars. These were even open to external students, often his own students from the Imperial University. He published theoretical and critical works on Marxism, historical and positive investigations on socialism, books on the ethical foundations of economics, on co-operation, on money, on the history of economic thought, and more than 150 other articles. The diversity of his interests is best embodied in his textbook, *Principles of Political Economy* (1909),[3] which provided stimulation for a generation of Russian economists who were to play key roles in the construction of the Soviet Union during the *NEP* (New Economic Policy) period within the *Gosplan* (State Planning Committee) and the *Narkomfin* (The People's Commissariat of Finance).

His publishing career, and especially his textbook, guaranteed him a source of income superior to his academic wages and a large visibility, which was increased by his participation in many debates, especially within the Russian Free Economic Society and in the cooperative movement. This popular success is to be set against a kind of isolation at the theoretical level among his colleagues in Russia; some of his ideas survived better abroad. He was accused of being a socialist within the university. Within socialist circles, he was accused of being an anti-Marxist, while he felt himself nearer to Marx than his Marxist opponents.

In theoretical terms, and in order to build a socialist society, it was necessary, for him, to distinguish two kinds of economic laws: those working *only* under capitalism and those operating *even* in the future socialist state. This research led him to study in depth the workings of a capitalist economy, in order to separate what is *historical* from what is *logical*, according to his terminology. His comparative study of capitalist economies and socialist economies reveals the key categories allowing their interaction: the notions of *value* and of *prices* (see Chapter 5). It is only within this economic typology that his synthesis of the theory of marginal utility and the labour theory of value makes sense.

Tugan-Baranovsky's system of political economy was not conceived as, and cannot be interpreted as, a coherent whole. Nevertheless, a fundamental principle can be found in his work: a typology of economic systems, in which capitalism and socialism represent the highest dual terms. He studied various concepts – money, production, value and prices – under both systems and tried to impose a synthesis on his conclusions. In the special case of value and prices, his critique of capitalism and recommendations for building a future socialist society proved particularly fertile.

This chapter explains why Tugan-Baranovsky's work was often perceived as pure eclecticism. It focuses on the methodological viewpoint used in his works and explains his use of categories. It then points out, from Tugan-Baranovsky's criticism of capitalism, the economic categories that are relevant for his typology of economic systems. It introduces the notions of *proportionality* and of *economic plan*, characteristic of his work on industrial crises, but also of his thoughts on socialism. His own critique of capitalism is contrasted with that of Marx, thus analysing Tugan-Baranovsky's position on Marxism. Finally, Tugan-Baranovsky's attempt to provide a definition of socialism, from *utopia* to the socialist economic plan, is exposed. This provides the link between Tugan-Baranovsky's ideas on socialism and his understanding of the notions of value and prices, which will be the subject of the next chapter.

Methodology of political economy

> In memory of François Quesnay – creator of the 'Tableau économique', Hermann Gossen – originator of marginal utility theory and Karl Marx – the most profound critic of the capitalist regime.
> (Tugan-Baranovsky 1909, Dedication of *Principles of Political Economy*)

Tugan-Baranovsky always showed a great interest in economic methodology. His position on that matter, as will be expounded in this section, owes much to German *Kathedersozialisten*, especially to the younger historical school representatives such as Sombart. Moreover, his long-standing interest in Kant's ethics (through neo-Kantian mediations) also impacted on his conception of what the task of a scientist should be. Finally, Tugan-Baranovsky's shifting attitude towards Marx certainly provoked some confusion about his own position, albeit this has more to do with the *perception* of his evolving attitude. Indeed, he had a habit of synthesising what others found incompatible. The dedication of his *Principles of Political Economy* (1909) to Quesnay, Marx *and* Gossen (see above) gives a good illustration of his often misunderstood eclecticism. In his biographical tribute to Tugan-Baranovsky, Kondratiev explained this characteristic as the result of his master's curious mind, keener on reacting to actual and contemporary debates than on the construction of a single, internally consistent economic system (Kondratiev [1923] 1998). An even more generous qualification is given by Shirokorad:

> M. I. Tugan-Baranovsky [...] falls into that rare category of prominent people contributing to the development of world culture who, like Picasso or Stravinsky, were influenced by various styles and trends and yet did not remain within those frames but chose to recast them and create something perfectly new on the basis of their synthesis that could be sometimes mistaken as eclectics.
>
> (Shirokorad 2006, 439)

Tugan-Baranovsky nevertheless gave an overview of his methodological positions in 1908 in the journal *Obrazovanie* (Education) and, in a more developed form, in two chapters of his *Principles of Political Economy*.[4] While the present reconstruction does not give a complete view systematically applied to his investigations, it nevertheless clarifies Tugan-Baranovsky's overall orientation and sheds light on many of his motivations, in particular on his attempted synthesis in the field of the theory of value.[5]

Tugan-Baranovsky's division of the sciences first distinguishes between theoretical and practical sciences. *Theoretical sciences*, according to him, have two main tasks: (i) describing and (ii) explaining phenomena. For their part, *practical sciences* are always a means to achieve an end: (iii) they use the theoretical understanding of reality in order to transform it. Practical knowledge is ruled by a practical interest: in medicine, for example, the interest is the good health of the human being. Theoretical knowledge is ruled by a theoretical interest: the classification of insects is done by species, and not, for example, by distinguishing between dangerous, harmless, useful or beautiful insects, which would have been of practical interest for human beings (Tugan-Baranovsky 1909, 43). Economic science has both elements: the theoretical part is political economy and the practical part is economic policy. Ideally, political economy discovers what *is* and economic policy states what *ought to be*. In fact, as Tugan-Baranovsky recognises, it is more complex than this.

Theoretical sciences are subdivided into abstract and concrete components. *Abstract science* deals with the explanation of observed phenomena. In social sciences, deduction is the main method, in contrast to the natural sciences where experiments are available. The good use of syllogism, observed Tugan-Baranovsky, should not overlook the need for verification through experiments (Tugan-Baranovsky 1909, 50–56). Against his detractors, Tugan-Baranovsky claims that the deductive method is less abstract than is often thought. In economic theory, the typical man is not entirely abstracted from his context: he is inserted into a historical type of economy – an exchange economy and within a legal order – the Roman law – in which private property exists (1909, 53).

Concrete science is concerned with the description of phenomena, and this is a complicated task, given the diversity of reality. The scientist does not describe reality as a photograph does; instead, like a painter, he chooses which aspects of that reality to describe. And in order to choose what to describe, the scientist constructs a classification of appropriate categories for the object under investigation. The classification helps in collecting facts, which in turn improves the classification. This classification cannot but logically be distinguished from the observed phenomena: in other words, there is no such thing as a description without a point of view. Which point of view is political economy supposed to embrace?

In this regard, Tugan-Baranovsky's noteworthy example on wages is emblematic: wages are seen by the worker as an income, while it is only one expense of production among others for the capitalist (Tugan-Baranovsky 1909, 46–47). These two practical interests, arising from two points of view, are in conflict, and therefore should both be rejected, as should each class-based interest. The only acceptable point of view, which does not undermine the scientific objectiveness of knowledge, is ethics:

> By taking the point of view of ethics, we have the chance to rise above contradictory interests and find the universal practical interest that is a requirement for all humans endowed with a normal moral consciousness. The central idea in contemporary ethics was formulated by Kant as the idea of the supreme value, and consequently the equal value, of human personality.
>
> (Tugan-Baranovsky 1909, 47–48)

This practical interest – Kant's supreme value of human personality – is the only possible foundation for political economy for Tugan-Baranovsky. There is therefore a clear primacy for the practical interest: not only practical economic science – economic policy – but also the description of phenomena is ruled by ethics.

For Tugan-Baranovsky, what *is* and what *ought to be* have their role in theoretical economic science, as long as they strictly keep to their place: abstract political economy explains what is on the basis of the descriptions of what is and what ought to be from concrete economic science:

> Idealist and objective elements have their place together in economic theory only as long as the distinction in their natures is always clearly stated, as with water and oil in the same receptacle, which will not mix even if they are immediate neighbours.
>
> (Tugan-Baranovsky 1909, 57)

This reference to Kant shows how closely interrelated *normative* and *positive* economics are in Tugan-Baranovsky's political economy. Tugan-Baranovsky read Kant as a high school pupil, and his understanding of Kant seems linked to his reading of Dostoyevsky.[6] His theory of knowledge is drawn from the neo-Kantian philosophers of the so-called Baden or Heidelberg School, Rickert and

Windelband, who were widely recognised in Russia.[7] Barnett explains Tugan-Baranovsky's concern with ethics as resulting 'from his adherence to the current of neo-Kantian philosophy that was influential in socialist circles at that time' (Barnett 2004, 83). Makasheva (2008, 76) sees in the revolution of 1905 the trigger for Tugan-Baranovsky's clean break from materialism for idealism. Zweynert unveils an interesting insight on Kant and Tugan-Baranovsky:

> In his [Tugan-Baranovsky's] interpretation of Kant, he approaches the position of Mikhailovsky. In postulating the absolute value of human personality as the foundation of social sciences, he arrives [...] at the anthropocentric position, characteristic of the intelligentsia of the Russian left, which has always, in the last analysis, had a religious nature.
>
> (Zweynert 2002, 331–332)

It is perhaps better to characterise Tugan-Baranovsky's position in his own words:

> Kant's ethical point of view cannot be reconciled with Marx's a-moralist point of view. On this point, the new theory should strongly reject Marx and go with Kant, but the fact is that Kant's ethical ideas became a justification for socialism, while at the same time Kant drew from them the necessity of private property [...]. Therefore, Vorländer [The author of *Kant und Marx*, translated by Tugan-Baranovsky into Russian] is rejecting the slogan 'back to Kant'. But his own slogan 'forwards with Marx and Kant' incorrectly characterises the problems of our time. The slogan of modern socialists should be 'forwards to a new theory of socialism', and Kant and Marx have to stay behind as surpassed stages of social thought.
>
> ('Kant and Marx', in Tugan-Baranovsky [1912] 1996)

Tugan-Baranovsky's categories rely on the work of previous economists (mainly Rodbertus, Wagner and Dietzel, but also Schmoller, Knies, Hildebrand, Simmel, Stammler, Philippovich and A. I. Chuprov). The main object of study of political economy is the 'national economy' (*narodnoe hozâjstvo*), composed of interacting 'individual economies' (*edinicnoe hozâjstvo*) and their economic activities. An economic activity always takes place between the two poles of the economy – man and nature – and is always directed towards nature, in order to satisfy man. The individual economy is ruled by a master: human will. The national economy has no master, and depends on the interaction of the individual economies, linked by exchange and the social relations appearing through exchange. One of the most important tasks of political economy is to discover and explain the links between the individual and the national economy (Tugan-Baranovsky 1909, 30–33).[8]

What is the nature of these links? Political economy is a historical science, since it deals with a specific economy, i.e. exchange economy (Tugan-Baranovsky 1903, 8), but at the same time there are 'natural laws' governing the interaction of individual will in the national economy (Tugan-Baranovsky 1903, 5). Tugan-Baranovsky uses the expressions 'hidden mechanism' and 'natural effect' as synonymous with 'natural law'. For him, there are thus laws which are universally valid for all economies, independent of place, time or characteristics (legal, social…), and there are historical laws, valid for a type of economy, which are historically and even nationally located. In these considerations, Tugan-Baranovsky explicitly borrows from Rodbertus the idea of 'logical' and 'historical' categories of the economy (from the Preface of Rodbertus's *Zur Beleuchtung der socialen Frage*, 1875). A logical category of the economy is a notion valid in ancient Greece, in capitalism and in a future socialist society. A historical category depends on the particular social structure in place. For Tugan-Baranovsky, value and costs (as defined by him) are typically logical categories of the economy while the concepts of prices and wages are historical categories par excellence (see Chapter 5).

The coexistence of historical and logical categories within Tugan-Baranovsky's system invited him to conduct both highly theoretical investigations *and* statistical and historical research, often on the same subject. Sometimes, the link between them was not obvious, and it was not possible to claim that he achieved a synthesis. For instance, in his work on *Industrial crises in England*, historical statistical, social and theoretical investigations are separated in dedicated chapters. Robertson, in a review of Tugan-Baranovsky's *Crises industrielles en Angleterre* (1913a) – the French edition of his book on industrial crises – complained that these parts were not clearly enough articulated:

> there is a certain sketchiness about each of the three parts into which the work is divided, as well as a certain lack of cohesion between them.
>
> (Robertson 1914, 82)

For his part, Schumpeter praises his methodology and, rejecting Tugan-Baranovsky's work as a whole, takes only the parts he is interested in:

> The methodological aspect of his [Tugan-Baranovsky's] work is particularly interesting: he did much historical work of high quality; but he was also a 'theorist'; and he combined, or welded into a higher unit, these two interests in a way which he had learned from Marx and which was by no means common. From Marx, too, he had learned to theorize, though he experienced the influence both of the English 'classics' and of the Austrians with the result that his theoretical work in the end amounted to a 'critical synthesis'. [...] The only [...] item that need be mentioned out of what no doubt was an imposing total is the most important of all, for this did make a mark and did exert influence far and wide, viz., his history of commercial crises in England [...]. *Again, the first and theoretical chapter is a distinctly poor performance. The rest stands in the history of our science.*
>
> (Schumpeter 1954, 1126, emphasis added)

And even the theory of crises was composed of several elements, as Besomi (2006) recalled. One of these, the theory of the market, was discussed in the literature only by Marxists or critics of Marxism, while another, his theory of the periodicity of crises, was discussed or commented on exclusively by non-Marxist academics. This schizophrenic attitude towards Tugan-Baranovsky's work, i.e. the dispersal of parts of his work into separate sub-disciplines (crises theory, Marxist political economy), can be imputed to his desire to position himself against Marx, and also to the combination of the empirical and the theoretical in his works, which is in turn a consequence of his logical/historical categories. This, together with his taste for eclecticism, did not help his contemporaries understand his political economy.

But this coexistence of historical and logical categories was instrumental in permitting Tugan-Baranovsky to stay within the then dominant historicist paradigm while, at the same time, emancipating himself from it. It allowed him to incorporate, within the Russian debates, such oddities as Gossen's laws so that he could understand the English crises at the same level as a historical account of Chartism. The articulation of these various levels of explanation was not often provided, and when it was, was not always successful. But a notable exception can be made for value (as a logical and ethical category), prices (as a historical category) and their synthesis.

Critique of capitalism

> capitalistic economy [...] condemns the proletariat to excessive work and a miserable life.
>
> (Tugan-Baranovsky 1913b, 118)

Tugan-Baranovsky condemns the exploitation of workers by idle capitalists and landowners. He retraces, in *Modern Socialism in its Historical Development* (1910a), the sources of this exploitation.[9] Starting from Proudhon, one of his favourite authors, Tugan-Baranovsky sees in the anarchy of production the source of all the misfortunes of the working class. Incidentally, and as a critique of the capitalist regime, more than half of his celebrated work on *Industrial Crises in England* (1894) is devoted to the social consequences of crises. It contains statistics on deaths and marriages, careful descriptions of periods of starvation and mass unemployment and an analysis of their social and political consequences in England: strikes, social movements and the organisation of the working class around political parties.

Crises in the capitalist economy are explained by the absence of an economic plan at the level of the national economy. Each individual firm has full control over its own production plan but takes decisions without exact knowledge of the needs of society, or of the aggregate supply:

> Society needs a determined quantity of bread, meat, textiles, iron, glass, wood, etc. If the quantity of iron, wood or meat produced is greater than that required, the residue is – relatively at least – superfluous. Under the conditions

that lie at the bottom of the capitalistic system of the present day, this proportionality of the productive powers is carried into effect by the complicated expedient of the market, by the fluctuation of market prices.

(Tugan-Baranovsky 1910a, 178)

The absence of 'proportionality of the productive powers' in the various branches of the economy or, alternatively, the absence of an explicit economic plan at the national level is the cause of all fluctuations in the capitalist economy. And the profound reason for this disproportionality is to be found in the antagonistic nature of capitalism as an economic system.

In his typology (see Table 4.1), economic systems are classified according to their harmonious or antagonistic nature. They are further organised according to their level of economic development. In a harmonious economic system, the interests of one individual are in harmony with the interests of the other individuals. Such is the case in the primitive economy, with only a few means of production and no notion of private property, where only a few exchanges take place. This is also the case in the 'mercantile society', composed of small independent producers, owners of their own means of production (it is here implicitly inspired by Sismondi, whose work was well known in Russia). And this will be the case, as will be seen later, in the socialist economy.

The opposite occurs under slavery: some individuals – the slaves – are the property of others – the owners – as their means of production. Under serfdom, the masters have a right to some part of the labour of their serfs. Under capitalism, albeit legally free, the worker is deprived of the means of production and has to sell his labour power to the owners of capital. The antagonism of capitalism lies in the fact that the economy serves the interests of capitalists, and functions as an end in itself, not as a means to satisfy *all* individuals' needs. Production is not driven by consumption, but is conducted for its own sake.

Tugan-Baranovsky even supplied a proof, based on a hypothetical example, that capitalism could be self-sufficient (i.e. with capital and without workers), without needing to fulfil any social demands: a single worker could operate machines that produce other machines, and so forth, without any trouble of outlet. In his example (see Table 4.2), Tugan-Baranovsky introduced the canonical three-sector model (I. means of production, II. means of subsistence, or workers' consumption goods, III. luxury goods, or capitalists' consumption goods), and computed a three-period numerical example, where c = constant capital, v = variable capital and s = surplus value.

Table 4.1 Typology of economic systems

Antagonistic	Harmonious
Slavery	Primitive economy
Serfdom	Mercantile society
Capitalism	Socialism

Source: Tugan-Baranovsky (1909, chap. VIII).

Table 4.2 Unlimited growth in sector I

First period								
I.	1,632 c	+	544 v	+	544 s	=	2,720
II.	408 c	+	136 v	+	136 s	=	680
III.	360 c	+	120 v	+	120 s	=	600
Total	2,400 c	+	800 v	+	800 s	=	4,000
Second period								
I.	1,987.4 c	+	496.8 v	+	828.1 s	=	3,312.3
II.	372.6 c	+	93.2 v	+	155.2 s	=	621.0
III.	360.0 c	+	90.0 v	+	150.0 s	=	600.0
Total	2,720.0 c	+	680.0 v	+	1,133.3 s	=	4,533.3
Third period								
I.	2,585.4 c	+	484.6 v	+	1,239.0 s	=	4,309.0
II.	366.9 c	+	68.9 v	+	175.5 s	=	611.3
III.	360.0 c	+	67.5 v	+	172.5 s	=	600.0
Total	3,312.3 c	+	621.0 v	+	1,587.0 s	=	5,520.3

Source: Tugan-Baranovsky (1905b, 224–225; totals added).

The following assumptions are required to compute the tables, given that the first period only is known:

- Capitalists are satisfied with a consumption value of 600. This explains why the total value produced by sector III is stable (600) over the periods. Since total surplus exceeds the production of luxury goods for the capitalists (and therefore their possible consumption), the excess is invested, according to the next assumption.
- Capitalists decide to reduce the value of wage (v) by 25 per cent each year. The proportions between constant and variable capital change accordingly. This regulates the proportions between sectors I and II, following the rules of expanded reproduction.
- The increase in labour productivity, due to wage cuts, accounts for the rise in the rate of surplus value. Determined in the third sector, this new rate is valid for the whole economy.

From Table 4.2, it appears that sector I is growing (21.78 per cent and then 30.09 per cent), that sector II is declining (−8.67 per cent and then −1.56 per cent) and that sector III is stable. This allows Tugan-Baranovsky to claim that infinite growth in the first sector (means of production) is compatible with a decline in the wage goods sector (subsistence goods), without breaking Say's law (that production creates its own demand).

Tugan-Baranovsky is famous in the Marxist literature for being the first, according to Howard and King (1989, 168–169), to make analytical use of Marx's reproduction schemes. He was the first to use them in the context of the transformation problem, and for the analysis of the law of the tendency of the rate of profit to fall. Thus he paved the way for the large amount of numerical and later algebraical uses of these schemes by various authors, from Bukharin to Bortkiewicz through Luxemburg (to evoke only contemporaries).

The example given in Table 4.2 first appeared in 1904 in the German journal *Archiv für Sozialwissenschaft und Sozialpolitik* (1904, 284–285), then in *Theoretical Foundations of Marxism* in both Russian (1905a, 205–206) and German (1905, 224–225) editions (the Russian edition contains typos on this very table).

Tugan-Baranovsky's intention in these schemes was only to dismiss *in abstracto* the Sismondist underconsumption theory which was popular in Russia at this time, and certainly not, as was often over-interpreted (see, for instance, Luxemburg [1913] 1951, chap. 23), to provide a realistic interpretation of the future of capitalist society doomed to machinery without human beings. With this example, among others, Tugan-Baranovsky alienated most Marxists. But for him, unlimited reproduction would only have been a theoretical possibility, *given that proportionality is enforced* between sectors I and II above.[10] Nothing guarantees that this would happen, since it requires more than simple coordination between capitalists; it necessitates *planning*:

> In my 'Theoretical Foundations of Marxism', I provide schemes on accumulation of capital on the hypothesis of an absolute reduction in social consumption. In the end, there are no excess products, for the reason that the reduced demand on the means of consumption is balanced by an increased demand for the means of production. One can ask what the use of these means of production will be, if the demand for consumption decreases. The answer is not difficult. Means of production will be used on the production of more and more new means of production. Let us suppose that all workers but one are replaced by machines. This unique worker will then drive the colossal mass of machines and he will produce with them new machines and means of production for the capitalist class. The working class would have disappeared, but it does not matter for the outlets for the capitalist industry products. [...]
>
> It is even possible that driven by their passion for accumulation, capitalists might want to reduce their own consumption. In this case, the production of means of consumption for capitalists will reduce, and an even larger part of social production will be composed of means of production designed for their subsequent extension of production [...].
>
> Production will have, in this case, the sole purpose of the accumulation of capital. The capitalist will be like the miser, who lays up treasures which he does not actually enjoy, but which he could use at any moment in time if he so desires. Whenever he wants, he can always stop this process of capital accumulation and enjoy the colossal productive forces at his disposal thanks to previous accumulation, and produce means of consumption for himself: palaces and silks instead of coal and iron. All this may seem weird, and one can find this absurd. This is possible. Truth is not always easily accessible to the mind; it is nevertheless the truth. Needless to say that by truth, I mean not this arbitrary assumption which does not correspond to reality, according

to which the replacement of the worker by the machine may cause the virtual elimination of the workers (I used this assumption to show that my theory holds true even in its most extreme deductions), but the thesis that, with a proportional distribution of social production, no reduction in social consumption can cause the formation of excess production.

(Tugan-Baranovsky 1913a, 216–217)

Therefore the key concept which explains why capitalism should not work in practice is *disproportionality*; and this internal contradiction creates the possibility of crises, which happen naturally and periodically in capitalist economies:

Crises are inherent in the very nature of capitalist economies. Their necessary nature results from three characteristics of the capitalist economic system: (1) it is antagonistic, in that the worker is a simple means of production for the capitalist firm; (2) unlike other antagonistic economic systems, it tends to unlimited expansion of production (as a means of capital accumulation); and (3) as a whole, it is a disorganized economy, in which a planned distribution of social production between the different industrial sectors is lacking. On the basis of these three characteristics of the economic system, capitalism inevitably provokes economic crises. The frequency of crises is due to the fact that free capital in capitalist economies does not accumulate initially in industry, but is first held up in the banks. During industrial recovery, banks have enough of it. When capital runs out, a crisis follows.

(Tugan-Baranovsky 1915, 353)

But crises are only cyclical deviations from equilibrium[11] and capitalism will not disappear because of them. Capitalism is not threatened by these internal and mechanical contradictions. Rather, it should be replaced by the human will – the power of the mind – because it does not follow the ethical ideal: capitalism does not allocate the productive forces according to human needs, but according to the interest of specific social classes, the owners of the means of production who are exploiting the working class. Capitalism causes disproportionalities and crises, and the working class suffers from this exploitation. Socialism, in contrast, should be consciously established in order to reconcile the constraints of production with the needs of society.

The decisive criterion for reconciling the economic interests of individuals is, for Tugan-Baranovsky, the ethical ideal of the equal value of human beings. Capitalism is mistaken, since it confuses the means and the end – whereas the economy should only be a means to achieve human ends. The economy is located between the two sides of life: the materialist forces – production, and the psychological forces – human needs, or demand. By postulating that the two forces, materialistic and psychological, drive history Tugan-Baranovsky moves further away from Marxism and paves the way for utopia to enter the stage.

Critical foundations of Marxism

But it must not be forgotten that Marxism was the chief formative influence on practically all the Russian economists of the age. Marx was the author they really tried to master, and the Marxist education is obvious even in the writings of those who criticized Marxism adversely. The most eminent of these semi-Marxist Marx critics was Tugan-Baranowsky.

(Schumpeter 1954, 879)

The relations Tugan-Baranovsky maintained with Marx are complex. For instance, his 1899 paper 'The Fundamental Error in Marx's Abstract Theory of Capitalism' (1899a) starts with a global appraisal of Marx: 'Marx's economic and sociological system should be fully recognised as the most outstanding product of humankind's thought on the understanding of social phenomena' (Tugan-Baranovsky 1899a, 973). But a few lines later, he calls for the necessity, after Sombart, to assess Marx's ideas from a scientific point of view: 'It is necessary to go beyond Marx, but by means of Marx, incorporating in the process all that he gave us' (Tugan-Baranovsky 1899a, 974). In the light of his first clearly polemical paper and also as a consequence of the following works, most notably the paper 'Labour value and profit' (1900) and the book *Theoretische Grundlagen des Marxismus* (1905a, b),[12] Tugan-Baranovsky was rightly ranked among the Marxist revisionists, or Legal Marxists. Among these academic thinkers, Tugan-Baranovsky was the one who looked with the greatest care at Marx's economic writings; the others were more concerned with his philosophy, history and politics. Tugan-Baranovsky's criticism falls into two broad domains: the materialist understanding of history and the theory of value.

Tugan-Baranovsky thought that Marx explained historical change by means of the materialist side of economic life and missed the psychological side. For him, living productive forces are not exclusively accounted for by a 'capacity to produce', but also have a developing social 'consciousness', that he did not find in Marx. Class struggle is intelligible only with the idea of a developing social and class consciousness, and people's needs are to be understood as the driving force of their production capacities. This omission, according to Tugan-Baranovsky, is at the source of the narrow view Marx took towards exchange compared with production. For Tugan-Baranovsky, production is the domain of the predilection of objective materialist forces, while exchange naturally expresses subjective psychological needs (Tugan-Baranovsky 1905a, b, chapters I–V).

More directly relevant to the present investigation, Tugan-Baranovsky gradually rejected Marx's labour theory of value in several steps:

1   He showed that ill-conceived notions of exploitation and labour productivity were at the basis of Marx's law of the tendency of the rate of profit to fall (Tugan-Baranovsky 1899a and 1900).
2   He showed that there was an incompatibility between the theory of value described in volume I of *Capital* with the theory of prices in volume III. Because his goal was to explain *prices*, he did not consider abandoning

volume III but proposed instead to abandon the labour theory of value and surplus value (Tugan-Baranovsky 1899a; 1905a, b, chap. VII).

3   He offered a new terminology (absolute value *vs* absolute costs, see Chapter 5) as a way to 'rescue' Marx's theory in a sociological – not economic – sense (Tugan-Baranovsky 1905a, b, chap. VI; 1909, chap. 3–4).

First, Tugan-Baranovsky established that the law of the tendency of the rate of profit to fall is flawed. The capitalist mode of production surely implies a tendency for the organic composition of capital to rise, i.e. for there to be a rising share of constant capital in the whole (constant + variable) invested capital. But for him this does not lead to a diminishing rate of profit. There is first 'common sense': why would capitalists replace workers with machines if this implies a decline in profit? Here Tugan-Baranovsky falls into the common error pointed out by Ziber (in Chapter 2 above): he confuses the individual with the social economy. But he has also an analytical argument, as shown in Table 4.3.

It should be noted that this example is based on nominal prices, but that Tugan-Baranovsky's terminology includes a rate of profit in value and a rate of profit in prices; a rate of exploitation in value and a rate of exploitation in prices. In Table 4.3, the replacement of workers by machines from period I to period II *does* increase labour productivity and, as a consequence, the rate of exploitation (from 100 to 200 per cent). The rate of profit remains constant (66.6 per cent) and Marx's implicit assumption of a constant rate of exploitation with a declining rate of profit does not hold. Therefore, the law of the tendency of the rate of profit to fall, present in volume III of *Capital* has to be abandoned. Tugan-Baranovsky has only one doubt: had Marx published this volume himself, would he have changed anything?

> I have only one doubt on this: did Marx believe in this? The manuscript of the third volume of *Capital* was not prepared for publication by Marx, and, in the first two volumes, there is apparently no single mention of this law. At the same time, if the law of the falling rate of profit was to be considered as correct, it would be so important that Marx would have used it in the first volumes of *Capital*. It seems to me most likely that Marx would not have included this law [...] because it opposes the labour theory of value.
>
> (Tugan-Baranovsky 1900, 620)

Table 4.3 The increasing rate of profit

Period	Constant capital	Variable capital	Profit	Total	Rate of profit	Rate of exploitation
I.	100	200	200	500	66.6%	100%
II.	200	100	**200**	500	66.6%	200%

Source: Tugan-Baranovsky (1899a, 979–982).

Note
These numbers and the rates are found in the text, not in the form of a table.

Second, Tugan-Baranovsky tackled the 'inverse transformation problem', which was so called by Bortkiewicz since it consists of finding a system of value and a rate of surplus value on the basis of a given system of prices together with a given uniform rate of profit. The inverse transformation problem transforms prices into values, which is exactly the reverse of what Marx was trying to do. Tugan-Baranovsky provided a solution to this problem that attracted Bortkiewicz's attention (Dostaler 1978, 100–105; Jorland 1995, 265–268). This solution was published in 1905 by Tugan-Baranovsky (Tugan-Baranovsky, 1905a, b, chap. VII), but a sketch of it was already present in his 1899 article (1899a). Table 4.4 contains the original system in prices, while Table 4.5 contains the transformed system in values.

In Table 4.4, the rate of profit in prices is equal for all sectors ($\pi = 25$ per cent) as required by Marx, and the rate of exploitation in prices is variable (100 per cent in sector I, 50 per cent in sector II, 41.6 per cent in sector III). Starting from this system in prices, Tugan-Baranovsky computed a system of value, as given in Table 4.5.

In Table 4.5, the rate of exploitation (in value terms) is equal in all sectors (66 per cent), and the rate of profit (in value terms) is again variable (19 per cent in sector I, 36.36 per cent in sector II, 42.86 per cent in sector III). Let us have a look at this solution in five points.

1 There are different organic compositions of capital, as in Marx's solution.
2 Tugan-Baranovsky ignored fixed capital (whereas Marx tried with difficulty to consider this point). This will be of no consequence to the reasoning, but this was not known at that time (Dostaler 1978, 100).
3 The two equalities (between total profit and total surplus value, and between total prices and total values) are not obtained. Bortkiewicz will eventually show that choosing sector III as numeraire would already solve one equality, and that the second could also be solved by accident, if correct numbers

Table 4.4 Original scheme in prices

I.	180 c	+	60 v	+	60 s	=	300
II.	80 c	+	80 v	+	40 s	=	200
III.	40 c	+	60 v	+	25 s	=	125
Total	300 c	+	200 v	+	125 s	=	625

Source: Tugan-Baranovsky (1905a, 155; also in 1905b, 171; totals added).

Table 4.5 Transformed scheme in values

I.	225 c	+	90 v	+	60 s	=	375
II.	100 c	+	120 v	+	80 s	=	300
III.	50 c	+	90 v	+	60 s	=	200
Total	375 c	+	300 v	+	200 s	=	875

Source: Tugan-Baranovsky (1905a, 157; also in 1905b, 173; totals added).

were chosen. More importantly, he will point out that these equalities are not a necessary condition for what they were intended to be: to show that the whole surplus value is distributed among capitalists in the form of profits (Bortkiewicz 1906–1907, II).

4   This is, as already mentioned, an inverse transformation procedure, which contradicts Marx's intentions to show that surplus value is hidden behind the appearance of profit.

5   Finally, Tugan-Baranovsky's original titles for the tables were 'Reproduction and distribution of the social income in monetary prices/labour value'. Therefore, and for the first time in the literature, the conditions of reproduction as stated in volume II of *Capital* are combined with the transformation procedure as described in volume III. The constraints of simple reproduction that Tugan-Baranovsky imposes on himself (in both tables, the sum of line i is equal to the sum of column i, for $i=1, 2, 3$), were not present in Marx. This implies that what is sold by one sector is bought by the three sectors at the same value (in the values scheme) and at the same price (in the prices system). Tugan-Baranovsky transformed all inputs, and not just profits, into surplus value here.[13]

With these elements, Tugan-Baranovsky shows that it is possible to have a consistent system of value and prices. But this system contains no explanation of the source of profit being surplus value and, more generally, it contains no assertion that labour value explains the real exchange relationship. Thus, for Tugan-Baranovsky, the labour theory of value does not explain exchange value, and is therefore only a *fiction*.

But, and this is the third point, it is a *useful fiction*. For Tugan-Baranovsky, value must, for etymological reasons, be linked to an *evaluation*,[14] which is exclusively subjective for him.[15]

The theory of exploitation and surplus value seems appealing, but cannot be integrated into economic theory. It is however extremely useful in the field of sociology, where there is distribution of social income. Exploitation is an empirical notion only and explains neither profit nor prices.

To sum up: if capitalism can survive with its internal contradictions, if the rate of profit is not a threat to its long term development since it will not necessarily fall, if exploitation is not linked to value and is unable to explain market prices, and if the labour theory of value does not survive, it seems that there remains almost nothing of Marx's critique of political economy.

But it will soon be seen that Marx is more present than Tugan-Baranovsky is ready to admit. The critique of the capitalist system remains. The capitalist system is unable to maintain a sound *proportionality*, giving an impetus to the 'psychological forces', which are themselves trying to move history forwards. The theory of socialism is not far away from a critique of the actual economic system, and Tugan-Baranovsky would even find a way to reintroduce a 'labour theory of value' with his notion of absolute costs, but does so in association with Kant, in line with his characteristic synthetic eclecticism.

Socialism: towards a better future

The book now put before the reader has another aim: a succinct critical exposition of the essential tenets of modern Socialism as a definite social doctrine. And taking into consideration that Marxism, as I strongly believe, does not embrace all the scientific elements of Socialism, my investigation necessarily assumed an historical character in so far as I was obliged to retrospect and introduce earlier, partly forgotten doctrines of the so-called *Utopian* category, which I consider deserving of the most serious attention and which in some respects are even more scientific than Marxism.

(Tugan-Baranovsky 1910a, vi)

At the turn of the twentieth century, various conceptions of socialism were encountered in Russia. Supporters of Marx were as numerous in the various strands of society as interpretations of the Prophet's writings. The conservative Populist Voroncov, for instance, saw in Marx's description of the nightmare of English capitalism an analytical instrument to help Russia avoid this difficult transition. He tried to establish the impossibility of the growth of capitalism in Russia, and advocated a promising agrarian socialism based on the mythic and deep-rooted rural collectivist community – the *obshchina*.[16] Against these ideas, considered by their opponents as primitive and ignorant of the materialistic forces of history, another reading of Marx proposed by (among others) Plekhanov and Lenin, promoted a proletarian revolution. Although they disagreed later on whether the proletarian revolution should be preceded by a bourgeois revolution (the famous Bolshevik–Menshevik divide), these authors were unified against the Populists. Around these mainstreams towards socialism, other conceptions of socialism coexisted in the Russian debates, including non-Marxist ones. Besides Bulgakov's Christian socialism and Kropotkin's anarchist socialism, Tugan-Baranovsky's ethical socialist system demonstrates interesting insights, in that it mixes economic theory and ideas of utopia.

Tugan-Baranovsky's first publications (especially his doctoral dissertation *The Russian Factory*, 1898) were directly intended to refute the Populists' argument that capitalism could not take root in Russia. He showed, in particular, that industrialisation had a longer history in Russia than was often thought and that, albeit the State was strongly implicated in that history, industry was not foreign to the Russian economy. In the aftermath of his master's thesis *Industrial crises in England* (1894), he even pointed out that fluctuations, which were the symptoms of an industrial state, were appearing in Russia, just as they did earlier in England (Barnett 2005). Tugan-Baranovsky was at that point a member of the informal group named 'Legal Marxism' (together with Struve, Bulgakov, Frank and Berdiaev), which, during the 1890s, was in the same camp as Lenin and his *Development of Capitalism in Russia* ([1899] 1960), united against the Populists. Later on, however, Tugan-Baranovsky evolved from Marxism to some kind of ethical socialism of his own: he borrowed, from his reading of Kant, the ethical idea of the supreme and equal value of all human personalities, and placed it at the heart of his system.

Tugan-Baranovsky's socialism has already been the object of careful investigations.[17] In this chapter, an interpretation of his ideas on socialism is drawn from the perspective of utopia to value theory.[18] It suggests investigating the nature of the relationship between utopia and science within economic theory as a first step, and locating the role of the theories of value and prices within socialism and economic planning as a second step. The present reconstruction of Tugan-Baranovsky's socialist system consciously follows the three-step plan prescribed by him:

> Every accomplished social system consists of three parts: of the criticism of the existing social conditions, of a determined conception of the future organization, and of considerations regarding the ways and means by which its principles are to be carried out in actual fact.
>
> (Tugan-Baranovsky 1910a, 185)

Accordingly, the previous sections of this chapter contained Tugan-Baranovsky's 'criticism of existing social conditions', i.e. his critique of capitalism as an antagonistic economic system. It outlined his distance from Marxism and revealed essential notions of his socialist system: the ethical ideal and proportionality in the economic plan.

Tugan-Baranovsky's attempt to define the nature and goals of socialism are first examined. His 'determined conception' of what the future system should be will be considered together with his sources of inspiration, which owe a heavy debt to the theme of *utopia*. His definition of socialism is therefore reconstructed in line with the three notions mentioned above. Then, the 'consideration of the ways and means by which its principles are to be carried out in actual fact' are examined.

Socialism between utopia and science

In his quest for a definition of socialism and for the design of a socialist system, Tugan-Baranovsky makes abundant use of the writings of so-called utopian socialists, that he considers 'deserving [of] the most serious attention and which in some respects are even more scientific than Marxism' (Tugan-Baranovsky 1910a, vi). He remarks that the *Communist Manifesto* is almost entirely composed of claims that were formulated by earlier – so-called Utopian – socialists. Science and utopia are complementary:

> The opposition of science and utopia is untenable in the sense that science and utopia are not necessarily contradictory concepts. Utopia is not absurd or ridiculous. Utopia is an ideal. Every ideal contains something unfeasible, infinitely distant and unattainable, a dream; some of our inherent spiritual nature has the desire to leave the limits of the possible, to rise above the world of phenomena. [...] An ideal is unattainable, because otherwise it would not be an ideal, but a simple empirical concept. [...] An ideal plays the role of a star, thanks to which a stray night traveller chooses his road

[…]. Far away, the beautiful star indicates the true path, but it does not replace the convenient and mundane lantern.

If an ideal can be compared with a star, science plays the role of a lantern. With a lantern, not knowing where to go, one does not find the true path, but without a lantern at night one risks breaking his neck. The ideal, as well as science, is equally necessary for life. The ideal gives us the supreme goal for our activities; science shows the means for implementing these objectives and provides us with a correct criterion for determining what is feasible in our goals, and to what extent.

(Tugan-Baranovsky [1912] 1996, 86)

The ideal implies a profound modification of actual society and, in his analysis of various utopian schemes, Tugan-Baranovsky shows that the utopian authors clearly understood that human nature is controllable: with their new plan of society, they try to build a new man. In Tugan-Baranovsky's *Modern Socialism in Historical Perspective* (1910a), the plans of Bellamy, Blanc, Cabet, Fourier, Godwin, Kropotkine, Owen, Pecqueur, Proudhon, Rodbertus and Saint-Simon are scrutinised. These works provide him with interesting material for thinking about the future society and its new man.

Cabet helps in understanding the idea of the boredom of a society composed of integrally equal men, while Godwin furnishes a better picture of the new man. Concerning the question of economic equality, the plans of Blanc and Owen are rejected by Tugan-Baranovsky, as they promote inequality and, therefore, do not achieve the socialist ideal. Saint-Simon requires 'such an iron discipline to which the labourer of our days, with his love and freedom, would by no means willingly submit' (Tugan-Baranovsky, 1910a, 116) and is, therefore, criticised. Rodbertus is equally criticised for his system of distribution. Tugan-Baranovsky shares with Fourier a faith in the increasing social productivity of labour but does not explain how this could be compatible with freedom. Kropotkine oscillates on this point between freedom and violence. Bellamy is the only one who offers interesting commentary on the 'choice' of a profession; and Proudhon explains his innovative idea of a new organisation of exchange. However, the author that gains the most support from Tugan-Baranovsky is Pecqueur and his most harmonious reconciliation between individual freedom and the social organisation of labour.

These authors are, however, often mistaken, according to Tugan-Baranovsky, when they forget to analyse a few of the significant external constraints that are particularly under the scrutiny of political economy. Utopia and the science of political economy must therefore converse, in order to approach the socialist ideal, which Tugan-Baranovsky defines as follows:

We […] define Socialism as the social organisation in which, owing to equal obligations and equal rights of all to participate in the communal work, as also owing to the equal right to participate in the produce of this work, the exploitation of one member of the community by another is impossible.

(Tugan-Baranovsky 1910a, 14)

Table 4.6 Typology of socialisms

Systems	A. Socialism	B. Communism
1. Centralist	A1	B1
2. Corporate	A2	B2
3. Federal	A3	B3
4. Anarchical	A4	B4

Source: Tugan-Baranovsky (1910a, 110).

The plan of the future society that will fulfil this ideal is the result of a discussion between the various plans described by the utopian authors, and the science of political economy. The discussion is arranged around the typology found in Table 4.6. The first distinction of this typology, between socialism (A) and communism (B), concerns the way in which society organises the distribution of the social product among its members. The second distinction (1. centralist, 2. corporate, 3. federal, 4. anarchical) concerns the way in which the productive forces are coordinated in the economy, in order to meet social needs.

On the first distinction between *socialism* (A) and *communism* (B), Tugan-Baranovsky rejects the explanation based on property rights, according to which under socialism there are collective property rights of the means of production and private property rights of the means of consumption; while under communism private property rights do not exist. This criterion is dismissed for practical reasons: how to conceive of the absence of property rights on clothes that are currently worn, or on the poet's pen? (see Tugan-Baranovsky 1910a, 14–17) As an alternative criterion, Tugan-Baranovsky proposed to distinguish socialism from communism with the economic notion of income:

- Under socialism (A), each individual disposes of an income, from which he may freely choose between the available consumption goods. Private property rights are therefore guaranteed on goods acquired with that income. Individual consumption is limited by what that income may allow to be bought at given prices, and by the availability of products on the market. That availability is possibly but not necessarily expressed in prices, depending on the system of price formation (market oriented or managed). The notion of income may be expressed in monetary terms or take any other form.[19]
- Under communism (B), the economic notion of income is absent. Therefore, individual consumption is no longer limited by income, nor by prices, which become useless. Two scenarios are encountered:
- In the first, there is no physical constraint, i.e. there are enough consumption goods for everyone. In this case, consumption is entirely free. Property rights would not be necessary, since taking something from someone does not deprive this person of that good. This is the ultimate goal of communism. Nevertheless, this requires a tremendous technological level to satisfy all needs.

- In the second, there is still a physical constraint, i.e. there are not enough consumption goods for everyone to be fully satisfied. In this case, communism consists of fixed consumption bundles chosen at the collective level. The individual has no choice of what to consume, but every individual receives the same allowance, or according to a physiological table of needs. This constrained communism is justified in the socialist literature as being only a temporary state, until technology allows the removal of this constraint.

The second level of distinction (1. centralised, 2. corporate, 3. federal or 4. anarchical) directly answers the following quest:

> A society, to be perfect, to have all that is requisite to its nature, must consequently be so organized that the widest possible personal freedom of the individual can go hand in hand with the greatest possible security of the interests of the community as a whole.
>
> (Tugan-Baranovsky 1910a, 180–181)

The ideal system should therefore guarantee two contradictory goals: the maximum freedom *and* the maximum order. For Tugan-Baranovsky indeed, order is not a prerequisite to freedom. Both concur simultaneously, attracting and repulsing each other.

A *centralist system* (1) offers the greatest possible security, since it allows the coordination of the whole process of production in order to follow predefined goals, such as to answer the needs of the society, through planning (see below in this chapter). A centralist system can be highly efficient, since the division of labour can be extended on a large scale. On the other hand, centralist systems are necessarily authoritarian, if not dictatorial, since they decide, among other things, the profession of the members of the society. Individual freedom is therefore in danger. These characteristics are encountered, for example, in the systems of most Saint-Simonists, Pecqueur, Bellamy and Cabet.

A *corporate system* (2), such as in Blanc's proposal, does not realise the socialist ideal, since coordination is only ensured at the corporate level, and not at that of the society. The latter is organised around professional unions and does not secure equal economic rights for the members of the society, but creates new social classes by occupation. Corporatism should be forgotten.

In contrast, a *federal system* (3) can achieve the socialist ideal regionally: it consists of self-sufficient independent small communities, loosely connected to their neighbours on a voluntary basis. The division of labour is less developed as compared to the centralist system, and therefore brings a lower level of productivity, but, at the same time, it secures greater individual freedom. The organisation of labour, and of income distribution, can differ greatly from one community to another. This system, proposed by Owen, Thompson and Fourier, could and should be used as a counterweight to any centralist system.

Finally, an *anarchical system* (4) is a society in which the individual is absolutely free from the point of view of economic labour, and independent from any social community. The individual is self-sufficient, and interacts with others only on a voluntary basis. This system, proposed by Godwin, Proudhon or Kropotkin, guarantees the greatest individual freedom, but would necessitate a tremendous level of technology in order to allow each individual to produce all his needs by himself.

There is no combination in this typology that corresponds to the absolute ideal. Practical concessions are unavoidable between the two conflicting objectives: freedom for the individual on one side, and proportionality in the economy on the other.

Regarding the first distinction between communism (B) and socialism (A), the social ideal would be free unlimited consumption (B.i), but due to present-day constraints (technology and, perhaps, human nature; B.ii), today's practical ideal is socialism (A), in which consumption, albeit limited, is at least free:

> The socialistic system, which regulates the earnings of the individual without laying any restraint on the freedom of choice, represents, therefore, an incomparably higher type of social union than Cabet's communistic plan, according to which it is not the income but the consumption of the individual which is subject to control.
>
> (Tugan-Baranovsky 1910a, 144)[20]

An improvement can be guaranteed with a mixed system (compare especially chapters IV, V and VI of Tugan-Baranovsky 1910b): where communism is possible, it should be applied. Education, health services, museums, libraries, transport ... should as soon as possible be freely available to all members of the society. The greater the social productivity, the larger the supply of such 'communistic' goods: non-luxury foods, lodging, etc.

Regarding the second distinction, only centralism (1) can achieve the greatest coordination, i.e. *proportionality* in Tugan-Baranovsky's terminology, and therefore efficiency, i.e. useful productivity for mankind. The productive forces can be governed in accordance with social needs. For Tugan-Baranovsky, in order to guarantee individual freedom, ingredients of both federal (3) and anarchical (4) systems must be introduced within the centralist system (1). In this regard, the utopian systems contain a full set of ideas that can be of some help: a few hours per day of compulsory socially useful labour may be sufficient to procure for the society its basic needs, and to give the right to all members of the society to participate in this social product. In the realisation of their own ideal, individuals could freely spend the remaining hours in activities that are not directly useful to the society's immediate material needs: leisure, craftwork, arts, literature, intellectual and scientific work, etc. Whether the individual would retain a private property right on the product of this work is no longer a question in a socialist society. Once the 'minimum of economic comfort' is guaranteed (and in an efficient socialist society it will be much more than the minimum since generous 'comfort and leisure' will be secured by a very few working hours), leisure work will provide a much more rewarding 'extra remuneration' in the form of 'honour, admiration, renown and love on the part of his fellow citizens' (Tugan-Baranovsky 1910a, 124).

In *Modern Socialism*, Tugan-Baranovsky compares the various Utopian novels in regards to working hours, and clearly favours the optimism of Owen, for whom the daily labour load diminishes to two hours of labour after five years of hard labour, over Bellamy's more arduous plans, where everyone is assigned to 24 years of forced labour. This clearly reveals a very optimistic vision of technological progress.

The issue of the distribution of the social produce among the members of the society under socialism is a central one. Should the society provide an equal income to all its members (which does not mean equal consumption), or should it guarantee an equal right to all individuals to the integral produce of their individual labour, in order to totally preclude the exploitation of an individual by society? In others words, should the individual be remunerated according to what he gives? Keeping his ethical position in mind, Tugan-Baranovsky supports the first system:

> A system of equitable distribution must aim not at warranting to every labourer the whole of his produce, but at the greatest possible agreement of the distribution of products with the fundamental ethical principles of Socialism – the idea of equivalence of the human personality.
>
> (Tugan-Baranovsky 1910a, 127)

There is no other ethical system of remuneration: the myth of labour paid according to its productivity is meaningless according to Tugan-Baranovsky. It should be recalled that, under capitalism, he rejected both classical theories of wage and the marginal productivity theory of wage, to support his 'social theory of wage' (see Tugan-Baranovsky 1910b and 1913c), according to which wages are in line with the relative forces of the workers and the capitalists in each sector. Therefore, for Tugan-Baranovsky, the capitalist notion of wage cannot serve as an indicator of the worker's productivity. A comparison of two different types of labour is impossible:

> By what standard, for instance, could the productive work of a judge, a physician, or a farmer be rated? How many working hours are included in the work of a poet, or what quantity of 'normal working time' is equal to his labour of one hour?
>
> (Tugan-Baranovsky 1910a, 127)

Therefore, for Tugan-Baranovsky, the only practical solution is an *equal* income for all members of the society, which better conforms to the socialist ideal by asserting the equal value of all humans.

Another central issue discussed by Tugan-Baranovsky concerns the nature and organisation of labour under socialism. In the anarchist society, each individual can choose his profession, but if everyone wants to be a poet, the society will soon disappear due to shortages of food. Tugan-Baranovsky is confident that, with equal income in all professions, the choice of a profession will become solely a question of taste, and that it will make it easier to give everyone a job they desire, even within an authoritative mode of production. Some arrangements will nevertheless be necessary: the toughest jobs could be compensated for by a shorter workload (but not by a higher salary). Tugan-Baranovsky has a strong belief that social productivity will rise under collective ownership of means of production, and once the basic needs are fulfilled, it will leave the individuals with a considerable amount of free time. The relation to labour will change, and members of the socialist state will satisfy other needs with new activities: arts, literature, science, luxury craftwork … that will contribute to the spiritual development of the socialist society. Some of these activities, such as science, will even contribute directly to the growth of human labour social productivity.[21] In all *these* activities, no authority should ever be applied; they *must* remain absolutely free in order to be useful to humankind.

Before this ideal picture of free choice of labour is ever reached, the socialist society should first organise itself in order to secure for its members the basic and soon-to-be non-basic consumption goods. This is the transition from utopian socialism towards scientific socialism, and this transition is achieved, for Tugan-Baranovsky, precisely through the economic plan.

The socialist economic plan

> But now history holds on its course and the mission of capitalism is achieved, social economy must rise to a higher degree, and the capitalist anarchy, bearing rule in the domain of social production, must be superseded by a socialistically planned organization.
>
> (Tugan-Baranovsky 1910a, 105)

The economic plan corresponds to the distribution of the productive forces between the alternative sectors of the economy. In a capitalist economy, the plan stands for the aggregation of the numerous individual plans made by firms, based on the allocation of various means of production (labour, capital, and land), and according to the price mechanism. These calculations do not realise the socialist ideal, since they are based on *costs of production*, a concept that considers the work of man as a resource among others, for purposes alien to the worker. The sum of these plans leads to *disproportionality* between the social output and social needs.[22]

In a socialist economy, the plan can be consciously developed: it must correspond to the distribution of human labour (the means) among the alternative sectors of the economy, for the social output to be in full proportionality with the needs of human beings (the ends). In this way, the economic plan realises the socialist ideal, based on the ethical principle of the equal value of human personality. Production in the socialist society should therefore be planned, according to two considerations: on one side, considering human labour as the only pertinent input variable; and considering human needs as the only pertinent target for the output variable. This is what Tugan-Baranovsky aims to achieve with his theory of value and prices (see Chapter 5).

From 1890 onwards, Tugan-Baranovsky developed his own synthesis of the theory of value (Tugan-Baranovsky 1890). After his initial step, Tugan-Baranovsky's synthesis approach to value theory was to become a 'tradition' among Russian economists (see Chapter 6). For him, theories of value were one-sided, and the misunderstanding between an 'old' labour-based theory and a 'new' theory based on marginal utility were to be understood through the following perspective: Ricardo places the labour of man at the centre of his understanding of value ('an objective moment'), while Wieser takes for granted that the process of evaluation – marginal utility – determines the value of goods ('a subjective moment'). Objective and subjective moments are not incompatible; they are reconcilable and even, on an ethical basis, both necessary.

In 1890, Tugan-Baranovsky gave an example (the 'simple synthesis') of how this reconciliation takes place. A community produces only two goods: A and B. These two goods provide this community with marginal utilities, as represented in Table 4.7. Tugan-Baranovsky saw in Menger's schemes (which he reproduced in 1890, 197; 1909, 66; and [1918] 1996, 390) the best illustration of the difference between total and concrete (marginal) utilities provided by different goods. In Table 4.7, the third unit of good A, for instance provides a marginal utility of 8. It should be noted that this notion of marginal utility is a social one, and, as such, the very notion of social marginal utility was unfortunately not discussed by Tugan-Baranovsky.

Suppose that the production of one unit of good A requires one day of labour, while two days are needed for the production of one unit of good B, and that the community has at its disposal 4 days of labour. Tugan-Baranovsky asks: 'How should labour be distributed so as to observe the economic principle – to reach with the least expense the biggest utility? (Tugan-Baranovsky 1890, 225). The ideal production plan requires all labour forces to be assigned to the production of 4 units of good A, contributing to a total utility of 34 (10+9+8+7).

If the society disposes of 8 days of labour, the ideal production becomes the following: 6 units of A and 1 unit of B (since every alternative repartition of labour is less efficient), for a total utility of 55 (10+9+8+7+6+5+10). The last unit of good A has a marginal utility of 5, and the last unit of B has a marginal utility of 10. At the same time, the production of A takes 1 day, and the production of B takes two days.

Table 4.7 Tugan-Baranovsky's schemes of marginal utilities

| A | – | 10 | 9 | 8 | 7 | 6 | 5 | 4 | 3 | 2 | 1 | 0 |
| B | – | 10 | 9 | 8 | 7 | 6 | 5 | 4 | 3 | 2 | 1 | 0 |

Source: According to Tugan-Baranovsky (1890, 197 and 225–227).

Note
In the original, the schemes were represented vertically.

From these ratios ($10/5$ vs $2/1$, or $10/2$ vs $5/1$), Tugan-Baranovsky concludes that 'The marginal utilities of produced goods are proportional to their costs of labour' (Tugan-Baranovsky 1909, 73). In other words,

> The utility of the last units of reproducible goods of every kind – their marginal utility – should be inversely proportional to the relative quantity of these goods produced during one unit of time of labour; or directly proportional to the costs of these goods. Only the fulfilment of this condition guarantees that the distribution of the production corresponds to the economic principle of the greatest utility.
>
> (Tugan-Baranovsky 1909, 72)

This illustration of Tugan-Baranovsky's synthesis in the theory of value shows how he conceived planning in a socialist economy: by building an economic plan based on theory of value, which allows the synthesis between the objective (production) and the subjective (needs) sides of his human–ethical economy:

> For the establishment of this [economic] plan, the socialist society will have two considerations in mind: on the one hand, it must take into account the marginal utility of each good, on the other hand, their labour costs. These are the two fundamental elements for the construction of the socialist economic plan.
>
> (Tugan-Baranovsky [1918] 1996, 390)

Many problems arise from this conception of planning, such as the collection of data on labour costs, and the estimation of marginal utilities (on this, see Barnett 2000). Moreover, marginal utilities are calculated at the community level, without considering any individual level or any issue of aggregation.[23] Finally, the whole reasoning is based on the 'under present technical conditions' hypothesis, which eschews the issues of capital accumulation and of inter-temporal consumption. Nevertheless, without any knowledge of Barone's approach, Tugan-Baranovsky proposed an ethical system of planning under socialism, which was supposed to surpass capitalism.[24]

Whether socialist planning should be organised at the national level (along a centralist scheme), on a regional level (within a community organised around the federal scheme), or with a mix of both is not specified by Tugan-Baranovsky. One can guess, according to his previously exposed principles, that he would have avoided too much centralism (authoritarianism) and too much regionalism (disproportionality and inefficiency). His later involvement in the cooperative movements may be considered as an indication of his preference for smaller communities, and therefore for liberty over planning in every aspect of human life:

> There is but one province of human activity in which unlimited freedom is possible and indispensable: it is the province of the higher intellectual creative

labour, where no authority can be tolerated [...] this sphere of labour does not require the maintaining or the observance of proportionality of production, which constitutes an imperative demand in economic adventures.

(Tugan-Baranovsky 1910a, 181–182)

Tugan-Baranovsky acknowledges the eventual necessity for the proletariat to take political power in order to establish the future society,[25] because most political parties and syndicates only envisage the improvement of the situation of the workers, and not the transformation of society. However, he shared a faith in the future developments of these economical and political entities: cooperatives, unions, cartels, political powers ... for they were potentially instrumental in preparing the transformation of society, and especially the economic sphere of society. Indeed:

There is no necessity whatever to introduce Socialism at once to its extreme limits. On the contrary, it is to all intents and purposes by far more rational to gradually remould the existing economic structure by slowly infusing into it the spirit of the new order. The land and enterprises of national importance such as railways, credit and insurance institutions, likewise all capitalistic associations, trusts, and syndicates which extend to large proportions, can immediately pass into possession of the State without any technical difficulties.

(Tugan-Baranovsky 1910a, 229)

However, Tugan-Baranovsky warned: complications will not come from the political sphere, but from the economic organisation of the new socialist society:

The most difficult task for Socialism will be to adjust supply to demand; in other words, to establish a proportionality between production and consumption. Under the actual reign of unrestricted industrial activity and private enterprise, this problem is being solved by the ruin of those undertakings, the products of which exceed the social demand and the rapid growth of such concerns, and the increasing profits they yield are due to the demand for their products being greater than the supply.

(Tugan-Baranovsky 1910a, 229–230)

But in the process of regulation, or approaching *proportionality* in the economic plan, market signals will still play an important role. Nevertheless, this role will be different under socialism than under capitalism:

However, the Socialist system will not wholly escape the regulating influence of the fluctuations of the market, in so far as under the reorganized State, commodities will be bought and sold at prices dictated by the ratio between social supply and demand. In the Socialist community, just so as in the capitalistic, the prices of a commodity will rise in the case of demand exceeding supply, and fall in the inverse instance. In this manner, the market prices of a product will serve as a graduator of the proportionality of social production with the society of the future, as it serves with the society of the present time. The difference will consist only in prices; retaining the quality of a regulator of social production and consumption, under the Socialist arrangement of economic life, it will cease to be the regulator of social distribution.

(Tugan-Baranovsky 1910, 230–231)

For Tugan-Baranovsky, under socialism, income distribution will no longer depend on economical relations, but will depend on social and political relations. This very fact will induce many changes in the life of the people, in relation to freedom and the absence of exploitation:

> Under the Socialist organization of production, the income of the labourer employed in a given branch will not bear any direct relation to the consumption of the return of his labour, his fixed income being at all events secured. The elementary forces of the capitalist system, the influences of the fluctuations of the market, must be replaced by a special mechanism to be introduced and worked by Socialism, in the form of most detailed statistical data regarding production and consumption, and the elaboration of a rigorous organization of the employment of labour in different branches of industry on a level with the social exigencies. This organization must, on one side, secure the proportionality of social production, and on the other hamper personal freedom as little as possible – the freedom of every individual to choose his profession according to his taste.

(Tugan-Baranovsky 1910a, 230)

This is the beginning of the socialist transformation of human beings, and this is where Tugan-Baranovsky ends his investigation.

From capitalism to socialism

Tugan-Baranovsky extended his critique of the capitalist system to the formulation of a new social system trying to resolve the contradictions inherent in the former system. Capitalism is condemned to fail, not because of contradictions related to its mode of production, but as a consequence of its immorality. The exploitation of men by other men is not the goal ascribed to the economic system of a human society. The economy should only be a means for humans to satisfy their needs, at the least of *their* expense.

Handling the economic concepts that were disputed among economists at the end of the nineteenth century, Tugan-Baranovsky offered an attempted synthesis within the theory of value in full agreement with his vision of the new socialist society. On the subjectivist side of the economy, he borrowed the notion of marginal utility, albeit on a social scale, in order to follow strictly the needs of the society. Production is thereby driven by no consideration other than social consumption needs. On the objectivist side of the economy, he constructed a notion of labour costs, half way between Marx's labour value and Ricardo's absolute value, in order to take into consideration exclusively the expense of man, i.e. labour (see next chapter). The difficulty of production is considered from the point of view of human labour, and disregards all capitalist notions such as those – wage, profit and rent – that form the costs of production. Both subjectivist and objectivist sides – which coincide only by accident under capitalism – are to be implemented in the new socialist society within the scheme of a conscious economic plan. With his example, illustrated above, he paved the way for economic planning. Yet he overlooked two important conditions required to bring his economic plan into action.

The first condition implies the need to know the social marginal utilities for all possible goods in the given society. These estimations would necessitate large-scale censuses, not to mention the difficulties encountered in the expression and in the comparison (and therefore aggregation) of all individual goods evaluations. The second condition concerns the calculation of labour costs. The latter supposes a full knowledge of present day (and future) technology in order to estimate the total amount of human labour embodied in a given good under present technical conditions, again not to mention the issue of scale of production. While these two conditions imply large censuses and the development of statistical techniques for calculating the national balance (in labour terms), and offered a full range of fieldwork for statisticians in the Russian empire, Tugan-Baranovsky was certainly authorised to believe in their feasibility, given the promising development of theoretical and empirical statistics at the beginning of the twentieth century in Russia.

Nevertheless, statistics are not a panacea. If planning could answer the materialist needs of life, it should not hide the other objectives of socialism: freedom and development of human personality. A centralist society alone could not realise these objectives. In order to guarantee the utmost human freedom, federal and anarchist ingredients should be incorporated. This wisdom, theoretical at least, that would not be followed by the Bolsheviks, crossed Tugan-Baranovsky's mind while he was reading, and taking seriously into account, the utopian authors – the stars by which the night traveller chooses his road...

Notes

1 For an account of his life and work, see the classical exposition of Nove (1970) or the recent interpretations of Zweynert (2002, Ch. 5.5) and Sorvina (2005). While much editorial work has been done in the last two decades on Tugan-Baranovsky, Amato (1980) remains the reference for the primary and secondary literature. For a biographical account, see his grandson's biographical essay (Tugan-Baranovsky 1997). The recent collection of Shirokorad and Dmitriev (2008) contains the latest archival discoveries concerning Tugan-Baranovsky.
2 See the case of Georgievsky (Dmitriev 2008).
3 Tugan-Baranovsky (1909, 760 pages). The *Principles* circulated as lecture notes ten years before the first 1909 edition. This popular textbook had a second edition in

1911, a third in 1915, a fourth in 1917 and a fifth in 1918. There were only two post-humous reprints in 1924 and in 1998, and scarce translations (a Czech one in 1918, an Ukrainian in 1919): Tugan-Baranovsky's most popular writing still remains today untranslated into other languages.

4 See Tugan-Baranovsky (1908 and 1909, chap. 1. Object of Political Economy; chap. 2. Methodology of Political Economy).

5 For alternative reconstructions of Tugan-Baranovsky's methodology, see Kondratiev [1923] 1998, 319–320), Zweynert (2002, 5.4.2–3), Barnett (2004) and Makasheva (2008, 78–79).

6 Tugan-Baranovsky's fascinating text 'Three Great Ethical Problems: Dostoyevsky's Moral Point of View', published in his book *Towards A Better Future* ([1912] 1996), shows how Kant's idea of the supreme value of human personality is illustrated in Dostoyevsky's novels.

7 Windelband introduced the distinction between *nomothetic* and *idiographic* sciences, found for example in Russian economic literature in Yurovsky's *Essays on Price Theory* (1919). Rickert developed this distinction for separating generalising sciences of nature and individualising sciences of culture. Tugan-Baranovsky did not strictly follow their teachings, notably by his introduction of practical interests into theoretical discussions. Neo-Kantianism inspired revisionists not only in Russia, but also in Germany. Schumpeter devotes a long note to these two philosophers for their damaging influence on German economists, such as Max Weber (Schumpeter 1954, 744–745). He ignored the point that they also had 'such' influence in Russia.

8 Here, Tugan-Baranovsky departs from Ziber's methodological viewpoint: he distinguishes the individual and social levels, but places at the centre of economic science the link between the two, and does not emphasise, as Ziber did, the social economy only.

9 The English edition (Tugan-Baranovsky 1910a) and the French edition (Tugan-Baranovsky 1913b) differ only slightly from each other, and from the original Russian edition (Tugan-Baranovsky 1906).

10 Tugan-Baranovsky's conclusions that sector I would grow and at the same time sector II would atrophy proved wrong. Colacchio (2005) showed that, after the third period, sector II starts to grow again, until both sectors (I and II) reached their steady state *positive* growth rate. Indeed, the size of sector II only reduces in relation to sector I. If sector I grows enough, sector II even grows in absolute terms. But this mistake, due to the initial conditions in the model, had not been discovered during Tugan-Baranovsky's time.

11 On the evolution of Tugan-Baranovsky's ideas from crises towards the cycle, see Allisson (2011).

12 There were *three* Russian editions of this book within the same year, 1905, because it rapidly went out of print; and one in German in 1905, edited by Tugan-Baranovsky himself.

13 This is a major difference since this argument invalidated, at least until the 1970s, Marx's approach to the subject. On this point, Dostaler recognises Tugan-Baranovsky's damaging influence for Marx's ideas as follows:

> Tugan thus reached the same conclusions as Bernstein or Croce, but in quite different ways, and by fixing once and for all the way of presenting the problem, in which we are still locked. As the first author of 'Marxian models', Tugan links the issues of reproduction and of transformation, reducing from five to three the number of sectors in Marx's schemes. In this manner, the transformation does not meet the conditions of reproduction, and this is the sign of Marx's error, not any contradiction between value and price. This mistake is the non-transformation of inputs (which is not in itself linked to the three sectors reproduction). Tugan then resolves the issue in the same way as all subsequent correctors will do, without,

however, giving a general algebraic solution. In transforming simultaneously inputs and outputs, he notes that aggregates are not maintained from one scheme to another. This does not seem to be in itself a serious problem. On the contrary, the consecutive failure to retain some fundamental ratios, such as the exploitation rate and the profits–wage ratio, leads him to question the Marxist theory of value and profit. Indeed, the rate of profit is not given by Marx's formula. This approach will be taken up again. The validity of Marxist theory is linked with the preservation of quantitative equalities. This approach is unacceptable. But this critique is, this time, much more subtle than the marginalists' critique, and no answer will be found.

(Dostaler 1978, 104)

In almost the same terms, Faccarello contests Tugan-Baranovsky's approach: 'The reason why Tugan-Baranovsky criticizes the Marxian transformation schemes is questionable: the conditions of simple reproduction of social capital have nothing to do with this matter' (Faccarello 2000, 181).

14 See Tugan-Baranovsky's contribution to the controversy around the translation of Marx's *Capital* into Russian. He defends the translation of *Wert* as *Cennost'* (same etymology as value – e-valu-ation), and not as *Stoimost'* (same etymology as costs), as it was defended by the Populists and by the future Bolsheviks (Tugan-Baranovsky 1899b).

15 This *subjective* reading of evaluation (and utility), on the opposite direction from Ziber's reading, comes from Tugan-Baranovsky's psycho-physical readings (Weber and Fechner, Wundt).

16 On Voroncov's economic ideas, see Masoero (1988).

17 Barnett (2000) offers an analysis of Tugan-Baranovsky's planning approach in the context of its reception among Soviet economists and of the socialist calculation debate. Barnett also outlines the Russian economist's vision of an international socialist economy, and the role played by an international paper money system. For her part, Makasheva (2008) details the ethical foundations of Tugan-Baranovsky's socialism.

18 These ideas are developed in his various writings, mostly but not exclusively the following books: *Socialism as a Positive Doctrine* ([1918] 1996), *Modern Socialism in its Historical Development* (1906 in Russian, 1910a in English, 1913b in French), *Principles of Political Economy* (1909) and *Towards a Better Future* ([1912] 1996).

19 Tugan-Baranovsky remarks in *Modern Socialism* (1910a) that authors of Utopias frequently invent non-monetary forms of income to free their reader from the traditional economical world. However, this does not change the fact that they maintain an economic notion of income.

20 Tugan-Baranovsky describes all the evil of Cabet's *Icaria* as the worst type of centralist communism, where members of the society have the same books on their bookshelves, and cannot choose even the colour of their clothes (Tugan-Baranovsky 1910a, 137–145).

21 Tugan-Baranovsky explains that machinery will no longer be seen as an enemy to the workers under socialism, since it will give them the opportunity to develop themselves.

22 Here again, Tugan-Baranovsky moves away from Ziber's conception: for Ziber, costs of production do not explain social relations, while for Tugan-Baranovsky, they explain *capitalistic* social relations.

23 This implies a real theoretical problem, since it assumes a full centralisation (vs anarchy) on the subjective side of the economic plan. On what basis the community chooses its *social* marginal utility is a subject not touched upon by Tugan-Baranovsky.

24 Barone's pioneering work in the socialist calculation debate, 'The Ministry of Production in the Collectivist State', was published in Italian in 1908 (see Barone [1908] 2004).

25 See especially chap. VIII (Practical programme of socialism) of *Modern Socialism* (Tugan-Baranovsky 1910a).

References

Allisson, François. 2011. 'From Crises to Cycles: Tugan-Baranovsky and the Brockhaus-Efron (1895–1915)'. In Daniele Besomi, ed., *Crises and Cycles in Economic Dictionaries*, chap. 17, 343–360. Abingdon, UK: Routledge.

Amato, Sergio. 1980. 'M. I. Tugan-Baranowsky (1865–1919): Ricerca bibliografica'. *Argomenti Storici*, III–IV.

Barnett, Vincent. 2000. 'Tugan-Baranovskii's Vision of an International Socialist Economy'. *European Journal for the History of Economic Thought*, 7: 115–135.

Barnett, Vincent. 2004. 'Tugan-Baranovsky, the Methodology of Political Economy, and the "Russian Historical School"'. *History of Political Economy*, 36: 79–101.

Barnett, Vincent. 2005. 'Tugan-Baranovsky and The Russian Factory'. In R. B. McKean and Ian D. Thatcher, eds, *Late Imperial Russia: Problems and Prospects: Essays in Honour of R. B. McKean*, chap. 6, 84–100. Manchester: Manchester University Press.

Barone, Enrico. [1908] 2004. 'The Ministry of Production in the Collectivist State'. In Roberto Marchionatti, ed., *Early Mathematical Economics, 1871–1915*, vol. 4, 227–263. London: Routledge. Original published in Italian.

Besomi, Daniele. 2006. ' "Marxism Gone Mad": Tugan-Baranovsky on Crises, their Possibility and their Periodicity'. *Review of Political Economy*, 18: 147–171.

Bortkiewicz, Ladislaus von. 1906–1907. 'Wertrechnung und Preisrechnung im Marxschen System (I-II-III)'. *Archiv für Sozialwissenschaft und Sozialpolitik*, XXIII: 1–50; XXV: 10–51 and 445–488. Parts II and III translated into English by J. Kahane. 1952. 'Value and Prices in the Marxian System'. *International Economic Papers*, 2: 5–60.

Colacchio, Giorgio. 2005. 'On the Origins of Non-Proportional Economic Dynamics: A Note on Tugan-Baranowsky's Traverse Analysis'. *Structural Change and Economic Dynamics*, 16: 503–521.

Dmitriev, Anton Leonidovich. 2008. 'P. I. Georgievsky kak opponent M. I. Tugan-Baranovskogo (Georgievsky as Tugan-Baranovsky's Contradictor)'. In Leonid Dmitrievich Shirokorad and Anton Leonidovich Dmitriev, eds, *Neizvestnyj M. I. Tugan-Baranovskij (Unknown M. I. Tugan-Baranovsky)*, 253–260. St Petersburg: Nestor-Istoriâ.

Dostaler, Gilles. 1978. *Valeur et prix. Histoire d'un débat*. Montréal: François Maspero, Presses Universitaires de Grenoble, Les presses de l'Université du Québec.

Faccarello, Gilbert. 2000. 'Les controverses autour du Capital (I): les débats autour de la loi de la valeur'. In Alain Béraud and Gilbert Faccarello, eds, *Nouvelle histoire de la pensée économique: Des premiers mouvements socialistes aux néoclassiques*, vol. 2, chap. XVIII, 171–201. Paris: La Découverte.

Howard, Michael C. and John E. King. 1989. *A History of Marxian Economics: Volume I, 1883–1929*. London: Macmillan.

Jorland, Gérard. 1995. *Les paradoxes du capital*. Paris: Odile Jacob.

Klejnbort, L. M. 2008. 'Vstreči. M. I. Tugan-Baranovskij (Meetings with Tugan-Baranovsky)'. In Leonid Dmitrievich Shirokorad and Anton Leonidovich Dmitriev, eds, *Neizvestnyj M. I. Tugan-Baranovskij (Unknown M. I. Tugan-Baranovsky)*, 181–237, text prepared by Chris Monday and Anton Leonidovich Dmitriev. St Petersburg: Nestor-Istoriâ.

Kondratiev, Nikolay Dmitrievich. [1923] 1998. 'M. I. Tugan-Baranovsky. Basic Features of his Scientific World-View'. In Natalia A. Makasheva, Warren J. Samuels and

Vincent Barnett, eds, *The Works of Nikolai D. Kondratiev*. London: Pickering & Chatto.

Lenin, Vladimir Ilich. [1899] 1960. *Development of Capitalism in Russia.* Volume 3 of V. I. Lenin *Collected Works*. Moscow: Progress Publishers.

Luxemburg, Rosa. [1913] 1951. *The Accumulation of Capital*. London: Routledge and Kegan Paul.

Makasheva, Natalia A. 2008. 'Searching for an Ethical Basis of Political Economy: Bulgakov and Tugan-Baranovsky'. In Vincent Barnett and Joachim Zweynert, eds, *Economics in Russia. Studies in Intellectual History*, chap. 6, 75–89. Aldershot, UK: Ashgate.

Masoero, Alberto. 1988. *Vasilij Pavlovic Voroncov e la cultura economica del populismo russo (1868–1918)*. Milano: Franco Angeli.

Nove, Alec. 1970. 'M. I. Tugan-Baranovsky (1865–1919)'. *History of Political Economy*, 2(2): 246–262.

Robertson, Dennis Holme. 1914. 'Review of "Les crises industrielles en Angleterre" by M. Tugan-Baranovsky'. *Economic Journal*, 24: 81–85.

Rodbertus, Karl Johann. 1875. *Zur Beleuchtung der socialen Frage*. Berlin: Puttkammer & Mühlbrecht.

Schumpeter, Joseph Aloïs. 1954. *History of Economic Analysis*. London: Allen & Unwin.

Shirokorad, Leonid Dmitrievich. 2003. 'Sušestvuet li rossijskaâ škola èkonomičeskoj mysli? (Is There a Russian School of Economic Thought?)' In Leonid I. Abalkin, ed., *Očerki istorii rossijskoj èkonomičeskoj mysli (Essays in the History of Russian Economic Thought)*, 51–61. Moscow: Nauka.

Shirokorad, Leonid Dmitrievich. 2006. 'Book Review of Vincent Barnett, *A History of Russian Economic Thought*'. *European Journal of the History of Economic Thought*, 13(3): 433–443.

Shirokorad, Leonid Dmitrievich and Anton Leonidovich Dmitriev, eds. 2008. *Neizvestnyj M. I. Tugan-Baranovskij (Unknown M. I. Tugan-Baranovsky)*. St Petersburg: Nestor-Istoriâ.

Sorvina, Galina Nikolaevna. 2005. *Mihail Ivanovič Tugan-Baranovskij: pervyj rossijskij èkonomist s mirovym imenem (The First Russian Economist with a World-Known Name)*. Moscow: Russkaâ Panorama.

Tugan-Baranovsky, Djuchy Mikhailovich. 1997. 'Tugan-Baranovsky M. I. Biografičeskij očerk (Biographical Essay)'. In Mikhail Ivanovich Tugan-Baranovsky, *Izbrannoe. Russkaâ Fabrika v proshlom i nastojashchem (Collected Words. The Russian Factory Past and Present)*, 6–64. Moscow: Nauka.

Tugan-Baranovsky, Mikhail Ivanovich. 1890. 'Učenie o predel'noj poleznosti hozâjstvennyh blag kak pričina ih cennosti (Study on the Marginal Utility of Economic Goods as the Cause of their Value)'. *Ûridičeskij Vestnik*, XXII(10/2): 192–230.

Tugan-Baranovsky, Mikhail Ivanovich. 1894. *Promyšlennye krizisy v sovremennoj Anglii, ih pričiny i vliânie na narodnuû žizn' (Industrial Crises in Contemporary England, their Cause and Influence on National Life)*. St Petersburg: Skorokhodov.

Tugan-Baranovsky, Mikhail Ivanovich. 1898. *Russkaâ fabrika v prošlom i nastoâšem (Russian Factory in Past and Present)*. St Petersburg: Panteleev.

Tugan-Baranovsky, Mikhail Ivanovich. 1899a. 'Osnovnaâ ošibka abstraktnoj teorii kapitalizma Marksa (The Fundamental Error in Marx's Abstract Theory of Capitalism)'. *Naučnoe Obozrenie*, 5: 973–985.

Tugan-Baranovsky, Mikhail Ivanovich. 1899b. 'Russkie perevody I toma 'Kapitala' Marksa. Zametka (Russian Translations of the First Volume of Marx's Capital. A Comment)'. *Mir Božij*, 8: 10–16.

Tugan-Baranovsky, Mikhail Ivanovich. 1900. 'Trudovaâ cennost' i pribyl'. Moim kritikam (Labour Value and Profit. To My Critics)'. *Naučnoe Obozrenie*, VII: 607–633.

Tugan-Baranovsky, Mikhail Ivanovich. 1903. *Očerki iz novejšej istorii političeskoj ekonomii (Essays in the Newest History of Political Economy)*. St Petersburg: Mir Božij.

Tugan-Baranovsky, Mikhail Ivanovich. 1904. 'Der Zusammenbruch der kapitalistischen Wirtschaftsordnung im Lichte der nationalökonomischen Theorie'. *Archiv für Sozialwissenschaft und Sozialpolitik*, 19: 273–306.

Tugan-Baranovsky, Mikhail Ivanovich. 1905a. *Teoretičeskie osnovy marksizma (Theoretical Foundations of Marxism)*. St Petersburg: Mir Božij.

Tugan-Baranovsky, Mikhail Ivanovich. 1905b. *Theoretische Grundlagen des Marxismus*. Leipzig: Duncker & Humblot.

Tugan-Baranovsky, Mikhail Ivanovich. 1906. *Sovremennyj socializm v svoem istoričeskom razvitii (Modern Socialism in its Historical Development)*. Moscow: Petrovskaâ.

Tugan-Baranovsky, Mikhail Ivanovich. 1908. 'Metodologiâ političeskoj èkonomii (The Methodology of Political Economy)'. *Obrazovanie*, 12: 1–19.

Tugan-Baranovsky, Mikhail Ivanovich. 1909. *Osnovy političeskoj èkonomii (Principles of Political Economy)*. St Petersburg: Slovo. Reprint of the fourth edition, 1998. Moscow: Rosspèn.

Tugan-Baranovsky, Mikhail Ivanovich. 1910a. *Modern Socialism in its Historical Development*. Translated by M. I. Redmount. London: Swann Sonnenschein.

Tugan-Baranovsky, Mikhail Ivanovich. 1910b. 'Social'naâ teoriâ raspredeleniâ (Social Theory of Distribution)'. *Russkaâ Mysl'*, 1: 100–114.

Tugan-Baranovsky, Mikhail Ivanovich. [1912] 1996. *K lučšemu buduŝemu (Towards a Better Future)*. Moscow: Rosspèn.

Tugan-Baranovsky, Mikhail Ivanovich. 1913a. *Les crises industrielles en Angleterre*. Translated by Joseph Shapiro. Paris: Giard and Brière.

Tugan-Baranovsky, Mikhail Ivanovich. 1913b. *L'évolution historique du Socialisme moderne*. Paris, Rivière. Translated by Joseph Shapiro from the original Russian edition, 1906.

Tugan-Baranovsky, Mikhail Ivanovich. 1913c. *Soziale Theorie der Verteilung*. Berlin: Julius Springer.

Tugan-Baranovsky, Mikhail Ivanovich. 1915. 'Krizisy hozâjstvennye (Economic Crises)'. In *Novyj ènciklopedičeskij slovar'*, vol. 23, 349–354. St Petersburg: Brockhaus and Efron.

Tugan-Baranovsky, Mikhail Ivanovich. [1918] 1996. *Socializm kak položitel'noe učenie (Socialism as a Positive Doctrine)*. Moscow: URSS.

Yurovsky, Leonid Naumovich. 1919. *Očerki po teorii ceny (Essays on Price Theory)*. Saratov, Russia: Saratov University.

Zweynert, Joachim. 2002. *Eine Geschichte des ökonomischen Denkens in Russland. 1805–1905*. Marburg, Germany: Metropolis Verlag.

5 Tugan-Baranovsky's synthesis

The name of Tugan-Baranovsky, when quoted by historians of the theory of prices, is often associated with his critical contributions to Marx's theory of value (e.g. his revisionist use of Marx's schemes of reproduction to invalidate the law of the tendency of the rate of profit to fall). Indeed, his *Theoretische Grundlagen des Marxismus* (Tugan-Baranovsky 1905b) appear in every survey about the transformation problem as a forerunner – besides Dmitriev's *Economic Essays* ([1904] 1974) – to Bortkiewicz's solutions (1906–1907; 1907). In these matters, it clearly appears that Tugan-Baranovsky's *critical* contributions put his own *positive* contributions in the shade.

His attempt at a synthesis, the first in Russia, between marginal utility theory and the labour theory of value did not initiate a school, but neither did it make only passing waves. It paved the way for the next generation of Russian economists, who like him tried to reconcile those theories that were at least partially conceived as contradictory. This investigation allows the identification of an important concept in Tugan-Baranovsky's thought: the 'economic plan' (*hozâjstvennyj plan*), whose meaning is examined further in this chapter, and in particular whose concept can be construed as a go-between – making sense of, and even resolving, the contradictions between value and prices. The economic plan also provides a key to understanding the articulation between the positive and the normative components of Tugan-Baranovsky's economic thought. This articulation provides an explanation for the odd fact that, some decades after the 'marginalist revolution', there is still a strong persistence (in Tugan-Baranovsky's analysis, but not exclusively) of the notion of *value*, while it has progressively been replaced elsewhere by *prices*.

As Tugan-Baranovsky's writings on value and prices theory are little known, the corpus under investigation is first presented. In these writings, several references are made to the synthesis, which broadly fall into two types: the 'simple story' that is often met in the writings (as a simple, unexplained and somewhat lucky arithmetical example; see also the previous chapter), and a more complex and less studied theory. The simple version is described using Tugan-Baranovsky's own words, before moving on to his more complex version of the synthesis, using Tugan-Baranovsky's own categories, as defined in the previous chapter, and using the three notions of costs, value and prices.

Tugan-Baranovsky welcomed the theory of marginal utility as a complete and operational theory (see Chapter 3), while he made laborious attempts to modify the classical theory of value, in order to rescue it from the inherent faults he believed it contained. His articulations between ethics and theory, between Marx and Ricardo, and between capitalism and socialism *within* the theory of value and prices are dealt with. His notion of costs, together with his economic plan, provide a way to construe the synthesis between marginal utility theory and the labour theory of value by way of a synthesis between value and prices. Finally, to prepare for the coming of the mathematical economists, Tugan-Baranovsky's own relationship to mathematics is reconstructed.

The road to the synthesis

As early as in his first paper (1890), Tugan-Baranovsky supported the idea of a synthesis in the theory of value:[1]

> The theory of marginal utility does not contradict the views of Ricardo or Marx but, on the contrary, represents, if well understood, an unexpected confirmation of their study on value. Menger and his school studied the subjective causes of value, Ricardo and his followers the objective causes.
>
> (Tugan-Baranovsky 1890, 228)

The 'objective causes', or the classical theory of value, were widely recognised in Russia at that time (see Chapter 2). For his part, Tugan-Baranovsky clearly favoured Ricardo to Smith:

> In his study on value, Smith highlights the labour of man, recognising it as the universal measure of exchange value. But, as pointed out by Ricardo, Smith mixes two distinct conceptions here: labour expended in the production of a good and labour acquired in exchange for this good. For this reason, Smith's theory of value is confused and ambiguous.
>
> (Tugan-Baranovsky 1900a)

By 1890, as far as the classical theory of value is concerned, Tugan-Baranovsky had in mind a labour theory of value, in the vein of Ricardo and Marx ('a faithful Ricardo follower'; at that time, he did not distinguish between them), in which the value of a good is regulated by the labour expended in its production (Tugan-Baranovsky 1890, 222).

At the same time, early warning signs of marginalism ('the subjective causes') were also available in Russia before 1890 (see also Chapter 3 above): (i) the link between value and utility (not *marginal*) was well represented in the Russian translations of the works of J.-B. Say, Garnier, Molinari and Rossi. Tugan-Baranovsky himself mentions in this respect Say and Storch (Tugan-Baranovsky 1890, 209–210); (ii) the mathematical method, if unpopular, already had its early supporters in Russia;[2] moreover (iii) some forerunners of marginalism, such as

Cournot, Thünen and Gossen, had left their mark.[3] Tugan-Baranovsky's marginalism is unmistakably Austrian. Generally speaking, he holds the Austrian school in high esteem, but he is not uncritical of their writings. Menger is presented mainly through his most distinguished disciples, Wieser and Böhm-Bawerk, whose works form the main source of Tugan-Baranovsky's 1890 paper. The Austrian school was the most widespread variant of marginalism in Russia,[4] and if Tugan-Baranovsky mentions Jevons and Walras, it is through the secondary literature.[5]

Tugan-Baranovsky's 1890 paper produced no direct reaction, while reactions to his first writings on Marx were instantaneous. In 1899, he published an article with the provocative title: 'The Fundamental Error in Marx's Abstract Theory of Capitalism'. Even though recognising Marx's sociological and economic system as the 'most outstanding product of human thought for the understanding of social phenomena' (Tugan-Baranovsky 1899a, 973), Tugan-Baranovsky felt the need to criticise Marx's economic theory: 'The increase in constant capital does not *by itself* lead the rate of profit to fall' (Tugan-Baranovsky 1899a, 975). Tugan-Baranovsky used the schemes of reproduction from the second volume of *Capital* in order to obtain a constant rate of profit in the case of substitution of workers by machines, through labour productivity. For him, Marx clearly disregarded the influence of the organic composition of capital on labour productivity, which led Marx to adopt the hypothesis of a uniform rate of surplus value (Tugan-Baranovsky 1899a, 982). For Tugan-Baranovsky, an increase in the share of constant capital, i.e. in the organic composition of capital, increases the surplus rate by increasing the productivity of variable capital, i.e. constant capital does more than just transmit its value to the product, it boosts variable capital.

The tendency for the rate of profit to fall is consequently a fallacy, which requires the very notion of surplus value to be re-thought. Here, Tugan-Baranovsky fully enters into Revisionism.[6] When criticisms came from all sides, Tugan-Baranovsky replied (in 'Labour Value and Profit'; Tugan-Baranovsky 1900b) with some arguments from his 1890 paper on the necessity of an objective and a subjective element in the theory of value, and by relegating profits outside the sphere of value. All these reflections were developed in a more mature form in Tugan-Baranovsky's book, *Theoretical Foundations of Marxism*, published in 1905 in both Russian and German (1905a; 1905b). Tugan-Baranovsky strengthens his criticism of Marx's notions of surplus value and absolute labour theory of value, while he develops his own theory: the distinction between costs and value, the content of the notion of value, and the divergence between absolute and relative costs (see below). At the same time, he shows an awareness of such authors as Jevons and Marshall (Tugan-Baranovsky 1905a, 143–144 and 147) and widens his interest in Rodbertus and Proudhon. His own theory takes shape, albeit still in relation to Marx.

In addition, Tugan-Baranovsky published several essays on major economists and schools (Smith, Malthus, Ricardo, Sismondi, Owen, Saint-Simon, Fourier, Proudhon, Rodbertus, Marx; the Historical school, *Kathedersozialisten*, and the Austrian school), eventually reissued as a book entitled *Essays on the Newest History of Political Economy* (1903). Each essay highlights only some aspects of their work (sometimes their theory of value), according to the following rule: 'I have not striven to be a systematic historian of the past: history interests me only insofar as it creates the present and prepares the future' (Tugan-Baranovsky 1903, iv). All in all, this book contains an interesting methodological introduction and many reflections on the theory of value. Besides this, his popular textbook (*Principles of Political Economy*, 1909), intended for both pedagogical and scientific purposes, constitutes the best place to find gathered together many areas of Tugan-Baranovsky's research that are otherwise only found in separate books and articles. From *Principles of Political Economy* (1909), the following materials are particularly relevant to the theory of value and prices: Section I, Chapter III on the logical categories of the economy (value and costs); Section I, Chapter IV on the historical categories of the simple exchange economy (exchange value) and of the capitalist economy (surplus value); and Section III, Chapter I on prices.

Therefore, as far as value and prices are concerned, the principal sources for this investigation are: the first paper on marginal utility (1890, *Study on Marginal Utility*), some essays (on Ricardo, the Austrians, Proudhon, Rodbertus and Marx) on the Newest History of Political Economy (1903, *Essays*), the critical book on Marx (1905a/b, *Theoretical Foundations of Marxism*) and the *Principles of Political Economy* (1909, *Principles*).[7] Some passages of his two books on socialism are also used: *Modern Socialism in its Historical Development* (1906a) and *Socialism as a Positive Doctrine* ([1918] 1996, chap. 9: Value, Costs, Prices and Money under Socialism).

The simple synthesis

Tugan-Baranovsky's attempt at a synthesis between marginal utility and the labour theory of value took various forms, which are here gathered together in two versions: the 'simple' and the 'complex' synthesis. The simple synthesis was already described in the previous chapter, as an example that resolves all contradictions in the theory of value by reconciling social marginal utilities with social labour costs.

According to Tugan-Baranovsky, contradictions in the theory of value are the result of a great confusion. For some economists, notably Wieser, labour explained value in primitive societies, in a way which is no longer true in modern societies. This historical interpretation of the transition from labour theories towards marginal utility is wrong, according to Tugan-Baranovsky. Labour was important in primitive *and* still is in modern societies; the process of evaluation played a role for the primitive *and* the civilised man:

> The divergence between Wieser and Ricardo is easily interpretable: Ricardo had in mind the objective causes of value, and in this sense claims that in today's society the value of economic goods is regulated by the labour expended in their production. On the other hand, Wieser understood as value the state of mind experienced during our evaluation of goods.
>
> (Tugan-Baranovsky 1890, 222)

Objective and subjective elements are reconcilable, and both are necessary: they show the interdependency between the economic subject (man) and the economic object (nature). Thus, Tugan-Baranovsky followed an objective and a subjective element in his attempt at synthesis. The feasibility of the synthesis was self-evident to him. He was even confident that this synthesis would show no calculation difficulties. On the one hand, marginal utilities could be more closely known through experiments in psychology (à la Weber–Fechner). On the other hand, the cost of labour can be accounted for as the direct labour expended in the production of the final good, together with the labour expended in the factories producing the means of production of this good, with the labour expended in the industries that produced these means of production, etc., until the industries that produce their own means of production. Therefore, it is possible to count 'the exact sum of labour necessary for the production of a good, under given technical conditions' (Tugan-Baranovsky 1890, 223–224).

After John Stuart Mill's unfortunate prophecy, Tugan-Baranovsky reaffirms, with his 'organic synthesis', the end of controversies in the theory of value (Tugan-Baranovsky 1909, 81).

The complex synthesis

> A proper and comprehensive theory of value must, as I said, be as subjective as it is objective. The starting point can be nothing less than the existence of human motivation: the psychical processes that determine our actions. There follows another step in the theory: the analysis of the objective side of the process, the influence of objective conditions of production on economic activity. And only after both sides of the process – subjective and objective – are considered and analysed as an indivisible whole, is the question of the economic theory of value solved.
>
> (Tugan-Baranovsky 1906b, 564)

The interpretation of Tugan-Baranovsky's value and prices theory supported in this book is summarised, using *his* terminology and categories (the 'complex synthesis'), in Table 5.1.[8] The two horizontal lines correspond to 'the two opposite sectors of the economy, between which economic activity takes place' (Tugan-Baranovsky 1909, 61). The first line accounts for the exchange sector of economic activities, i.e. the accommodation of nature to human needs (*subjective and objective value*). The second line corresponds to the production sector, i.e.

Table 5.1 The complex synthesis

categories	logical	historical
exchange subjective cause	**subjective value** *marginal utility*	**objective value** *exchange value (prices)*
production objective cause	**absolute costs** *labour costs*	**relative costs** *expenses of production*

the human expense of labour with the view to achieving these ends (*absolute and relative costs*). The two columns differentiate logical categories, valid in any economic regime, with historical categories, valid only in the exchange capitalistic economy in which Tugan-Baranovsky lived.[9]

Subjective and objective value

For Tugan-Baranovsky, *value* is a fundamental notion, not only in political economy, but also in philosophy, psychology, etc. Political economy deals only with derived values, which are just means to reach more fundamental values, such as happiness, beauty, fame, virtue.... Value (*cennost'*) is the result of the process of evaluation (*ocenka*), which is itself the outcome of human will. Value is therefore only a form of human will.

Subjective value is determined by human will and is a logical category of the economy, since the evaluation of the ability of goods to satisfy needs exists for each human being in every society, independently of its regime. Needs can be satisfied to different degrees, with different scales, as is perfectly represented in Menger's schemes. Decreasing marginal utility is the representation of the general process of evaluation of which the psycho-physical law of Weber–Fechner is only one application (Tugan-Baranovsky 1909, 60–68). The theory of marginal utility explains, once and for all, the problem of subjective value:

> Only the theory of marginal utility explains the dependence between the value of goods and their ability to satisfy our needs to different degrees, in a way that is in full agreement with facts.
>
> (Tugan-Baranovsky 1890, 221)

It is also possible to explain the value of intermediate goods by the value of the final goods they produce (clearly, Tugan-Baranovsky refers here to the Austrian theory of imputation). But, according to this theory, the value of a good is a function of needs and of the quantity of goods available, which is problematically postulated as given. For Tugan-Baranovsky, marginalist authors did not resolve this question (or resolved it wrongly), and there is an obvious explanation for this fact: marginal utility restricts itself to the subjective causes of value, and therefore cannot claim to be a complete and final theory (Tugan-Baranovsky 1890, 200 and 208). It is characteristic of Russian economists of that time to fail to recognise a theory of production in the marginalists' works. (On the example of Walras's theory of production, neglected by Dmitriev, Shaposhnikov, Bukharin and Yurovsky, see Chapter 3.)

Objective value, or exchange value in the exchange economy, is the purchasing power of a good – in other words, its price (1890, 195). Objective value is a historical category of the economy, since it takes place in the exchange economy. It emerges from subjective value, since: 'the human being is the only personality of the economy and it is from the interaction of the different individuals that all phenomena of the national economy emerge'. (Tugan-Baranovsky 1909, 63).

Buyers and sellers, with their unequal subjective evaluation and their desire to earn the greatest advantage through exchange, form the market. The appearance of a unique price as the result of their subjective evaluations is illustrated by Tugan-Baranovsky using Menger's schemes (Tugan-Baranovsky 1909, 248–249), and Böhm-Bawerk's famous marginal pair in the horse market example (Tugan-Baranovsky 1890, 204–209). It seems to Tugan-Baranovsky that there is no complication in the transition from the individual to the national economy.[10] Once again, prices[11] depend on both subjective factors (individual evaluations), and objective factors (goods supply) (Tugan-Baranovsky 1909, 250), which belong to the other sector of the economy. The relation between the two sectors of the economy is bi-directional:

> From the subjective point of view, the product's value is the cause, and the value of its means of production is the consequence. [...] From the objective point of view, the expenses of production are the cause, the value of the product is the consequence.
>
> (Tugan-Baranovsky 1890, 218)

First, marginal utility determines the value of economic goods. Second, the distribution of labour in the different spheres of production (costs) determines the level of production and subsequently the level of marginal utility. Marginal utility is the first cause of value, whereas costs of production are an indirect, secondary cause of value. But before digging further into this synthesis, it is necessary to dwell upon Tugan-Baranovsky's notions of costs.

Absolute and relative costs

The category of costs, as an independent category from the category of value, represents the objective causes of economic activities, on which 'man has no influence' (Tugan-Baranovsky 1890, 224). In 1905, Tugan-Baranovsky recognised three types of labour theories, or labour costs: absolute, relative and idealistic (in the vein of Proudhon and Rodbertus) (Tugan-Baranovsky 1905a, 121–123). In 1909, only two types remain: absolute and relative costs. But it will soon be clear that the idealistic theory has not disappeared from Tugan-Baranovsky's sight.

Absolute costs are the labour costs expended in the production of an economic good, under given technical conditions. This logical category is necessary:

> [T]he economic process is a human activity, directed towards obtaining the material means to meet our needs. The economic category of value relates to it, but the economic activity of man itself is not included in the category of value. This is why the scientific understanding of the economic process involves, another independent category, next to the category of value, representing the labour costs, or absolute costs.
>
> (Tugan-Baranovsky 1909, 76)

In agriculture, man, field, horse, seed and sun are mechanical and biological forces contributing to the production of corn. But since in the human economy the point of view is that of the man, 'human labour is the only substance of absolute costs' (Tugan-Baranovsky 1909, 78). This is why 'the category of labour costs is an archetypal social category: it is even a bridge between political economy and general social science, because social progress is based on the growth in the productivity of social labour' (Tugan-Baranovsky 1909, 80). The productivity of human labour naturally depends on the technical conditions of production, the progress of sciences, etc., 'in short, to the degree of power of man on nature' (Tugan-Baranovsky 1890, 220). Therefore,

> [T]he whole of economic life, despite its extraordinary complexity, fits into these two main categories of the economy [value and costs], in the same way that the operations of a company, whatever they are, are entered in its accounts in two categories – assets and liabilities.
>
> (Tugan-Baranovsky 1909, 61)

Absolute costs have nothing to do with the absolute labour value: Marx gave an absolute labour theory of value; however, 'labour is not the absolute substance of value, but it can practically be counted as the absolute substance of costs' (Tugan-Baranovsky 1906a, 57). Labour is just one of the many determining factors of value (as a component of the value of the product, as Ricardo holds), and therefore cannot be the substance of value itself (Tugan-Baranovsky 1906a, 53). The categories of value and of costs should not be confused, as Marx erroneously did.[12]

There was much confusion between value and costs at that time. Russian economists, and especially Marxists, used the words value (*cennost'*) and costs (*stoimost'*) as synonyms. The first translation of the first volume of Marx's *Capital* translated the German *Wert* by the Russian *stoimost'*. In 1899, three different translations of the same book were printed. Their main differences consist in the translation of *Wert*: sometimes *cennost'*, sometimes *stoimost'*. Tugan-Baranovsky, who devotes a whole article to these three translations (Tugan-Baranovsky 1899b), definitely favours *cennost'* for value. *Cennost'*, in Russian, has the same etymology as *ocenka*, *rascenka* (evaluation), and even *cena* (price).[13] Unfortunately, according to Tugan-Baranovsky, costs as an independent category was not well recognised in the literature, the rare exceptions to this rule being Wagner, Lexis and Dietzel.

Relative costs, in contrast, are the historical manifestation of costs. In a capitalist society, costs are represented by the expenses of production. These expenses of production are value, not seen as an end, but as the means to obtain another value. From the point of view of the whole society, the only costs are labour costs. All other goods – forest, land, minerals, etc. – are gifts from nature. From a historical point of view, which is that of the individual capitalist firm, every input implies an expense, and is therefore a cost: labour is seen as one means of production among others (Tugan-Baranovsky 1909, 78–79).[14]

The relation between absolute and relative costs is trivial according to Tugan-Baranovsky. Absolute costs, as a logical category encompassing only human labour, are *not* value (Marx's error). Relative costs, as a historical category encompassing the remuneration of all means of production, *are* value, in the capitalist economy:

> Expenses [*izderžki*] of production are inherently the capitalistic conscious form for the costs [*stoimosti*] of production. It is precisely for this reason that contemporary economic thought turns away from the idea that only labour represents costs in its absolute form. But labour keeps the only absolute costs even in the capitalist economy, as in every other economy, because the capitalist economy is still a human economy.
>
> Let's stand aside for a moment from the private owner-capitalist and look at the case from the point of view of the whole society. What are the social expenses in the process of social production? Obviously, they are not composed of the 'expenses of production' – the sums paid by members of the society to other members of this same society for this or that commodity. With regard to the material goods expended in the process of production, they enter into the composition of the costs of production only to the extent that these means of production have themselves costs of labour, i.e. that they are the product of past labour. Spending them, we are spending crystallised social labour, according to Marx's figurative expression. But gifts of nature are not an element of absolute costs. [...] It is true that land has value, for the whole society, as well as for the individual. However, value is not costs.
>
> (Tugan-Baranovsky 1909, 254)

It is in this very distinction, between value and costs, that Tugan-Baranovsky believed he had rescued Marx from his mistakes. Here, the parallel with Ziber, who Tugan-Baranovsky regularly quotes, is striking, as illustrated in Table 5.2. In Tugan-Baranovsky's system, the notions of relative and absolute costs coexist (see next section to figure out how), in the same way that, in Ziber's system, labour value and costs of production coexist. This coexistence in Tugan-Baranovsky's system is no surprise, given the hegemonic theoretical understanding of the classical theory of value provided by Ziber (see Chapter 2). But there is a notable difference, and it is in this difference that Tugan-Baranovsky feels confident in his proximity with Marxism. While Ziber considers labour value as

Table 5.2 Comparison between Ziber's and Tugan-Baranovsky's categories

	Labour time embodied	*Wages + profits + rent*
Ziber	labour value (*social economy*)	costs of production (*individual economy*)
Tugan-Baranovsky	absolute costs (*logical economy*)	relative costs (*historical economy*)

the only pertinent point of view and rejects the usefulness, *from a social point of view*, of even considering costs of production, Tugan-Baranovsky considers both notions from the same social point of view.

Indeed, in agreement with Ziber, Tugan-Baranovsky considers absolute costs (i.e. Marx's labour value) as the only pertinent costs, but from an *ethical* social point of view.

And in contradiction with Ziber, Tugan-Baranovsky considers that relative costs (i.e. Ricardo's costs of production or Marx' prices of production), are pertinent to explain costs from an actual social point of view in a capitalist economy, where the capitalist point of view, albeit individual (vs social), overwhelms the other points of view.

It is on this basis, Tugan-Baranovsky writes in his *Principles* (1909) four years after he published his *Critical Foundations of Marxism*, that one cannot criticise Marx for an internal contradiction in his system. Marx's error, of course, is that he wanted to express two ideas in one: costs and exchange value by *value* alone. And value in Marx's work is nothing other than absolute costs in Tugan-Baranovsky's terminology. Marx's error was not terminological, but that he did not separate the sphere of exchange (which objectifies all relations of power and dependencies related to exchange, and not only labour) from the sphere of production (which objectifies labour relations). In the exchange sphere, exchange value is an abstract foundation for prices. And in the production sphere, labour costs are the foundations for studying the struggle between man and nature, the social relations between workers and owners of the means of production, in short, for studying the production world. Marx was interested in finding the hidden social relations in capitalist society, and it is normal that he chose to begin his investigation in the sphere of production, but he thought that this sphere was sufficient to explain prices, and this explains, *in fine*, that what he called *value* was in fact *costs* (Tugan-Baranovsky 1909, 81–83). In short, and in Tugan-Baranovsky's own words:

> My theory of value and costs as two separate categories provides the chance to save the social content of Marx's theory of value, eliminating the erroneous economic conclusions to which Marx came due to his misidentification of the categories of value and costs.
>
> (Tugan-Baranovsky 1909, 82–83)

From this viewpoint, the transformation problem is no longer a problem: there is no need to and no possibility of transforming absolute costs into relative costs. However, once the distinction is acknowledged, a dialogue seems possible.

Value and prices

Four categories have been reviewed in the previous section (see Table 5.1): two correspond to the production/objective side of the economy (a logical category – absolute costs, and a historical category – relative costs) and two correspond to the exchange/subjective side of the economy (a logical category – marginal utility, and a historical category – exchange value). Tugan-Baranovsky's *historical categories* are concepts that are closest to the prices actually observed in a historically and spatially located market. They are *prices*. His *logical categories* represent more abstract and remote constructions of the mind. They are *value*. With these newly defined categories of value and prices, and keeping Tugan-Baranovsky's historical and logical categories in mind, there is no need for a transformation of value into prices: *prices are the historical manifestation of the logical category of value.* Table 5.3 sums up these categories so far.

The category of *prices* is the result of the *synthesis* between exchange value (II) and expenses of production (IV). Exchange value (II) is derived from the marginal utility of individuals (I) and the expenses of production (IV) from the capitalists' understanding of costs. Both categories are observable in the market, and represent together the subjective (exchange) and objective (production) elements of the *synthetic* notion of prices. This synthesis is similar to the neoclassical synthesis à la Marshall, where marginal utility together with Ricardo's relative theory complement each other.

The category of *value* is the result of the *synthesis* between marginal utility (I) and labour costs (III). Marginal utility (I) is the subjective notion of the individual that represents his needs in the sphere of exchange. Labour costs (III) represent the objective conditions necessary in the national economy to meet these needs. In order to achieve this synthesis, labour costs should be proportional to marginal utilities (remember the 'simple synthesis').

In the simple version of the synthesis, however, marginal utility was that of a society, and not of individuals, and the distribution of labour was done as if there were no other means of production. In contrast, in the capitalist economy, prices (and therefore expenses of production) are the regulator of the whole exchange economy, according to which the distribution of labour between the alternative sectors is carried out. In a capitalist economy, nothing guarantees that the distribution of labour costs (III) is done proportionally to the marginal utility of goods (I), according to the economic principle. *Indeed, nothing guarantees that the synthesis in value is possible under capitalism.*

In Smithian terms, this last sentence would become: '*Only* in the early and rude state of society which precedes both the accumulation of stock and the appropriation of land *would* the proportion between the quantities of labour necessary for acquiring different objects *be* the only circumstance which can afford any rule for exchanging them for one another'. In Marxian terms: 'Commodities are *usually* not sold at their labour value.' In neoclassical terms: 'If the production function has *one single input*, labour, then the marginal productivity

Table 5.3 Value and prices according to Tugan-Baranovsky

Value	Prices
I. marginal utility	II. exchange value
III. labour costs	IV. expenses of production

of labour accounts for the whole production, and therefore prices resolve entirely into wages'.

The existence of a category of value next to a category of prices is a necessity for Tugan-Baranovsky. It places the man at the centre of the economy: as a consumer (striving for the greatest happiness...) *and* as a producer (...with the least expense to himself). The synthesis in the category of value, i.e. between marginal utility and labour costs, is the only way to follow the economic principle, under the assumption that man in the economy is always an end, and never a means, following his interpretation of Kant's ethics. His synthesis, in the logical sphere of the economy, is not an attempt at understanding reality; it is an idealised reality.

In this sense, and taking for granted that Tugan-Baranovsky is in fact only interpreting Marx, his approach bears some similarity to Croce's, as defined by Dostaler:

> Value, in Marx, serves as a term of comparison between today's society and the 'ideal' or 'typical' society in which there is neither private ownership of capital nor of labour power. Therefore, for Croce, there is no transformation problem – be it historical or logical – of value into prices, but a logical comparison between value and prices
>
> (Dostaler 1978, 93)

and by Potier (quoting Croce's terminology):

> The law of value would then be specific to the 'working society' [*società lavoratrice*] and would realise only in a fragmentary manner in 'economical societies' historically located. Marx, in establishing the principle of labour value as a 'type', is only proceeding to an 'implicit' or 'elliptical' comparison, between the capitalist (economical) society and a part of it considered independently, the 'working society'.
>
> (Potier 1986, 167)

Tugan-Baranovsky's synthetic theory of value takes a normative status, wherein the ethical principle of the supreme value of human personality prevails as the reference to follow. The notion of value as distinct from prices is required by its idealistic character. And Tugan-Baranovsky is not alone in Russia to call for the necessity of a notion of value. While Struve as an exception rejects the necessity of a notion (value) that nothing distinguishes from that of prices, the necessity of a notion of value is generally acknowledged in Russia: 'The anthropocentric tradition in Russian spiritual history inclined the majority of Russian economists to support the labour theory of value' (Zweynert 2002, 336).

The economic plan

The nature of this idealistic reality, or logical economy, is that production in an ideal society strictly follows the economic principle:[15] 'under a rational distribution of production, the marginal utility of goods must be proportional to their labour costs' (Tugan-Baranovsky 1909, 74). This rational distribution of labour in the economy is what Tugan-Baranovsky calls the *economic plan*. This notion, of which he already had a hint in 1890, originates from his theory of crises. It takes here a dual nature: it describes the distribution of labour in an ideal world, but it also allows the description and understanding of the real-world distribution of labour and the measurement of the distance between the ideal and the actual economic plan. The *ideal economic plan*: 'is at best an economic ideal, towards which it [the distribution of production] tends but never reaches. A perfect coincidence of the labour evaluation and the marginal utility evaluation is possible only at the ideal' (Tugan-Baranovsky 1909, 74). At the same time, there exists an economic plan in the actual – capitalist – economy: 'The economy requires a defined plan, a determinate distribution of labour between the alternative sectors of the economy' (Tugan-Baranovsky 1909, 30), and although 'the national economy does not follow any conscious plan … it yet behaves as if such a plan existed' (Tugan-Baranovsky 1909, 32). The capitalist economy, in which nobody dictates how many potatoes to plant or how many trousers to sew, does not lead to chaos, but naturally finds a kind of proportionality (through prices, the visible barometer). The mechanism works, even with tremors (crises), but it works as if there was a plan (Tugan-Baranovsky 1903, 4).[16] The absence of a real plan, however, is visible in the capitalist economy: it is here that Marx's critique of capitalism preserves its scientific meaning: as long as the ideal economic plan is not implemented, the economy is not ruled by humans for humans, but for other purposes, whose consequences include the exploitation of man by man, and not, as they ought to be, the exploitation of nature by man *for* man.

Tugan-Baranovsky saw in socialism the *historical* manifestation of this ideal society. In one of his last books, *Socialism as a Positive Doctrine* ([1918] 1996), he complains that socialists, though they did much to criticise capitalism, did very little to find the basis of the new socialist society. By 1918, this was certainly a crucial necessity. It is precisely in a socialist society that marginal utility will coincide with labour costs of goods, since the economic plan will be consciously established:

> For the establishment of this [economic] plan, the socialist society will have two considerations in mind: on the one hand, it must take into account the marginal utility of each good, on the other hand, their labour costs. These are the two fundamental elements for the construction of the socialist economic plan.
>
> (Tugan-Baranovsky [1918] 1996, 390)

The example given in the simple version of the synthesis takes on a new significance here: the organic synthesis of marginal utility and labour costs is possible only in the socialist economy, because only in this case are the two fundamental logical categories of the economy (value and absolute costs, in Tugan-Baranovsky's terminology) fully apparent. Under capitalism, costs are visible in their relative version only: the expenses of production. This explains the impossibility of transforming value into prices under capitalism: there is no direct relation between labour costs and capitalist prices: labour cannot be the substance of value in capitalism. The direct relation between labour costs and value is apparent only in socialism.[17]

To sum up, the economic plan, defined as the distribution of labour among the different productive sectors, contains two main significations. For capitalism, it constitutes an ideal reference from which the antinomy between expenses of production and labour costs is understandable. It shows the misappropriation of economic activity, not as an end for human needs, but as an unethical activity, which confuses the means with the end, and alters the true aim of human labour. For socialism, the economic plan provides the basic principle according to which planning should be done. The ideal reference it constitutes in capitalism becomes reality in socialism.

In the theory of value, the economic plan is the medium of reconciliation of the two sectors of the economy: exchange (marginal utility) and production (labour costs). An organic synthesis emerges only when the two categories are in full agreement, when 'the leading ethical idea of political economy', Kant's 'supreme and therefore equivalent value of human personality', is not only recognized in theory, but in practice. Nevertheless, it should be remembered that for Tugan-Baranovsky, 'the ethical foundation of labour costs does not undermine the scientific significance of this notion, but proves how intimately related are, in political economy, the categories of what is [*suŝij*] and what ought to be [*dolžnij*]' (Tugan-Baranovsky 1909, 81). Therefore, Tugan-Baranovsky had in mind a scientific synthesis within the theory of value, in which an important role is attributed to ethics.[18]

The economic plan connects the two spheres of the economy, relates the subjective evaluation to the objective process of production, allows for the distinction between socialism and capitalism, defines socialism as a practical science through planning, and is precisely the notion connecting the positive and the normative in Tugan-Baranovsky's economic theory. The economic plan, with its idealistic and realistic parts, is both a positive *and* a normative notion, acting as a platform for the reconciliation of labour costs and marginal utility (a synthesis in value) and of exchange value and expenses of production (a synthesis in prices). The transformation of value to prices is not possible in capitalism, where the actual economic plan does not match the ideal economic plan, while it becomes unnecessary in socialism, where the actual and the ideal economic plans coincide and value and prices become one.

Tugan-Baranovsky divides his analysis twice: once by the logical/historical dichotomy; once by the exchange/production dichotomy. The first division (logical/historical) is necessary for him to distinguish the economic mechanisms dependent on the economic order (capitalism) from those independent of any economic order (to discover those at work even under socialism). The second division (subjective evaluation or exchange and objective conditions of production) is necessary to separate what *is* from what *ought to be* so that their reunification, through the economic plan, preserves its scientific prominence, but at the same time contains an idealistic element. Herein precisely lies Tugan-Baranovsky's originality: not in new elements concerning the understanding of value or prices, but in the ethical status of his economic plan, which was intended to help building the road towards a better future.

In this particular sense, one can see in Tugan-Baranovsky's synthesis a resurgence of Engels's historical interpretation of the transformation debate, but (once again) in the reverse order: in future utopian socialist societies, commodities *will* be exchanged at their value.

Throughout his career, from his very first article in 1890 introducing marginalism in Russia up to his last socialist thoughts in 1918, Tugan-Baranovsky had always been interested in developing a synthetic theory of value and prices. Unlike Marx, he called *costs* the amount of labour embodied in a commodity. Unlike Marx, he considered that *value*, as the foundation of *prices*, is the result of the synthesis between marginal utility and of supply (under capitalism as under socialism). Supply corresponds to the *economic plan*, i.e. the distribution of labour among the various branches in the economy.

In a capitalist economy, the economic plan is chaotic because it does not follow the economic principle of maximising social output under the constraint of the least human labour costs. On the contrary, it follows the interests of the capitalists, who make individual economic plans according to their expenses of production (wages, profits and rent). *Prices* are in this system the result of the synthesis between *costs of production* (or relative costs, i.e. the materialist side) and *marginal utility* (the psychological side).

Tugan-Baranovsky's terminology was considered by most of his contemporaries either as unhelpful or harmful in that it deviated from Marx. But this is precisely what allowed him to introduce within the theory his ethical concept of the supreme value of human personality, borrowed from his reading of Kant. Indeed, Tugan-Baranovsky sees the advent of socialism as coinciding with the end of capitalist exploitation; by setting human beings at the centre of the economy, choosing their needs *and* efforts, the economy should be at the service of humankind, and not the other way round. Tugan-Baranovsky's contribution to the building of the new society consists in his idea of planning: labour, for ethical reasons, should be distributed among the economic sectors according to the needs of society, taking into account only the expenses of human labour itself, or absolute labour costs, which results in a synthesis between absolute labour costs and marginal utility. Beyond the terms employed, it is a synthesis between marginal utility and labour value in the Marxian sense that Tugan-Baranovsky accomplished. And it is at the basis of his socialist economic plan.

In the end, Tugan-Baranovsky observed an insurmountable gap between value and prices in the capitalist economy. He tried to fill this gap. He eventually reached a synthesis between value and prices under the condition that a socialist economic plan is consciously applied.

Fascinated by the blind economic forces at work in the modern industrialised economies, Tugan-Baranovsky first studied the English economic crises and then

Russian industrial history to figure out the workings of a capitalist economy. He reached conclusions that did not fit with his Marxist convictions, and he progressively moved away from Marxism. This distance from Marx took two forms. First, he rethought the theory of socialism without Marx and started the journey from scratch with Utopian socialists. Second, he reworked Marx's labour theory of value, in order to integrate his ethical component.

On this latter point, he started with a criticism of Marx's way of transforming labour values into prices of production. However, his theory of socialism, based on the economic plan, eventually reaches a synthesis between value and prices. In the end, and half-way between Croce and Engels, *value* regulates exchange relations in his ideal society (reminiscent of Croce's *società lavoratrice* – working society) and prices transform into value within the socialist economic plan (this reverses the direction of history in Engels's *historical* transformation). But Marx's own transformation problem ends, in Tugan-Baranovsky's terminology, in an incompatibility between absolute and relative costs.

In his highly analytic synthesis between marginal utility and labour value, Tugan-Baranovsky was followed by some of his students. They were, however, not interested in his inclination for ethics. Like Tugan-Baranovsky, they produced attempts at synthesis between marginal utility and labour value. Like Tugan-Baranovsky, they tackled the Marxian transformation problem. But unlike Tugan-Baranovsky, they were mathematicians. Will the language of mathematics simplify Tugan-Baranovsky's terminological issues, or will it lower the level of the debate? Retrospectively, textbooks on the history of economic thought remember Dmitriev's equations, but forget Tugan-Baranovsky's synthesis. The last chapter of this book takes an interest in these issues.

Ethics without mathematics?

But before starting the analysis of the transformation of the Russian synthesis by so-called Russian mathematical economists, and in order to facilitate the transition to the next chapter, it is important to briefly clarify Tugan-Baranovsky's views on mathematics.

In Tugan-Baranovsky's synthesis, the relation to ethics is explicit. In his system of thought, ethics enters into consideration not only in economic policy (applied science) but also in the theory of political economy (abstract science), through the point of view of observation of economic life, so that normative and positive parts of his system interact. In his synthesis, the choice of absolute costs, or human labour costs as the only pertinent social costs (or value) is motivated by ethics. In other words, *in the theory*, *value* as the synthesis between social labour costs and social marginal utility represents the normative component of his analysis, while *prices* as the synthesis between marginal utility and the capitalists' costs of production represent its positive counterpart. *On the practical side*, the objective of economic policy is to move *prices* towards *value* in order to follow the ethical ideal, which is what socialism is designed for.

In his system, the key notion articulating the objective and subjective elements is the 'plan', either capitalist or socialist, and the tendency towards an 'ideal' proportionality. An adequate proportionality happens when the productive forces are distributed within the different productive sectors according to the needs of the society. This idea of proportionality is expressed *mathematically* in Tugan-Baranovsky's writings in his 'simple synthesis' example, where the marginal utilities of each good are proportional to their labour costs. His reproduction schemes and Menger's schemes represent most of the mathematics in Tugan-Baranovsky's work. In addition, he makes considerable use of statistical tables for a descriptive work. And, sometimes, reasoning is expressed with a ratio a/b. While he was reluctant to use mathematics in his work, his prose is impregnated with mathematics. He wrote:

> If in this numerical example we had chosen other numbers, then we could not obtain a strict proportionality. This is explained by the fact that a strict proportionality can be reached only at the margin [*predel'*] – under the hypothesis of a possible infinitely small increase of the production of each good – but in concrete cases, it reaches only an approximation of this proportionality. It is also explained by the fact that, in real life, the last unit of time is used in the production of goods with various, i.e. not equal, marginal utility. In the above example of the [self-]production of stoves, the production stops with the first stove, with maximal marginal utility; the second will not be produced, since it is not needed. Because of this, the production ends in the last unit of time in different activities of labour with unequal levels of utility, although this contradicts the principle of seeking the greatest utility. All this must be borne in mind, to understand the conditional and purely abstract meaning of the principle of the gravitation [*tâgotenie*], established in the text, of marginal utilities towards proportional labour costs.
>
> (Tugan-Baranovsky [1909], third edition 1915, 56)

It appears from the above passage that Tugan-Baranovsky was not only aware that his numerical example was well chosen but also that proportionality only holds at the margin. He clearly understood the difference between continuous and discontinuous utility curves, and between discrete and continuous goods. Moreover, he not only had an intuition about derivatives, but also the knowledge of them. In fact, on 11 February 1902, the Kiev mathematician Stoliarov gave a conference at the Kiev Physico-Mathematical Society, entitled 'Analytical Proof of the Politico-Economic Formulae Proposed by M. Tugan-Baranovsky: Marginal Utility of Freely Produced Goods Proportional to their Labour Costs', in which he showed that Tugan-Baranovsky's proposition can be deduced with the use of differential calculus. Similarly, one of Tugan-Baranovsky's students, Girshfeld, offered in 1910 another – algebraic – expression for Tugan-Baranovsky's synthesis, entitled 'Theorem of the Proportionality of the Marginal Utility of Goods with their Labour Costs'.[19]

Tugan-Baranovsky had been trained in mathematics during his studies in natural sciences at Kharkov University, and he was not opposed to the use of mathematics in political economy, especially in pure economics. Two reasons may account for his parsimonious use of mathematics.

First, Tugan-Baranovsky wanted to convince his audiences. In order to do so, he took seriously into account the pedagogical part of his activity, and he anticipated the negative reactions of his colleagues. His lectures were popular, and his textbook was a best seller. He was not prepared to wait for years to find a publisher ready to print a mathematical political economy book, like Dmitriev did. In 1913, his textbook *Principles of Political Economy* was submitted for the Greig Prize. This prize was an exceptional award of 1,000 roubles left by the late Greig, former Minister of Finance, and granted every five years to the best book on political economy and public finance written in Russian (Shirokorad and Dmitriev 2008, 118–123).

An influential member of the selection committee, Yanzhul, wrote to Tugan-Baranovsky that he was very happy with his book, his only complaint being Tugan-Baranovsky's 'abuse of the mathematical method'. In an attempt to justify himself, Tugan-Baranovsky wrote to him:

> One of the objections formulated in your letter is the 'misuse of the mathematical method'. Evidently, you have in mind my schemes in the chapter devoted to the theory of market. I am well aware of the awkward and heavy apparatus of my schemes, and would prefer to do without them, in particular in a work of such general character as my textbook. Unfortunately, I did not see another way to give sufficient accuracy to my presentation. [...] Mathematical formulations have a more precise nature. I have recourse to them, well aware of all the inconvenience of their exposition.
>
> [...] I mean that mathematical constructions cannot help to establish new propositions, but can merely help to prove these propositions, once they are derived through inductive generalisation and logical deduction. My theory of crises was derived in an inductive way – I reached it by studying facts on the development of English industry – mostly through the study of price movements of different commodities [...]. From here, step by step, I constructed my theory of crises, and then my theory of the market.
>
> I exposed my theoretical views on the subject in the reverse order: [...] because it is only possible to bring the logical proof to completion by means of deduction.
>
> So I think that the mathematical method in political economy is unusable for the discovery of new truths, but in some cases it is the only possibly method of demonstration.
>
> (Letter from Tugan-Baranovsky to Yanzhul, 30 July 1913. In Shirokorad and Dmitriev 2008, 125–126)[20]

It is rather paradoxical for the first author who made an analytical use of Marx's schemes of reproduction, and ample use of Menger's schemes, to claim that new ideas could not be discovered with the help of the mathematical method. This may be explained by the fact that, willingly or not, Tugan-Baranovsky restrained his use of mathematics in order to reach a greater public and to please his older colleagues, before considering his taste and capacities for mathematics. This reason should not be underestimated. Not unrelated to what has just been said, Tugan-Baranovsky won the Greig Prize in 1913.

The second reason why Tugan-Baranovsky was parsimonious with his use of mathematics, although he was not explicit about it, is equally important. While mathematics are useful in demonstrating the 'simple synthesis', they are helpless to reflect the richer dimensions of the 'complex synthesis', and especially the nature of categories. It is from the distinction between historical and logical categories that Tugan-Baranovsky could extract his socialist ideas on planning.

Tugan-Baranovsky did not find mathematics incompatible with his synthesis. He even considered that the application of the mathematical method in political economy was necessary in some cases. But he probably would have found the mathematical method insufficient to express his synthesis. He could have concluded: 'Mathematics are useful, but only at the margin'.

Notes

1 This first paper is based on Tugan-Baranovsky's diploma, obtained in 1889 at the University of Kharkov. The title of the diploma was 'The Causes of Value'. Unfortunately, it was not possible to locate a copy of this unpublished dissertation. In the same vein, Tugan-Baranovsky wrote a dissertation (probably lost as well), the same year, for his grade in natural sciences. The theme of this dissertation was, intriguingly enough, the phenomena of two-headed animals. However, Tugan-Baranovsky never used such a biological analogy to describe his synthesis.

2 On mathematical economics in Russia before 1890, see Dmitriev (1908, 24–26), Shukov (1988) and Belykh (2007, chap. 1).

3 Vernadsky made the first mention in Russia of Gossen's work (Vernadsky 1858, 161–162) and Slonimsky presented Thünen and Cournot's works (Slonimsky 1878).

4 Menger's *Grundsätze der Volkswirthschaftslehre* were translated into Russian (see Menger [1871] 1903) and an authorised translation of Böhm-Bawerk's *Kapital und Kapitalzins* was supervised and prefaced by Tugan-Baranovsky himself in 1909.

5 Tugan-Baranovsky read Jevons's *Theory of Political Economy*, but certainly not Walras's *Éléments d'économie politique pure*. This conclusion is drawn, not on the issue of command of the French language, which Tugan-Baranovsky mastered, but on the absence of textual evidence: (i) every single word written by Tugan-Baranovsky on Walras is found in Wieser's own writings; (ii) in some places, only Gossen, Jevons and Menger are called the founders of a new school of political economy. Therefore, it is difficult to agree with Nove's statement, according to which Tugan-Baranovsky 'read Menger, Jevons *and Walras* and took them very seriously' (Nove 1970, 247, emphasis added).

6 On Russian Marx revisionists (or 'Legal Marxists' as they are misleadingly labelled), see Kindersley (1962) and Zweynert (2002, chap. 5). On their contributions against Marx, see Howard and King (1989, chap. 10; 1995).

7 The following three versions of the *Principles* have been consulted: the first edition (1909), the second (1911), the third (1915) and the 1998 reprint of the fourth edition (1917). The most relevant chapters on value and prices underwent only small changes (stylistic changes and shortenings, updated bibliography). Unless otherwise stated, all quotations are taken from the 1998 edition.

8 Tugan-Baranovsky's theory of value and prices has already been the object of various interpretations. Among them, in chronological order, see Stoliarov (1902), Danielson (1902), Shaposhnikov (1909), Dmitriev (1909), Girshfeld (1910), Bukharin ([1919] 1927, Appendix), Kondratiev ([1923] 1998, 323–324), Seraphim (1925, 74–87), Gringauz (1928, chap. IV), Gotz (1930, chap. I.2), Timoshenko (1954), Kindersley (1962, 155–172), Kowal (1965, chap. IV), Nove (1970, 119–121), Amato (1984), Howard and King (1995), Barnett (2000), Rogachevskaya (2001, 150–155), Zweynert (2002, 332–337), Schütte (2002, 37–43), Klimina (2008, 5–7), Nenovsky (2009), and Makasheva (2008, 79–82). Kowal (1965), Barnett (2000) and Makasheva (2008) are the first, as far as it could be ascertained, to interpret Tugan-Baranovsky's theory of value from more than two sources (his *Study on Marginal Utility, Principles* and *Socialism as a Positive Doctrine*). The present interpretation pursues further their effort in that direction. It is different from them in that the central emphasis is on the notion of an economic plan.

9 Tugan-Baranovsky had in mind two rather different reference economies – end of nineteenth-century England and Russia – on which he conducted detailed economic historical studies.

10 Equally, Girshfeld (1910) sees only advantages in the social, or national, level: it cancels out individual anomalies.

11 The distinction between retail and wholesale prices, the recognition of routine in consumption and of all other exceptions to the economic principle are of great importance for the study of *concrete* prices, as in Tooke's *History of Prices* (1838–1857). In Tugan-Baranovsky's methodology, it belongs to the *concrete* (descriptive, not explanatory) science.

12 Rubin explicitly rejects Tugan-Baranovsky's transformation of labour value, i.e. his *costs*, into a purely logical category (Rubin [1928] 1972). Howard and King (1990, 93–95), for their part, reject Tugan-Baranovsky's critique of Marx and treatment of value theory as the weakest point of his revisionism.

13 The controversy carries on. In 2007, two regular papers were published in the same issue of *Voprosy Ekonomiki* (Problems of Economics), with the words *cennost'* and *stoimost'* in their title to designate the same notion. See Chekhovsky (2008).

14 Tugan-Baranovsky observes that the same applies to banknotes: while they are considered in the household as wealth, it is no longer the case from the point of view of the national economy (Tugan-Baranovsky 1909, 79).

15 The notion of 'economic principle' is borrowed from either Hermann (on this, see Kirzner 1960, chap. 3.3) or Menger, both of them quoted in Tugan-Baranovsky's 1890 paper.

16 Barnett (2000, 120) comments: 'This meant that for Tugan capitalism involved 'planning' in a specific sense.'

17 At this stage, it is difficult to follow Klimina, according to whom:

> It is interesting to note that if initially Tugan-Baranovsky tried to reconcile a labour theory of value with neoclassical utility analysis (1890, 1909), later on, in his final methodological article on the question ([1919] 1977), cited above, he fully allied himself with marginalism and its focus on rational individuals and attained equilibrium states.
>
> (2008, 5)

The mentioned methodological paper, published posthumously (Tugan-Baranovsky [1919] 1977) shows no association with neoclassical analysis: its focus is indeed on marginal utility, and on the strong link between marginalism and socialism, but in the same vein, and even with the same words as in his *Principles* (1909). Therefore, Tugan-Baranovsky was still trying to 'reconcile a labour theory with neoclassical utility analysis' in his 1918 book on socialism and even when he wrote his last 1919 paper.

18 Zweynert sees in the synthesis the expression of Tugan-Baranovsky's two sides: scientific–rational (marginal utility) and ethical–socialist (labour value) (Zweynert 2002, 328).
19 This work was published in 1910, together with other students' and professors' work, in one of the collective volumes, *Problems of Social Sciences*, edited non-periodically by Tugan-Baranovsky and his colleagues, notably as a platform to publish students' seminar works.
20 These kinds of arguments between scholars on the use of mathematics in political economy are more and more frequent after the 1870s. On the case of Menger and Walras on mathematics as a means of exposition vs a means of deduction, see their correspondence, analysed by Garrouste (1994).

References

Amato, Sergio. 1984. 'Tugan-Baranovsky's Theories of Markets, Accumulation and Industrialization: Their Influence on the Development of Economic Thought and Modern Historiographic Research'. In Iwan S. Koropeckyj, ed., *Selected Contributions of Ukrainian Scholars to Economics*, 1–59. Cambridge, MA: Harvard University Press.
Barnett, Vincent. 2000. 'Tugan-Baranovskii's Vision of an International Socialist Economy'. *European Journal for the History of Economic Thought*, 7: 115–135.
Belykh, Andrej Akatovich. 2007. *Istoriâ Rossijskih èkonomiko-matematičeskih issledovanij (History of Russian Mathematical-Economic Investigations)*. Second edition. Moscow: LKI.
Böhm-Bawerk, Eugen von. 1909. *Kapital i pribyl' (Capital and Interest)*. Authorised translation from the second German edition by L. I. Forbert, under the supervision and with a preface by Mikhail Ivanovich Tugan-Baranovsky. St Petersburg: Rozen.
Bortkiewicz, Ladislaus von. 1906–1907. 'Wertrechnung und Preisrechnung im Marxschen System (I–II–III)'. *Archiv für Sozialwissenschaft und Sozialpolitik*, XXIII: 1–50; XXV: 10–51 and 445–488. Parts II and III translated into English by J. Kahane. 1952. 'Value and Prices in the Marxian System'. *International Economic Papers*, 2: 5–60.
Bortkiewicz, Ladislaus von. 1907. 'Zur Berichtigung der grundlegenden theoretischen Konstruktion von Marx im 3. Band des Kapital'. *Jahrbücher für Nationalökonomie und Statistik*, 34: 319–335. Translated into English: 'On the Correction of Marx's Fundamental Theoretical Construction in the Third Volume of Capital'. In Paul M. Sweezy, ed., *Karl Marx and the Close of His System*, 199–221, 1949. New York: Kelley.
Bukharin, Nikolay Ivanovich. [1919] 1927. *Političeskaâ èkonomiâ rant'e (Economic Theory of the Leisure Class)*. London: Martin Lawrence.
Chekhovsky, V. 2008. 'O perevode Marksova "Wert" na russkij âzyk (On the Translation of Marx's Wert in Russian)'. *Voprosy èkonomiki*, 1: 154–157.
Danielson (pseudonym Nikolay-on), Nikolay Francevich. 1902. 'Teoriâ trudovoj stoimosti i nekotorye iz ee kritikov (Theory of Labour Value and Some of Their Critics)'. *Russkoe Bogatstvo*, 2–3: 31–69, 31–65.
Dmitriev, Vladimir Karpovich. [1904] 1974. *Èkonomičeskie očerki (Economic Essays)*. Moscow: Rikhter. First essay published in 1898, Moscow: Moscow University. Second and third essays published in 1902, Moscow: Rikhter. English edition by Domenico Mario Nuti. 1974. London: Cambridge University Press.
Dmitriev, Vladimir Karpovich. 1908. 'Teoriâ cennosti. Obzor literatury na russkom âzyke (Value Theory. Review of the Literature in the Russian Language)'. *Kritičeskoe Obozrenie*, VII: 12–26.

Dmitriev, Vladimir Karpovich. 1909. 'Novyj russkij traktat po teorii političeskoj èkonomii [M. I. Tugan-Baranovskij. Osnovy političeskoj èkonomii. Spb., 1909 (xii+760s., cena 3 rublja.)] (A New Russian Treatise in the Theory of Political Economy. Tugan-Baranovsky's Fundamentals of Political Economy, 1909)'. *Russkaâ Mysl'*, 30: 102–125.

Dostaler, Gilles. 1978. *Valeur et prix. Histoire d'un débat*. Montréal: François Maspero, Presses Universitaires de Grenoble, Les presses de l'Université du Québec.

Garrouste, Pierre. 1994. 'Léon Walras et Carl Menger à propos de l'utilisation des mathématiques en économie politique'. *Economies et sociétés, série PE (Œconomia)*, 20–21: 11–27.

Girshfeld, V. 1910. 'Teorema o proporcional'nosti predel'nyh poleznostej blag ih trudovym stoimostâm (Theorem of the Proportionality of the Marginal Utility of Goods with their Labour Costs)'. In Mikhail Ivanovich Tugan-Baranovsky and Pavel Isaakovich Lyubinsky, eds, *Voprosy obshchestvovedenija (Problems in Social Sciences)*, vol. 2. St Petersburg: Slovo.

Gotz, Wulf. 1930. *Zum ökonomischen System Tugan-Baranovskys*. Ph.D. diss., referent: Prof. Dr. Karl Diehl. Freiburg im Breisgau: Albert-Ludwicks-Universität.

Gringauz, Samuel. 1928. *M. I. Tugan-Baranowsky und seine Stellung in der theoretischen Nationalökonomie*. Riga: Salamandra.

Howard, Michael C. and John E. King. 1989. *A History of Marxian Economics: Volume I, 1883–1929*. London: Macmillan.

Howard, Michael C. and John E. King. 1990. 'Tugan-Baranovsky, Russian Revisionism and Marxian Political Economy'. In Donald E. Moggridge, ed., *Perspectives on the History of Economic Thought, Vol. III. Classicals, Marxians and Neo-Classicals*. Hants, England: Edward Elgar for the History of Economics Society.

Howard, Michael C. and John E. King. 1995. 'Value Theory and Russian Marxism before the Revolution'. In Ian Steedman, ed., *Socialism and Marginalism in Economics: 1870–1930*, 224–257. London: Routledge.

Kindersley, Richard. 1962. *The First Russian Revisionists: a Study of 'Legal Marxism' in Russia*. Oxford: Clarendon Press.

Kirzner, Israel M. 1960. *The Economic Point of View: An Essay in the History of Economic Thought*. Princeton, NJ: Van Nostrand.

Klimina, Anna. 2008. 'On Misuse of the Term "Institutionalist" in the Analysis of Russian Academic Economics of the Late Nineteenth and Early Twentieth Centuries: the Case of Michail Tugan-Baranovsky (1865–1919)'. *Economics Bulletin*, 2: 1–9.

Kondratiev, Nikolay Dmitrievich. [1923] 1998. 'M. I. Tugan-Baranovsky. Basic Features of his Scientific World-View'. In Natalia A. Makasheva, Warren J. Samuels, and Vincent Barnett, eds, *The Works of Nikolai D. Kondratiev*. London: Pickering & Chatto.

Kowal, Lubomyr Mariana. 1965. *Economic Doctrines of M. I. Tugan-Baranovsky*. PhD diss. Urbana: University of Illinois.

Makasheva, Natalia A. 2008. 'Searching for an Ethical Basis of Political Economy: Bulgakov and Tugan-Baranovsky'. In Vincent Barnett and Joachim Zweynert, eds, *Economics in Russia. Studies in Intellectual History*, chap. 6, 75–89. Aldershot, UK: Ashgate.

Menger, Carl. [1871] 1903. *Osnovaniâ političeskoj èkonomii (Principles of Economics)*. Translated by R. M. Orzhencky. Odessa: Hakalovskij.

Nenovsky, Nikolay. 2009. 'Place of Labor and Labor Theory in Tugan Baranovsky's Theoretical System'. *The Kyoto Economic Review*, 78: 53–77.

Nove, Alec. 1970. 'M. I. Tugan-Baranovsky (1865–1919)', *History of Political Economy*, 2(2): 246–262.

Potier, Jean-Pierre. 1986. *Lectures italiennes de Marx. Les conflits d'interprétation chez les économistes et les philosophes (1883–1983)*. Lyon: Presses universitaires de Lyon.

Rogachevskaya, M. A. 2001. 'M. I. Tugan-Baranovskij – vydaûŝijsâ russkij èkonomist (Tugan-Baranovsky: Eminent Russian Economist)'. *Eko*, 9: 135–155.

Rubin, Isaak Ilich. [1928] 1972. *Essays on Marx's Theory of Value*. Translated by Miloš Samardźija and Fredy Perlman from the third Russian edition. Detroit, MI: Black and Red.

Schütte, Frank. 2002. *Die ökonomischen Studien V. K. Dmitrievs*. Ph.D. diss., Technische Universität Chemnitz. Available at: http://monarch.qucosa.de/fileadmin/data/qucosa/documents/5136/data/start.html (accessed on 5 August 2014).

Seraphim, Hans-Jürgen. 1925. *Neuere russische Wert- und Kapitalzinstheorien*. Berlin and Leipzig: Gruyter.

Shaposhnikov, Nikolay Nikolaevich. 1909. 'Review of Tugan-Baranovsky's Principles of Political Economy (1909)'. *Kritičeskoe Obozrenie*, 5: 48–53.

Shirokorad, Leonid Dmitrievich and Anton Leonidovich Dmitriev, eds. 2008. *Neizvestnyj M. I. Tugan-Baranovskij (Unknown M. I. Tugan-Baranovsky)*. St Petersburg: Nestor-Istoriâ.

Shukov, N. S. 1988. 'Mathematical Economics in Russia (1867–1917)'. *Matekon*, 24: 3–31.

Slonimsky, Lûdvig Zinovevich. 1878. 'Zabytie èkonomisty. Tjunen i Kurno (Thünen and Cournot: Forgotten Economists)'. *Vestnik Evropy*, 9: 5–27.

Stoliarov, Nikolay Aleksandrovich. 1902. *Analitičeskoe dokazatel'stvo predloženoj g. M. Tugan-Baranovskim politiko-èkonomičeskoj formuly: Predel'nye poleznosti svobodno proizvedennyh produktov proporcional'ny ih trudovym stoimostâm (Analytical Proof of the Politico-Economic Formulae Proposed by M. Tugan-Baranovsky: Marginal Utility of Freely Produced Goods Proportional to their Labour Costs)*. Lecture at the Physico-Mathematical Society of Kiev, 11 February 1902. Kiev: Kuk'ženko.

Timoshenko, Volodymyr Prokopovich. 1954. 'M. I. Tuhan-Baranovsky and Western European Economic Thought (Speech on the 5th Anniversary of his Death)'. *The Annals of the Ukrainian Academy of Arts and Sciences in the US*, 3: 803–823. First published (without the addendum) in Ukrainian in 1925.

Tooke, Thomas. 1838–1857. *A History of Prices and of the State of the Circulation from 1793 to 1856.* 6 volumes (vol. 5–6 co-written with William Newmarch). London: P. S. King & Son.

Tugan-Baranovsky, Mikhail Ivanovich. 1890. 'Učenie o predel'noj poleznosti hozâjstvennyh blag kak pričina ih cennosti (Study on the Marginal Utility of Economic Goods as the Cause of their Value)'. *Ûridičeskij Vestnik*, XXII(10/2): 192–230.

Tugan-Baranovsky, Mikhail Ivanovich. 1899a. 'Osnovnaâ ošibka abstraktnoj teorii kapitalizma Marksa (The Fundamental Error in Marx's Abstract Theory of Capitalism)'. *Naučnoe Obozrenie*, 5: 973–985.

Tugan-Baranovsky, Mikhail Ivanovich. 1899b. 'Russkie perevody I toma 'Kapitala' Marksa. Zametka (Russian Translations of the First Volume of Marx's Capital. A Comment)'. *Mir Božij*, 8: 10–16.

Tugan-Baranovsky, Mikhail Ivanovich. 1900a. 'Adam Smith'. In *Ènciklopedičeskij slovar'*, vol. 60. St Petersburg: Brockhaus and Efron.

Tugan-Baranovsky, Mikhail Ivanovich. 1900b. 'Trudovaâ cennost' i pribyl'. Moim kritikam (Labour Value and Profit. To My Critics)'. *Naučnoe Obozrenie*, VII: 607–633.

Tugan-Baranovsky, Mikhail Ivanovich. 1903. *Očerki iz novejšej istorii političeskoj ekonomii (Essays on the Newest History of Political Economy)*. St Petersburg: Mir Božij.

Tugan-Baranovsky, Mikhail Ivanovich. 1905a. *Teoretičeskie osnovy marksizma (Theoretical Foundations of Marxism)*. St Petersburg: Mir Božij.

Tugan-Baranovsky, Mikhail Ivanovich. 1905b. *Theoretische Grundlagen des Marxismus*. Leipzig: Duncker & Humblot.

Tugan-Baranovsky, Mikhail Ivanovich. 1906a. *Sovremennyj socializm v svoem istoričeskom razvitii (Modern Socialism in its Historical Development)*. Moscow: Petrovskaâ.

Tugan-Baranovsky, Mikhail Ivanovich. 1906b. 'Subjektivismus und Objektivismus in der Wertlehre'. *Archiv für Sozialwissenschaft und Sozialpolitik*, 22: 557–564.

Tugan-Baranovsky, Mikhail Ivanovich. 1909. *Osnovy političeskoj èkonomii (Principles of Political Economy)*. St Petersburg: Slovo. Third edition, 1915. Petrograd: Pravo. Reprint of the fourth edition, 1998. Moscow: Rosspèn.

Tugan-Baranovsky, Mikhail Ivanovich. [1918] 1996. *Socializm kak položitel'noe učenie (Socialism as a Positive Doctrine)*. Moscow: URSS.

Tugan-Baranovsky, Mikhail Ivanovich. [1919] 1977. 'The Influence of Ideas of Political Economy on the Natural Science and Philosophy'. *The Annals of the Ukrainian Academy of Arts and Sciences in the US*, XIII: 189–208. Posthumous English translation from the Russian.

Vernadsky, Ivan Vasilevich. 1858. *Očerk istorii političeskoj èkonomii (Essay on the History of Political Economy)*. St Petersburg: Èkonomičeskij Ukazatel'.

Zweynert, Joachim. 2002. *Eine Geschichte des ökonomischen Denkens in Russland. 1805–1905*. Marburg, Germany: Metropolis Verlag.

6   The mathematicians' syntheses

For more than half a century, there has been a new trend in political economy, which is associated with the application of mathematical method to the analysis of economic issues. The founder of this trend is the famous mathematician Auguste Cournot, who published in 1838 a book in which he applies higher mathematical theorems for the first time to the study of several economic issues. Despite its novelty and originality, this book went unnoticed, and its author fell into oblivion. However, the idea of the possibility and fruitfulness of applying the mathematical method to political economy had not been abandoned. A number of scholars appeared, more or less successfully pursuing this goal: Gossen, Thünen, Walras and others. The number of supporters of the mathematical method has grown each year, especially from the 1870s and 1880s, even creating a whole school of mathematical-economists. This trend did not remain unknown to Russian scientists. Recently, a book appeared in our country, whose author, V. K. Dmitriev, is a strong and ardent supporter of the mathematical method.

(Shaposhnikov 1905, 75)

Tugan-Baranovsky's *synthesis*, which was referred to in the literature as a 'synthesis', a 'formula', or 'conciliation', was rapidly either criticised or imitated in the Russian economic literature.

The critical point of view was almost always directed against Tugan-Baranovsky's methodology. Bukharin provides the best example of such a critique in an appendix to his *Economic Theory of the Leisure Class* ([1919] 1927).[1] This appendix, entitled 'The Policy of Theoretical Conciliation (Tugan-Baranovsky's Theory of Value)', attacks Tugan-Baranovsky on the basis that he did not understand both Marxism and marginalism: the first is a social, objective, historical theory concerned with production conditions, the second is an individualist, subjective, a-historical theory concerned with consumption only. And Tugan-Baranovsky's approach of mixing both, is either the result of a serious misconception or, as Bukharin stated himself: 'To maintain that a quantity that is applicable only in the field of an individualistic economy is proportional to another quantity applicable only in the field of social economy, is equivalent to "grafting telegraph poles onto pockmarks"' (Bukharin ([1919] 1927, Appendix). On the positive side, several economists were attracted by the implicit mathematical formulation behind Tugan-Baranovsky's synthesis: proportionality between cardinal marginal utilities and labour costs expressed in a quantifiable quantity of hours. These economists were educated according to new standards, shaped by the growing demand from the Imperial government for mathematically literate economists. The number of new chairs of political economy *and statistics* within law faculties reflected this trend. These students were no longer attending law lectures together with a few introductory lectures on political economy. Instead, they had a substantial curriculum in political economy (including lectures by Tugan-Baranovsky in St Petersburg), together with lectures in statistics. From the 1890s onwards, theoretical statistics was developing at a fast pace, incorporating the works of the Russian school of probability theory, and giving birth to the Russian school of mathematical statistics, of which A. A. Chuprov and Slutsky were the brilliant representatives in the 1910s.[2] As a product of this shift in education policy, and as there were no dominant schools in Russia, as there were in France, or in Great Britain, the mathematical school could develop more freely. It can even be asserted that formalism was considered as a means of communication between the various ideas that were developing in the numerous schools.

The first Russian mathematical economists were born. Dmitriev, Bortkiewicz, Slutsky, Shaposhnikov and Yurovsky followed Tugan-Baranovsky's ground-breaking tracks by offering their own attempts at synthesis of the theory of value. Their successive works gradually transformed and reduced the scope of the original project. During this process, one can still find a strong will to find a synthesis between classical political economy and the marginalist school, and an almost persistent will to keep a link between labour and value. But the link between value and prices declines through the successive attempts at synthesis and, more significantly, the interest in ethics entirely disappears. The new generation emancipated itself from the older one, and established a new relationship between political economy and mathematics.

This last chapter shows the successive transformations to which the original synthesis project was subjected. First, brief overviews of the syntheses of Dmitriev, Bortkiewicz, Slutsky and others are given. Then, the focus is on Shaposhnikov, as the finest observer of the recent developments in mathematical political economy in Russia. He was indeed the first to appreciate the pioneering works of his later-celebrated contemporaries, Dmitriev and Bortkiewicz. Unlike them, his work is not well known, and is here taken as representative of his generation: the second generation of the Russian synthesis, composed of mathematical economists. Finally, Yurovsky's position is set out, as the last episode of the Russian synthesis, giving the opportunity to assess its evolution.

Dmitriev, Bortkiewicz, Slutsky and others

The mathematical economists were the first in Russia to have a deep and up-to-date knowledge of the economic literature, both classical and marginalist. In their economic works, they all *more or less* intended a synthesis within the theory of value, with the aid of mathematics.

This section handles several authors. The first two, Dmitriev and Bortkiewicz, are supplemented by Shaposhnikov's comments on their works. He was aware of belonging to this new school of political economy and wanted to share his conviction. He was one of the very first to consider and appreciate the works of Dmitriev and of Bortkiewicz. And he was aware that the mathematical character could put a damper on the development of this science. Indeed: 'Dmitriev's book requires from his readers a habit of mathematical notation, and some knowledge of higher mathematics' (Shaposhnikov 1905, 75). This is why, in an early review of Dmitriev's *Economic Essays* ([1904] 1974), Shaposhnikov feels the necessity to explain without technicalities the content of the 'talented scholar''s books, since the latter 'could pass unnoticed because of its form' (Shaposhnikov 1905, 75).

Dmitriev's Economic essays

Vladimir Karpovich Dmitriev was born in 1868 in Smolensk province. In 1888, he started medical studies at the University of Moscow, but soon changed to political economy at the law faculty. From 1896, he held a tax controller position 'in an obscure province'. He returned to near St Petersburg three years later because of tuberculosis, which had exhausted all his resources, both intellectual and financial. On recovering, he continued to study economics, and taught until the end of his life at the Polytechnical Institute of St Petersburg. He died in 1913 in Gatchina, near St Petersburg.[3]

Dmitriev was not a prolific author. In all, he published two books ([1904] 1974; 1911), two review articles – one on value theory (1908), the other on theoretical statistics (1909a) – and several book reviews in the journals *Russkaâ Mysl'* (Russian Thought), *Russkoe èkonomičeskoe obozrenie* (Russian Economic Review) and *Kritičeskoe obozrenie* (Critical Review). His 1911 book is a statistical investigation on alcohol consumption in Russia. And his main work is his 1904 book, his celebrated *Economic Essays* ([1904] 1974). The subtitle of the work, 'An Attempt at an Organic Synthesis Between Labour Theory of Value and the Theory of Marginal Utility', announces his project: the 'first Russian mathematical economist', according to Shaposhnikov's expression, intended a synthesis with his three essays: on Ricardo's theory of value, on the theory of competition, and on the theory of marginal utility.

In his first essay, 'The Theory of Value of David Ricardo: An Attempt at a Rigorous Analysis' (first published independently in 1898), Dmitriev offers a formalisation of Ricardo's theory of value, with many innovations to his credit.

One such innovation is the mathematical formulation of the total sum of labour (current and past) embodied in a good. Let good i ($i = 1, 2, \ldots, n$) require a_i units of direct labour and $1/m_{i,j}$ units of good j ($j = 1, 2, \ldots, n$). The coefficients of production $1/m_{i,j}$ represent the given technical conditions. The total amount of units of labour A required to produce one unit of good i, is

$$A_i = a_i + \sum_{j=1}^{n} \frac{1}{m_{ij}} A_j \qquad (6.1)$$

This gives a system of n simultaneous equations with n unknowns (A_1, A_2,... A_n). Once the total sum of labour is known, Dmitriev is able to formulate the equations for prices of production:

$$p_i = A_i \cdot l \cdot (1+r)^{t_i} \tag{6.2}$$

where p_i is the price of production of one unit of good i, A_i is the total sum of labour embodied in good i, as determined in equation (6.1), l is the nominal wage for one unit of labour, r is the profit rate in the economy and t_i is the duration of the production process of good i. This gives a set of n equations, but with $(n+2)$ unknowns ($p_1,\ldots, p_n$, l, r). Since only relative prices are of concern here, one of the goods is taken as numeraire ($p_g=1$). At that stage, the system is not yet determined. This is precisely why the Austrians and Walras accused Ricardo of circular reasoning: explaining the prices of goods (p_i) by other prices (r and l). Dmitriev shows that this accusation is unfair. Under the assumption that real wage is given – by considerations that fall outside the scope of economic theory – nominal wage can be rewritten as:

$$l = k \cdot p_k \tag{6.3}$$

where k is the wage good for one unit of labour, and p_k is the price of the wage good. By introducing the equation (6.2) for $i=k$ in equation (6.3), this gives the rate of profit (6.4).

$$l = k \cdot p_k = k \cdot l \cdot A_k \cdot (1+r)^{t_k} \Rightarrow r = \sqrt[t_k]{\frac{1}{k \cdot A_k}} - 1 \tag{6.4}$$

The system is determined (under the criteria that the number of equations equals the number of unknowns), and the profit rate comes from the sector of the economy that produces the wage good (see Dmitriev [1904] 1974, First essay; and Shaposhnikov 1905, 78–80).

Dmitriev further examines several complications in his first essay, such as the determination of profit, of wages (involving Thünen) and the phenomena of rent. He went on to the case of real wage being composed by more than one good. But his main contention against the classical theory of value, according to Smith and Ricardo, is that the 'relationship between the number of competing individuals and price' is not clear (Dmitriev [1904] 1974, 94). According to Dmitriev, prices of production as determined above are valid under constant return to scale and free competition as defined by Cournot.

This led him to his second essay: 'The Theory of Competition of Augustin Cournot: The Great Forgotten Economist' (first published in 1902). In a detailed analysis of Cournot's theory of competition, and of all the ancient and recent literature on the subject, including the impact of technical progress, Dmitriev arrives at an original idea. He rejects the fact that free competition lowers prices to the costs of production. He suggests instead a theory of competition in which there is a rationale for producers to overproduce and maintain inventories, which leads to the reverse effect: costs grow up to meet prices. This new competitive framework makes Ricardo's theory of value insufficient to determine prices, and it opens the door to demand-side explanations.

Dmitriev's third essay, 'Theory of Marginal Utility', is devoted to this theory, from historical, mathematical and psychological points of view. Tugan-Baranovsky, quoted by Dmitriev, explains that Austrian economists have solved the problem of subjective value (i.e. have solved all economic consequences of this problem, leaving other tasks for disciplines like psychology, physiology and biology). In his historical investigation, Dmitriev gives more credit to older economists:

> An impartial analysis must lead to the conclusion that *the Austrian school* as such (Menger, Böhm-Bawerk, von Wieser and others) *added very little* (unless much significance is given to the introduction of new terms) *to what had been done* before them *for the solution of the problem.*
>
> (Dmitriev [1904] 1974, 181)

The third essay therefore opens with historical research on the ancestors of the theory of marginal utility from Galiani to Gossen, through Senior, Dupuit, and many others, offering comparisons with Austrian economists. The essay then describes the theory of marginal utility in its developed form, i.e. with Walras's exchange equations. It ends with the psychological law of diminishing marginal utility.

We will not enter here into the detailed analyses to which Dmitriev invites his – few at the time – readers. See the excellent introduction to the English edition of Dmitriev's *Economic Essays* by Nuti (1974) for more details (see also Samuelson 1975; Schütte 2002), to see its merits. Shaposhnikov himself saw Dmitriev's greatest theoretical merit in his first essay, with his innovative mathematical analysis of the total amount of labour, and its formulation of prices of production and of the rate of profit. But another merit is the way in which his essays articulate to form a complete theory of value (Shaposhnikov 1905; 1914). In Dmitriev's own words: '*These first three essays,*[4] which are united by a common plan, *constitute a complete theory of the general elements of value*' (Dmitriev [1904] 1974, 213). For Shaposhnikov, this complete theory is Dmitriev's synthesis:

> In his *Economic Essays*, the attention of Dmitriev is concentrated on the main problem of economic theory, the theory of value. Exchange value, or the proportion of exchange is, according to V. K. Dmitriev, the product of a number of different factors, irreducible to each other, both objective and subjective. It depends on the conditions of the demand, on the utility of the commodity – the subjective moment – and on the objective conditions of its production. The conditions of consumption determine the demand; the conditions of production determine the supply of the good.
>
> (Shaposhnikov 1914, 1)

Shaposhnikov found that the only weakness in Dmitriev's synthesis was that it was centred on his particular notion of competition, which he criticised in 1905 (Shaposhnikov 1905).

But was there a synthesis in Dmitriev's *Economic Essays*? There clearly was an intention to provide such a synthesis, as the subtitle of the work reminds the reader. But the way in which the three essays are articulated makes it difficult to see its result. The first essay on labour value and prices of production contains room for the theory of competition and leads to the second essay. The second essay contains room for the theory of marginal utility. And the third essay essentially contains an historical investigation. The short conclusion does not go further than giving mere ideas about the connections between the three essays. The equations in the first and the third essays are not compared.

Dmitriev's synthesis was only a hint. This hint nevertheless pursues the investigation in the direction taken by Tugan-Baranovsky.[5] Moreover, these *Economic Essays* provided the tools needed by the next Russian mathematical economists involved in the Russian synthesis, in the first place Bortkiewicz.

Bortkiewicz's three-fold episode

Shaposhnikov is the link between Dmitriev and Bortkiewicz. He knew Bortkiewicz personally, considered him more as a mentor than a colleague. They had discussions about value, the synthesis, and Dmitriev. Bortkiewicz became aware of Dmitriev's *Economic Essays* through Shaposhnikov's review (1905). When Shaposhnikov had to produce a memorial discourse in honour of Dmitriev (Shaposhnikov 1914), Bortkiewicz was aware of it:

> Recently, due to a sad occasion, I had to address once again the issues that you raised in your articles about Marx. Perhaps you know the news that Vlad. Karpovich Dmitriev died in September. We want to arrange at the Chuprov Society a meeting dedicated to his memory. There, I will have to talk about his theoretical work and of course mostly about his equations, which gave the possibility of determining the level of profit.
> (Letter from Shaposhnikov to Bortkiewicz, 14.11.1913)

And when Shaposhnikov discussed his own version of the synthesis with Bortkiewicz, one can realise that they had different versions of it:

> Let me return to the conversation we had about my book [Shaposhnikov 1912a]. You pointed out to me that when talking about the reconciliation of the costs of production theory with the marginal utility theory, I should have referred to Walras, and that I should not have attributed this part to Marshall, Dmitriev, *et al.* Of course, we found in Walras a perfectly correct representation of the role of utility and costs of production, but to attribute to him the merit of the reconciliation of the theory of marginal utility and the theory of costs of production is unlikely to be correct. Walras, if I am

not mistaken – I do not yet have his book at hand – emphatically contrasts his theory with the theory of the classical school.

(Letter from Shaposhnikov to Bortkiewicz, 12.7.1913)

Bortkiewicz was himself also engaged in an attempt at synthesis; although his position is perhaps less explicit than that of Shaposhnikov, Dmitriev or Tugan-Baranovsky, the theme of the synthesis is present throughout Bortkiewicz's main contributions on value theory. Three episodes of Bortkiewicz's scientific activity, which are rarely considered together, are relevant to understand his position: his youthful but deep interest in the theories of Walras around the 1890s; his contributions to the transformation problem in 1906–1907; and his 1921 article on objectivism and subjectivism. Shaposhnikov was aware of Bortkiewicz's Walrasian episode through Bortkiewicz himself, and he read the 1906–1907 papers (Bortkiewicz 1906–1907, 1907). But it is not yet ascertained whether he was aware of Bortkiewicz's 1921 paper.

Bortkiewicz published a review of the second edition of Walras's *Éléments d'économie politique pure* in 1890, in which he shows his full agreement with Walras's general equilibrium system. It should be added that Walras and Bortkiewicz corresponded and met, and that Bortkiewicz wrote the aforementioned review at Walras's initiative, who sought a defender against Edgeworth's attacks (on this episode, see Marchionatti 2007; Bridel 2008). Considered alone, Bortkiewicz appears as an adherent to the subjective mathematical school, yet he already praises the relationship between Walras's theory of exchange and production and costs: 'I think that a good theory of political economy shall reckon with the equality of selling prices with costs, and I think also that Mr Walras's system fully satisfies this requirement' (Bortkiewicz 1890, 83). Sixteen years later, in 'Value and Price in the Marxian System' (1906–1907), Bortkiewicz develops a highly technical Ricardian theory of prices in a mathematical framework (with the help of Dmitriev's algebra). There is nevertheless still a Walrasian imprint behind this construction:

> Modern economics is beginning to free itself gradually from the successivist prejudice, the chief merit being due to the mathematical school led by Léon Walras. The mathematical, in particular the algebraic, method of exposition clearly appears to be the satisfactory expression for this superior standpoint, which does justice to the special character of economic relations.
>
> There is thus a decided advantage in the fact that Dmitrieff has recourse to algebraic procedure.
>
> (Bortkiewicz 1906–1907, II, 1952, 24)

Later in the text, the idea of synthesis attests its presence:

> The mathematical method, however, achieves still more: by its means, the costs of production theory can, without any difficulty, be brought into harmony with the law of supply and demand or with the determination of

prices by the subjective valuations of buyers (and, if need be, of sellers). Following the example of Walras, this is done by inserting the costs equations into a more comprehensive set of equations, in which regard is also paid to those subjective valuations.

(Bortkiewicz 1906–1907, III, 1952, 54)

Here lies the continuity between his 1890 and 1907 contributions. But at that stage, it was the simultaneous character of general equilibrium that appealed to Bortkiewicz, and not the notion of subjective demand. Marchionatti and Fiorini arrived at the conclusion that this provides a unique 'Dmitriev Bortkiewicz model' (2000, 179). In their words, the latter's intentions are well captured:

it lies in an original programme of application of the mathematical method to the Ricardian–Marxian theory of prices; the resulting model had to be conceived, according to Bortkiewicz, as a part of the wider setting formed by the Walrasian general equilibrium analysis.

(Marchionatti and Fiorini 2000, 173)

A few years later, in 1921, Bortkiewicz published in German a paper entitled 'Objectivism and Subjectivism in the Theory of Value', in which he consolidated his views on value, introducing both objective and subjective elements as causes of value. His views are summarised in Table 6.1, which shows the effect of an increase/decrease of costs and utility on the equilibrium quantity and exchange value, in the case of constant (a) and of increasing costs of production (b).

Table 6.1 shows that Bortkiewicz was interested in highly theoretical developments and in the application of mathematics to political economy. He had a high reputation as a qualified Ricardian and a qualified Walrasian, and held himself as taking an intermediate position:

[T]he task of the present study is only to show that costs and utility, or more generally, the objective and the subjective factors of exchange value, demand the same consideration in the theory and that, when one follows the

Table 6.1 Bortkiewicz's synthesis

Cause		Permanent effect		
		Quantity	*Exchange value*	
Cost	increases	−	+	
	decreases	+	−	
			a	b
Utility	increases	+	ø	+
	decreases	−	ø	−

Source: Bortkiewicz (1921, 20).

terms of their interaction, it does not mean syncretism, but *the attempt at a synthesis*.

(Bortkiewicz 1921, 22; emphasis added)

Thus Bortkiewicz arrived, though via a different path from Tugan-Baranovsky and Dmitriev, at his own concept of the synthesis. Dmitriev's and Bortkiewicz's analyses will be instrumental in the design of Shaposhnikov's synthesis.

Slutsky's master's dissertation

In his master's dissertation, *The Theory of Marginal Utility* (1910), Slutsky had already outlined the main ideas of his forthcoming papers (on Slutsky more generally, see Kljukin 2010a; Barnett 2011). As can be seen from the table of contents of this dissertation (see below), Slutsky's celebrated paper on budget theory (Slutsky 1915) was already largely contained in Part IV (and especially its chapter IV) of the dissertation. The same is true for Slutsky's paper on praxeology (Slutsky 1926), which was already partly present in Part II, and for Slutsky's paper on the critique of Böhm-Bawerk's theory of value (1910, Part III, chap. III; 1927). In contrast, some themes of this dissertation were not worked upon further by Slutsky. This is the case for all the psychological content of the dissertation, which is discarded in his 1915 paper, and of the synthesis. Here is the table of contents of Slutsky's *The Theory of Marginal Utility* (1910):[6]

Part I. Introduction
Chapter I. Classical psychological phenomena
Chapter II. A critique of hedonism
Chapter III. The theory of Ehrenfels

Part II. Elements of a theory of action
Chapter I. Linear systems of urges. Basic concepts
Chapter II. The power of urges. The relationship between urges and linear systems
Chapter III. Deviations from the basic types. The concept of interest
Chapter IV. Measurability of the power of urges

Part III. Value and utility. Critique of the concepts
Chapter I. Objective–subjective value
Chapter II. Wieser's concept of value
Chapter III. The concept of value in Menger and Böhm-Bawerk
Chapter IV. Establishment of the terms value and utility

Part IV. Theories of complex systems of interest (theory of budgets)
Chapter I. Introductory remarks
Chapter II. Theory of instantaneous systems
Chapter III. Theory of long-run systems

Indeed, chapter V of Part V is entitled 'Synthesis of the theory of costs of production and the theory of marginal utility', and is preceded by a chapter on costs of production (chapter III) and another on marginal utility (chapter IV). In his chapter on 'The theory of costs of production', Slutsky starts like Dmitriev with the determination of labour values, as the sum of direct and indirect labour embodied in a good under present-day technical conditions, using simultaneous equations like Dmitriev. In a footnote, Slutsky explains that he arrived independently at the same equation derived earlier by Dmitriev, without knowledge of it (Slutsky [1910] 2010, 352). From these labour values, he expresses prices of production, introducing a formulation for the rate of profit similar to Bortkiewicz (also quoted by Slutsky). The system is underdetermined when Slutsky, invoking Cournot, uses different equations for each producer, in order to take into account the type of prices he reaches (monopoly, free competition): the number of unknowns exceeds the number of equations (Slutsky [1910] 2010, 358–359). This provides him with the transition to his next chapter.

Chapter IV on 'The theory of marginal utility' describes how to get supply and demand functions for consumption goods starting from utility functions and budget equations (the latter are analysed by Slutsky in his Part IV). Following the Austrian ideas on imputation, he shows how the theory of marginal utility can give prices for goods of higher order (i.e. production goods).

Finally, in his chapter V on the 'Synthesis of the theory of costs of production and the theory of marginal utility', Slutsky wants to 'dispel the prejudices from supporters of the theory of marginal utility against the use of the equations of production costs' (Slutsky [1910] 2010, 371). He maximised utility functions under a budget constraint that included initial endowments that embody production functions (i.e. consumers have means of production, and can produce with them). Solving this maximising problem gives the functions of production costs (Slutsky [1910] 2010, 369–371 and 373–376). His resolution explicitly 'takes into account the changes occurring to goods, not only in the exchange process, but also in production' (Slutsky [1910] 2010, 371).

Slutsky remarks that the first economist to introduce the equations of expenses of production into supply and demand functions was Walras in his theory of production. This is not, according to him, an eclectic assembly of antagonistic principles, but the simple resolution of a general problem.

Eventually, Slutsky underlines the importance of the method of resolution of the problem of determining prices: the interdependence of variables is taken into account only with this method, and this result would not have been possible without the help of mathematics (Slutsky [1910] 2010, 377).

Significantly, Slutsky studies the particular case of free competition in which costs of production are proportional to the output produced. In this case, the solution of the problem contains only the technical conditions of production. Costs of production are sufficient to determine prices. But when the scale of production matters, synthesis enters the stage (Slutsky [1910] 2010, 376–377).

Slutsky's synthesis is not neoclassical. He starts with the determination of the total amount of labour embodied in a good, i.e. from a labour theory of value. He continues with the incorporation of profit to get prices of production. For the next step, Cournot was essential, as it was in the case of Dmitriev: costs of production may depend on demand, which implies the consideration of marginal utility. Finally, and following Walras, consideration of the costs of production and marginal utility is undertaken with simultaneous equations. And, as Walras did, Slutsky counts the unknown and the equations to make sure that the problem is solved. The synthesis results from his investigation, and is not contained in his initial hypothesis.

And some others

Stoliarov is perhaps the most interesting of those who directly followed Tugan-Baranovsky, without however adding much to him – Zalesky (see 1893, 120) and Girshfeld (1910) being the two others. Mathematically, Girshfeld brought an algebraic development, while Stoliarov used a differential method. Without casting doubt on Tugan-Baranovsky's synthesis, Stoliarov brought a further proof that the latter's theorem was true, i.e. that marginal utilities are proportional to labour costs. Taking labour costs as given (exactly as Tugan-Baranovsky, without deriving them as would be done by Dmitriev), and taking an aggregate case, Stoliarov considered as given the total amount of labour costs available as N:

$$T_1 x_1 + T_2 x_2 + \cdots + T_n x_n = N \qquad (6.5)$$

where x_i represent the number of good i produced, T_i represent the total amount of labour costs required for the production of one unit of good i. Equation (6.5) represents the labour constraint. Then, he derives a total – additive – utility function U (again, this is social utility):

$$U = u_1(x_1) + u_2(x_2) + \cdots + u_n(x_n) \qquad (6.6)$$

where $u_i(x_i)$ indicates the utility derived from consumption of x_i units of good i. In order to prove Tugan-Baranovsky's synthesis (the simple version, see Chapter 4), he uses Lagrange's method in order to maximise total utility (6.6) subject to the available labour constraint (6.5):

$$M = U + \lambda(T_1 x_1 + T_2 x_2 + \cdots + T_n x_n) \tag{6.7}$$

Solving the first and second order conditions on (6.7) gives a maximum of utility if and only if:

$$\lambda = \frac{u_1'(x_1)}{T_1} = \frac{u_2'(x_2)}{T_2} = \cdots = \frac{u_n'(x_n)}{T_n} \tag{6.8}$$

Equation (6.8) is the exact mathematical formulation of Tugan-Baranovsky's simple synthesis: the maximum of utility is reached when labour costs are proportional to marginal utilities. Stoliarov did not go further than giving an example (equations 6.5 to 6.8 are exactly as found in Stoliarov 1902, 15–16), since the goal of his conference at the Kiev physico-mathematical society was simply, as explained in its title, to give an *Analytical Proof of the Politico-Economic Formulae Proposed by M. Tugan-Baranovsky: Marginal Utility of Freely Produced Goods Proportional to their Labour Costs*.

Frank was for his part engaged with his *Marx's Theory of Value and its Meaning* (1900) in a critical study, in which he also subjected to criticism the subjective theory of evaluation, i.e. marginalism. He reached the conclusion that both evaluations coincide: 'The subjective value of the products of labour [...] coincides with their labour value, i.e. is the result of the evaluation of the good proportionally to the labour expended in its production' (Frank 1900, 234). But this was only a short note, and Frank, a former Legal Marxist like Tugan-Baranovsky, equally lost interest in economic theory, and devoted his time to philosophy and theology afterwards. But, interestingly enough, Frank was more aware than others of the *social* character of this coincidence:

> subjective value of these goods [of all freely reproducible goods] will be proportional to the relative expense of labour in their production only from the point of view of their *social evaluation*, i.e. if it comes from the representation of national economy as a whole, as if they were evaluated by an organ of the whole society.
>
> (Frank 1900, 257; emphasis added)

Bilimovic published a large study entitled *On the Question of the Evaluation of Economic Goods* (1914). This book is an impressively exhaustive methodological and theoretical survey of the literature on subjective and objective value (in the Russian, German, French, Italian and English languages). There is a clear accent on mathematical economics. The first two chapters of the book are devoted to subjective value and utility, demonstrating direct acquaintance and deep understanding of authors like Gossen, Pareto, and Jevons. It explores complex issues for the first time in Russian economic literature, in the fields of the measurability of utility (he believes that it is not possible in absolute terms), the impossibility to apply interpersonal utility comparison, etc. The third and last chapter is devoted to price and objective exchange value, and discusses its issues (notably the non-existent invariable standard of measure of value). It contains an impressive bibliography at the end of the book. He describes his task as follows:

> [T]he guiding principle of our investigation is the desire to avoid a mistaken one-sidedness, like in the pure–subjective theory of value or in the pure–objective theory of value. *Following the example of authors, who already aspired to this principle,* we try to build a theoretical scheme of evaluation which adequately takes into account the two elements – subjective and objective.
>
> (Bilimovic 1914, vi; emphasis added)

Here, Bilimovic clearly shows his intention to follow the steps *of authors, who already aspired to this principle*. Albeit not mentioned explicitly, it is possible to believe that he refers here to the authors, present in his text and bibliography, that attempted to take into account both objective and subjective moments in the theory of value: Tugan-Baranovsky, Dmitriev, Bortkiewicz, Shaposhnikov, Slutsky. Bilimovic speaks of 'collaboration':

> Independently of the intentions of the individual works of research, this work is the result of a complex collaboration between various schools and currents in the study of the evaluation of economic goods: thoughts on the link between the value of goods and utility, which were revived anew in the theory of marginal utility on one side; the remarkable fact of the dependence of value on the conditions of production on the other side; finally the old theory of demand and supply which tries to unite the various factors of value on a third side. All these, by pointing to disparate doctrines, are mutually reinforcing each other with shares of the truth.
>
> (Bilimovic 1914, v)

Bilimovic did not reach such synthesis in his book. The absence of a general conclusion to the three chapters is perhaps the best indication that, for him, the state of research did not allowed (yet) for such a synthesis. But the intention was there.[7]

Shaposhnikov

The Russian economist Nikolay Nikolaevich Shaposhnikov (1878–1939) was a student of Tugan-Baranovsky. He set himself the challenge of becoming a specialist in the newest theories of value and distribution, and wrote a dissertation entitled *Theory of Value and Distribution* (published in 1912). This work is mentioned in the literature as a valuable source of information 'in the Russian language' on value and distribution theories by authorities such as Bukharin, Rubin, Yurovsky and Gelesnoff. His synthesis in the theory of value is very different from Tugan-Baranovsky's approach, as he already captures the spirit of his time, which was made up of the ideas of Dmitriev and Bortkiewicz. However, as will be presently shown, Shaposhnikov *does not* develop a technical analysis. He borrows Dmitriev's and Bortkiewicz's analyses and discusses them, but he does not elaborate them further. He was one of the first to recognise Dmitriev's achievement and acted as a populariser of Walras in Russia. His stature within Russian economic thought was overshadowed by Dmitriev, and until recently he was mentioned almost exclusively for having coined the expression 'Vladimir Karpovich Dmitriev, the first Russian mathematical economist'. In order to correct this sorry state of affairs, this section attempts to rehabilitate a part of his economic thought.[8] After the analysis of Shaposhnikov's work, a comparison between Tugan-Baranovsky's and Shaposhnikov's attempts at synthesis is offered.

Shaposhnikov's writings and network

Nikolay Nikolaevich Shaposhnikov was born in 1878.[9] In 1901, he entered the law faculty at the University of Moscow where, just after graduating in 1906, he was appointed as *dozent*. He then spent the customary three to four years abroad completing his studies, mainly in Berlin (where he is likely to have met Bortkiewicz), and returned to Russia in 1910, where he occupied various positions of *dozent*. Besides his previous position at the University of Moscow, Shaposhnikov was appointed to the Petersburg Political Institute in 1910, and the Petersburg Polytechnical Institute in 1912. The submission of his dissertation, *Theory of Value and Distribution* (1912a), enabled him to become professor at the Moscow Institute of Commerce, a position he held from 1913 to 1927 (renamed Plekhanov's Institute of National Economy in 1917). Additionally, in 1917–1918, he gave lectures on political economy and statistics at the law faculty at the State University of Moscow and at the Shanyavksy Moscow City's People University (lectures for women).

During these pre-revolutionary years, Shaposhnikov showed an early and active interest in value and distribution theories. Just before completing his studies, in 1905, he published what is apparently his first work, entitled 'Free Competition and the Price of Goods' (Shaposhnikov 1905). In this paper, Shaposhnikov critically reviews Dmitriev's recently released *Economic Essays* ([1904] 1974). He describes Dmitriev as a 'fervent and convinced follower of the mathematical school' (Shaposhnikov 1905, 76). In 1906, he published a booklet on Böhm-Bawerk's theory of profit. While abroad, he collaborated with the Russian journal *Kritičeskoe Obozrenie*, in which he published numerous short reviews on recent economic literature (on Sombart, Tugan-Baranovsky, and Woytinsky).[10] In 1909, he published a booklet on Thünen's natural wage (Shaposhnikov 1909b). The following years were devoted to his dissertation

Theory of Value and Distribution (1912a), his main pre-revolutionary work, which contains his previously published booklets on Böhm-Bawerk and Thünen, to which he added a chapter on Clark's marginal productivity theory, one on distribution theory, and two on value theory. In the same year appeared his entry on Walras in the second edition of the Russian encyclopedia *Brockhaus-Efron* (1912b), and a shorter version of the same entry in the *Granat Encyclopedia* (1912c). Soon after Dmitriev's death in October 1913, Shaposhnikov read a paper in his memory at the Chuprov Society: 'The first Russian mathematical-economist V. K. Dmitriev' (published in 1914). The expression 'Russian mathematical-economist' was born, and Shaposhnikov was later to be considered the second on this list, after Dmitriev. Still prior to the revolution, Shaposhnikov published a book on *Protectionism and Free Trade* (1915) and an article defending the 'Scientific Value of Abstract Theory' (1917).

It is useful to complete this pre-revolutionary picture by briefly mentioning Shaposhnikov's relations with his contemporaries. He was clearly interested in the latest developments in the application of mathematics to political economy, and to the newest marginal utility theory, and was therefore close to some of their specialists. Shaposhnikov most probably met Bortkiewicz during his stay in Berlin. Bortkiewicz settled for good in Berlin in 1901, but kept many relations with Russian economists and statisticians. Many young Russian economists passed through Berlin to visit Bortkiewicz and seek his advice. He knew the economic theories of Marx, Ricardo, Walras, Böhm-Bawerk,... well and was in particular concerned, in 1906–1907, with the transformation of value into prices problem, for which he used Tugan-Baranovsky's and Dmitriev's constructions. Shaposhnikov exchanged letters and offprints with Bortkiewicz between 1910 and 1913, and between 1918 and 1928. Moreover, Shaposhnikov visited Bortkiewicz at Christmas, and during his summer holidays in Austria. Their correspondence reveals, among other things, that Bortkiewicz examined the chapters of Shaposhnikov's 1912 dissertation (concerning Walras, Ricardo, Böhm-Bawerk and Clark); they also had several discussions about economists, including Dmitriev, Walras, Clark, and Lexis.

Shaposhnikov gave a special seminar on value and distribution at the University of Moscow in 1909–1910 and had Bukharin among his students (Belykh 2007, 11). He was certainly the first to teach the young Bolshevist the doctrines of Walras and Böhm-Bawerk.[11]

During his pre-revolutionary period, Shaposhnikov acted mainly as a critic of others' theories (Dmitriev, Walras, Thünen), and was keen to teach state-of-the-art economics to his students. Compared to the older generation of academic economists, Shaposhnikov was up to date with the latest developments in his discipline: he was one of the first to read Dmitriev and to spread his ideas; he promoted the work of Walras with the very first encyclopedic entries on him in Russia. In a sense, he shares much in common with Bortkiewicz: a fine critic, but not himself an original thinker.

During the Soviet period, and besides teaching, Shaposhnikov was involved, like many of his colleagues, in various bureaucratic committees and policy-oriented research institutes. His scientific interests shifted from value and distribution towards more applied subjects: foreign trade and tariff policy, monetary and credit policy, industrialisation and business cycles. In 1922, he worked on the establishment of a new Soviet tariff. From 1923, he was vice-president of the monetary and credit section at the Economic Institute of the *Narkomfin* (People's Commissariat of Finance), and in this capacity was adviser at the Gosplan. From 1924, he handled the economic part of the construction conglomerate, *Dneprostroya*. During the 1920s, he was one of the three top consultants (with Vainshtein and Slutsky) at Kondratiev's Conjuncture Institute. He actively participated in the Institute's debates and wrote papers for the Institute's journals.[12] During these years, Shaposhnikov published many articles, theoretical and policy oriented, and a book on tariff policy.

At the end of the 1920s, his career slowed down sharply. Economists like Shaposhnikov, who believed in some of the virtues of the market economy (such as information contained in market prices), could work easily under the NEP (New Economic Policy). But once Stalin drove the Soviet Union down the forced industrialisation road, their researches became useless and were stopped. In 1928, Kondratiev was removed from his seat as director of the Conjuncture Institute. Many of its 'bourgeois' elements were dislodged, including Shaposhnikov. For its part, the Narkomfin fired a fifth of its employees, including Shaposhnikov. During the 1930 Moscow Trials, many 'bourgeois spies', accused of trying to restore capitalism in Russia, were condemned and, later, executed (in 1937–1938). Shaposhnikov was imprisoned for seven months in 1930. From 1931, he worked as chief economist at the *Glavenergo* (Central Conglomerate of Electricity) but had to leave in 1936. He entered the foreign information office at *Narkomfin* for a few months, but had to leave once again. He received a university pension in 1937, and died of lung cancer in 1939 at the age of 61.

Shaposhnikov's synthesis

Shaposhnikov's *Theory of value and distribution* (1912a) had the ambition to investigate the then latest developments in distribution theory. He has, however, to start with the theory of value:

> Given the close links that exist according to many economists between the problems of value and distribution, value analysis is the inevitable introduction to the theory of distribution. Many economists regard the contemporary theory of distribution as a sub-division of the theory of value. Wages, profits and rents are nothing other than the prices of labour, capital and land. The law of supply and demand determines these values. Therefore, we must explain what are the supply and demand, what determines them, and what influence they may have on prices.
>
> (Shaposhnikov 1912a, 4)

The first chapter of the book is devoted to the analysis of demand and the second is devoted to the analysis of supply. As the result of his investigation, Shaposhnikov

Table 6.2 Shaposhnikov's synthesis

1. the marginal utility of the good	*demand*
2. the marginal utility of all other goods	
3. the monetary purchasing power	
4. the quantity of labour embodied in production	*supply*
5. the duration of the production process	
6. the rate of wage	
7. the rate of profit	

Source: composed according to Shaposhnikov (1912a, chapters 1 and 2).

reaches the conclusion that, in order to know the price of one good, the law of demand and supply has to be decomposed into simpler elements.

Table 6.2 reveals the seven elements that are necessary for a complete under-standing of the price mechanism: 1–2–3 account for the demand side, and 4–5–6–7 for the supply side. According to Shaposhnikov, economic theory was not successful in reducing the explanation of prices to a single factor (utility or labour), but instead pointed out numerous factors. Some of them are beyond the scope of economic theory, and may be considered as given. Thus, the satisfac-tion afforded by consuming a certain quantity of goods (1 and 2), the amount of necessary labour embodied (4) and the duration of the production process (5) belong to other fields (psychology, physiology and technical sciences). What remains to economic theory is to study the purchasing power, which is nothing but buyer's income (3), the wage rate (6) and the profit rate (7). In other words, the theory would arrive at a complete economic understanding of prices when the question of distribution of national income between wages and profits is solved (1912a, 48–50).

For Shaposhnikov, the demand for a certain quantity of a good at given prices depends on its subjective decreasing marginal utility, on the prices of the other goods and on the buyer's purchasing power. The buyer's budget is divided into numerous 'special funds', one for each good. The level of each fund is deter-mined according to the maximum happiness principle, which, following Gossen, requires equal marginal utilities (Shaposhnikov 1912a, 6–7, 9, 14). This leads to a negative functional relationship between prices and quantity demanded, where the marginal buyers' evaluation, together with the number of goods supplied determine prices. The demand for intermediate goods depends on the prices for final goods. Using Menger's schemes, Shaposhnikov gives examples to convince his readers (1912a, 5, 8). While he uses the Austrians' language and representa-tion tools, he is critical of their achievements:

Any theory that does not consider the interdependence between the prices of goods cannot lay claim to scientific completeness. We are entitled to raise this warning against many theorists, especially against the representatives of the Austrian school. Only Walras, and representatives of the mathematical school around him, has devoted to this issue the attention it deserves, and has raised the question of value in its entirety. In this lies the importance of Walras's work.

(Shaposhnikov 1912a, 11)

According to Shaposhnikov, Walras is the most accomplished theorist of the marginal utility theory, being the first to offer a 'general solution' to the problem of value, taking care of the 'interdependence of the variables': 'Many economists have described similar solutions to the question of value, but all had in mind special cases with two tradable goods: they have arbitrarily reduced their task. Walras provides a general solution to this problem' (Shaposhnikov 1912b). Walras's general solution is his exchange equations, on which Shaposhnikov writes nothing but compliments. Moreover, Shaposhnikov discusses several complications in the theory of demand, such as the implication of discrete and continuous goods for utility functions,[13] the elasticity of the demand for various commodities (production vs consumption goods), the case of complex goods which serve various purposes (around Clark's law), and a justification for partial vs general analysis in some applied cases, when an approximation is sufficient.

But generally speaking, for Shaposhnikov, these prices are only *demand prices*. They are prices 'only if we look at the problem of pricing as unrelated to production' (Shaposhnikov 1912a, 10). They give an indication of the prices at which buyers are ready to buy a given quantity of goods. And this quantity is determined on the supply side.

For Shaposhnikov, the supply of goods in the market depends on their costs of production. Below these costs, which include expenses (wages and intermediate goods) and profit at the normal rate in the country, the product is still sold, but no longer produced. Therefore, for him, what matters in the long term is the notion of 'costs of reproduction'. As regarding the latter, and following Cournot, Shaposhnikov distinguishes the case of monopoly from that of free competition. Under monopoly, costs of reproduction do not play the same large role as in the case of free competition, but the scale of costs (decreasing, constant or increasing) influences the choice of the net income maximising quantity (Shaposhnikov 1912a, 26–28). Under free competition, prices match costs of reproduction and, in static equilibrium, costs of production. In reality, there are some branches of industry where the assumption of free capital mobility is illusory. When capital moves slowly and with difficulty (in the railway industry, for example), the influence of costs of (re-)production on prices is only gradual and progressive. Therefore, prices may stand still for a while above (or below) their necessary costs. Changes in the prices of input or in wages, however, act more quickly: as soon as prices do not cover these costs, production ceases promptly (1912a, 28–33).[14]

Once the influence and the limits of the theory of costs of production are known, it remains to define their components. According to Shaposhnikov, the classical school, and especially Ricardo in the first two chapters of his *Principles of Political Economy*, have resolved this issue. Shaposhnikov adds to this 'the researches of two Russian economists, Dmitriev and Bortkiewicz, which clarified and developed some aspects of Ricardo's doctrine' (1912a, 39). Thus, according to Shaposhnikov, Ricardo's starting point is the Smithian division of prices into the incomes of all those – the worker, the capitalist and the landowner – involved in production: wages, profits and rent. Rent being excluded by Ricardo from the analysis of prices, there remains wages, which depend on the quantity and value of labour, and profits, which depend on the amount of capital and the duration of the production process. According to their costs of production, the relative prices of two goods (*m* and *n*) can be represented as

$$\frac{P_m}{P_n} = \frac{A_m L_m (1+r_m)^{t_m}}{A_n L_n (1+r_n)^{t_n}} \tag{6.9}$$

where P_i is the price of product *i* ($i=m, n$), A_i the total sum of labour embodied in the production of good *i*, L_i the wage rate, r_i the profit rate and t_i the duration of the production process. This equation can be simplified, if one accepts the assumption of free competition and its consequences: uniform rates of profit and of wage. In this case, differences in prices are explained only by the total sum of labour expended and by the duration of the production process. The relative prices of two goods with the same duration of production depend only on the amount of labour embodied in their production. In order to understand Shaposhnikov's costs of production theory, two notions are still needed: the total sum of labour (A_i) and the role of fixed capital.

By labour costs, Shaposhnikov has in mind, like Dmitriev, direct and indirect expenses of labour, i.e. the expenses that are directly involved in the production of a good and, recursively, are indirectly involved in the production of all its means of production. With a system of simultaneous equations, Dmitriev showed that, without any need for an infinite historical regression back to the first human tool, it is possible to determine the total amount of labour used in the production of a good, under present technical conditions.

The role of fixed capital is different in Ricardo and in Marx: both authors agree that the duration of the production process can cause a deviation between labour costs (labour value) and costs of production (prices of production), as seen above. But Marx adds another element: the organic composition of capital, i.e. the influence of fixed capital on relative prices. Here Shaposhnikov endorsed Bortkiewicz's remarks that the organic composition of capital does not affect relative prices, since fixed capital is considered as past labour. Shaposhnikov gives an algebraic example, where the production of a good is vertically integrated with a variant where an industry buys fixed capital from another, to show that fixed capital does not influence relative prices. For Shaposhnikov, Marx would impoverish Ricardo's doctrine, which must be considered as the most advanced theory of the costs of production, taken together with the additions of Dmitriev and Bortkiewicz (Shaposhnikov 1912a, 39–48).

The synthesis offered by Shaposhnikov is based on the idea that demand (subjective evaluation) and supply (objective conditions of production) are both necessary to provide a complete theory of value. The theory of demand is able to determine the prices reached in the market *for a given quantity supplied*. On the other side, costs of production depend on production scale, which depends on demand (Shaposhnikov 1912a, 35–36). In other words:

> The classical school, which has done much for the theory of value, mainly in the shape of Ricardo, has hardly touched this issue [the demand]. The consumer–purchaser interests him only a little, and attention is directed to the seller, the analysis of the conditions of supply of goods. This shortcoming of the classical theory has been filled by the marginal utility theorists, establishing in detail the analysis of the evaluation of goods by buyers and their influence on prices.
>
> (Shaposhnikov 1912a, 4–5)

The Austrians are known for having accused the classical school of creating a vicious circle: to explain prices (of goods) by other prices (costs of production of productive services) and vice-versa. Shaposhnikov condemns this accusation:

> Which is the cause and which is the consequence? The link between these phenomena is not expressed in the form of a cause and an effect, or in the form of a determinant and a determined, but in the form of reciprocal determination and relationship [...] Bortkiewicz rightly observed that it is Walras that has begun to consider this properly.
>
> (Shaposhnikov 1912a, 38–39)

Interdependency is the keyword of Shaposhnikov's synthesis. This does not mean, however, that all the above-mentioned factors affecting prices have the same importance (1912a, 36–39, 48–49). First of all, there are special cases: when costs of production are constant, prices do not depend on demand; when two goods are produced in equivalent conditions (e.g. duration), these elements neutralise each other; sometimes a modification in prices may have almost no effect on the price of another good. More generally,

> We should follow Ricardo when he states that the effects of profit and labour are not the same. Modifications in labour expenses influence prices more seriously than modifications in the rate of profit. Thus, undoubtedly, labour is the dominant factor in value.
>
> (Shaposhnikov 1912a, 49)

This statement somewhat weakens Shaposhnikov's synthesis, but does not undermine its foundations: marginal utility and costs of production are compatible. The last step in Shaposhnikov's investigation is to discover the laws of distribution, or to understand the origin of profits and of wages:

> Two main streams can be identified among the theoreticians of distribution: some see the source of non-labour income in the private ownership of means

of production, which leads to inequalities between social classes. Profit and rent are not logical categories of the economy, but historical categories – this is the main idea found in Rodbertus. For the representatives of the other stream, the source of non-labour income is not to be found in the historical conditions of the economic activity, but in their natural and eternal conditions.

(Shaposhnikov 1912a, i)

In the remaining four chapters of his *Theory of Value and Distribution* (1912a), Shaposhnikov provides a critical analysis of the theories of distribution belonging to the second stream: Ricardo and Thünen's differential rent analysis, Thünen's natural wage and profit doctrine, Böhm-Bawerk's interest theory, and the theory of marginal productivity of Clark and the American school. These analyses are often accompanied by comparisons with the social theories of Rodbertus and Tugan-Baranovsky. At the end of his investigations on distribution, which will not be covered here, Shaposhnikov reaches the conviction that:

no contemporary theory of distribution is able to accomplish this task [to explain the source of non-labour income]. The assumption of free competition, which is so fruitful in the theory of value, is sterile in the theory of distribution. Hence, the question of the very possibility of an abstract–deductive theory of distribution unwillingly arises. Should we adhere to Struve's consideration that 'We cannot establish any abstract position or law on distribution … [and that] the problem of distribution belongs to inductive sociology' (Russian Thought 1911, 121)? Struve's statement seems very close to truth: the possibility of an abstract–deductive solution to the problem of distribution seems seriously doubtful.

(Shaposhnikov 1912a, ii)

Shaposhnikov's analysis of the theory of value in his book is the following: a follower of the 'mathematical school' (albeit he himself makes parsimonious use of symbols), he is enthusiastic about the subjective theory of marginal utility, in which he sees a complement to the classical school costs of production theory. His synthesis is motivated by the will to offer the most complete theoretical explanation of the phenomenon of prices, which, for historical reasons, he calls value.

From Tugan-Baranovsky to Shaposhnikov

In a review of the first edition of Tugan-Baranovsky's *Principles of Political Economy* (1909) (three years before he published his *Theory of Value and Distribution*), Shaposhnikov welcomed the idea of a synthesis in the theory of value:

In his book, he [Tugan-Baranovsky] wants to show the possibility of a new direction, consisting to some extent of the synthesis of these two theoretical currents [Marxism and the school of marginal utility]. We can only welcome Tugan-Baranovsky's aspiration for a synthesis. At this junction in the development of economic thought, such a direction of research seems to us the most appropriate.

(Shaposhnikov 1909a, 49)

Shaposhnikov explains in the same review that Tugan-Baranovsky does not see a contradiction between the theory of marginal utility and the theory of *costs of production*. The latter blames the Austrians for not taking into account the theory of production. And Shaposhnikov blames Tugan-Baranovsky for not acknowledging Walras:

> It is true that the Austrian school almost completely neglected this issue [production], but apart from Menger, Böhm-Bawerk and Wieser, there are other theoreticians of marginal utility. Walras, one of the founders of this theory, has already shown that the production of individual goods must be distributed so that their value (marginal utility) equals their costs of production.

(Shaposhnikov 1909a, 50)

He goes further, accusing Tugan-Baranovsky of simply rehashing Walras: 'Tugan-Baranovsky's thesis is nothing else, in essence, than a paraphrase, in his own words, of Walras's famous theory of production'(Shaposhnikov 1909a, 50). It should be taken into account that, by mentioning Walras's theory of production, Shaposhnikov does not have in mind the idea that Walras *had* a theory of production. He just meant that there is a place for a (classical) theory of production in Walras's pure exchange economy (see Shaposhnikov 1912a, chapter 1; 1912b, 1912c).

As far as Tugan-Baranovsky is concerned, therefore, Shaposhnikov concludes that there is no great originality in his thought on value. But there is a misunderstanding, and it clearly appears in the following passage of Shaposhnikov's review: 'In the case where costs of production are only composed of labour – and it is not always the case, as Tugan-Baranovsky himself recognises (pp. 361f.) – the marginal utilities must be proportional to the labour expended in the production' (Shaposhnikov 1909a, 50). The misunderstanding lies in the fact that Tugan-Baranovsky had two attempts at synthesis in his 'complex story' (which are merged into the 'simple synthesis'): the capitalist synthesis, implying costs of production, and about which Shaposhnikov wrote; and the socialist synthesis, implying only labour costs.

Shaposhnikov mixed these two syntheses, and took Tugan-Baranovsky's category of labour costs (or absolute value) as a historical category – as in Smith's 'early and rude state of society' – instead of, as it should be in Tugan-Baranovsky's mind, as a logical category. This misunderstanding, intentional or not, may be explained by Shaposhnikov's approach to political economy in general, and to the theory of value in particular.

In his *Theory of Value and Distribution* (1912a), Shaposhnikov is concerned by the *theory* of political economy. Shaposhnikov described himself as a follower of the 'modern' mathematical school (Walras, Pareto, Dmitriev) and therefore defines theoretical, or pure political economy, following Walras, as a *mathematical* science, since it deals with relations and interdependencies between different measurable magnitudes. Given this definition, there is no room *within the theory* for ethics, which is clearly ruled out by mathematics. Therefore, there is no mention of ethics in Shaposhnikov's writings. Theories are not fair or unfair; they are successful in explaining their objects and resolving their issues, as in the field of value. Or they are unsuccessful, as in the field of distribution. In the latter case, for Shaposhnikov, this opens the door to ethical considerations, but outside the theory of political economy.

Whether Shaposhnikov simply ignored Tugan-Baranovsky's ethical thought, considering it as outside the field of theoretical political economy or whether he really thought that Tugan-Baranovsky was writing on the historical significance of labour costs is another question.[15]

What can be ascertained is that the synthesis underwent a transubstantiation and a transformation between Tugan-Baranovsky and Shaposhnikov: it was stripped of its ethical component, in order to don a strictly mathematical form.

Shaposhnikov was convinced by the necessity to apply mathematical methods in theoretical political economy. His main influences were clearly Walras, Ricardo and Tugan-Baranovsky. As an astute observer of his contemporaries, he already perceived that the leading researchers in value theory were Dmitriev and Bortkiewicz. Thus, the research programme of synthesis was followed by Tugan-Baranovsky, Dmitriev, Bortkiewicz, Slutsky, Zalesky, Stoliarov, Girshfeld, Frank, Bilimovic and Shaposhnikov, each in their own way. Tugan-Baranovsky certainly gave the impetus for such development. His synthesis includes an ethical principle, which is not present in the others. They favoured instead an 'engineering approach', using the mathematical method as a way to encompass the interdependency of economic variables. These authors supported various conceptions of free competition (Dmitriev rejected the classical concept of free competition, for instance), and maintained different ideas on the question of distribution. But they all considered that objective factors alone (the conditions of production or supply) or subjective factors alone (consumers' evaluations or demand) could only provide part of the understanding of the phenomena of value and prices.

The demand side was borrowed by these Russian economists from Walras (for Bortkiewicz, Dmitriev, Slutsky and Shaposhnikov), Menger (Tugan-Baranovsky, Zalesky), Wieser (Tugan-Baranovsky) and Böhm-Bawerk (Tugan-Baranovsky, Dmitriev, and Shaposhnikov), and they accepted the marginalist theory almost without criticism (except for Bilimovic). The supply side, in contrast, was drawn from Ricardo (for most of the positive part) and Marx (for most of the critical part). They investigated and handled various notions such as labour value and costs of production, absolute value and relative value, and production and reproduction costs, *in order to extend and develop an unfinished but not dead classical theory.*

In this sense, Tugan-Baranovsky, Dmitriev, Bortkiewicz, Slutsky, Shaposhnikov and others represent a Russian tradition in economic thought, that of a synthesis: an attempt at synthesis between marginalist and classical theories, between labour and value and between value and prices. The last two elements, which were strong in Tugan-Baranovsky's work, are less affirmed in the works of his followers. The transformation of Tugan-Baranovsky's synthesis had started. And it continued with Yurovsky.

Yurovsky

> One can consider that Jevons established a different science from Ricardo's, and Gossen could think that he was the Copernicus of social sciences, but we will examine the evolution of economic thought from a different perspective than those of the economists of the middle and the late nineteenth century. The line of development seems almost continuous: in Edgeworth and Cournot, in Marshall and Jevons, and in Böhm-Bawerk and Menger, we turn to Ricardo, Senior, J. B. Say, J. S. Mill, Hermann and Thünen, finding in the classical authors the sources of the contemporary achievements and methods.
>
> (Yurovsky 1919, iii–iv)

This section shows how the Russian synthesis evolved after Shaposhnikov. It is argued that Yurovsky's *Essays on Price Theory* (1919) represent the peak of this line of research in Russia. Yurovsky's *Essays* summarise and conclude the pre-revolutionary Russian research on value and prices in the realm of synthesis. At the same time, it imposed a radical transformation on the synthesis that marked the end of its Russian-specific character. For this reason, Yurovsky's attempt is called *the last synthesis*.

Yurovsky's *Essays on Price Theory* (1919)

> Despite the many controversies about theoretical issues, disputes between economists – at least among most economists – are not as great as a cursory review of the literature would suggest. During the last one hundred and fifty years, political economy has experienced many productive and creative periods and successions of schools of thought producing new ideas and rejecting the old ones. But if we leave aside the few remaining on the wrong track or sneaking into dead ends, we can say that all theorists have worked on the very same building. The work of predecessors is more often taken and changed than subjected to destruction. It seems that no one defends this view with such eloquence and conviction as Alfred Marshall.
>
> (Yurovsky 1919, iii)

The Russian economist Leonid Naumovich Yurovsky (1884–1938) is known to Soviet monetary historians as the architect of the Soviet monetary reforms in the

1920s.[16] In the pre-revolutionary period, he received an economic education in St Petersburg and had Tugan-Baranovsky as a professor. He even published his lectures notes two years before the latter published his famous textbook (see Yurovsky 1907). He then studied in Germany, wrote a dissertation on the exportation of Russian corn, and obtained a PhD in 1910 at the Ludwig-Maximilian University of Munich under the supervision of Brentano. The title of the dissertation is *Der Russische Getreideexport: Seine Entwickelung und Organisation* (Yurovsky 1910). After a career as a journalist (in China and Siberia), and before settling in Moscow in 1921, he spent three years at Saratov University (1918–1921), where he published his *Essays on Price Theory* (1919).[17]

The first of his *Essays* (Economy and Economic Value. Object of Political Economy) is devoted to the definition of economics as a science, and contains an appendix on the theory of marginal utility. It discusses the various definitions of political economy, stresses its relative character, and addresses the issue of the measuring of psychological states and the principles of maximisation of satisfaction. The essay shows a wide knowledge of the marginalist literature, with competent and up to date references to Western (Cournot, Jevons, Walras, Pareto, Marshall, Edgeworth, Thünen, Böhm-Bawerk, Auspitz and Lieben) and Russian (Tugan-Baranovsky, Dmitriev, Shaposhnikov and Bilimovic) authors.

The second essay (Value and Prices as Functions of the Quantity of Goods and the Equations of Exchange. The Principal Issue and the Method of Political Economy) discusses the nature of pure economics, and its mathematical method. It analyses in depth Walras's exchange equations and argues that the method of the marginalist economists is the same as the one used by Ricardo in his theory of rent. The legacy of Thünen and Cournot as forerunners of the new theories is positively assessed.

The third essay (Main Cases of Equality between Supply and Demand. Economic Statics and Dynamics) discusses the notion of equilibrium in political economy and introduces a typology of economic theoretical systems (see especially Yurovsky 1919, 161–162). This essay distinguishes between economic statics (A) and economic dynamics (B). Static equilibrium studies the relation of supply and demand, while dynamic equilibrium additionally incorporates the relation between production and income distribution.

The task of the theory of *economic statics* (A) is to discover 'static equilibrium prices', or average market prices. This is the equilibrium obtained through the mechanism of demand and supply, as in Walrasian equilibrium prices. The task of *economic dynamics* (B) is divided by Yurovsky into three successive steps:

1 Theory of the stationary economy
2 Theory of economic evolution
3 Theory of economic cycles

The task of the theory of the stationary economy (B1) is to determine 'dynamic equilibrium prices'. Yurovsky defines these as 'static equilibrium prices' for which long term Ricardian costs of production are taken into account. The task of the theory of economic evolution (B2) is to extend the explanation of prices to considerations of income distribution, population growth, change in technique and organisation, etc. Finally, the task of the theory of economic cycles (B3) is to take into account the variations of prices in the various phases of the cycle: crises, depression, and recovery.

The fourth and final essay (Imputation and Capitalisation of Income. Problems of Distribution) discusses the issue of distribution of income as being inextricably linked to the problem of value and prices. In opposition to Tugan-Baranovsky, Yurovsky thought that the theory of distribution must have its place in the theory of prices, a place that still needs to be found. The essay consists essentially of a discussion on the role of time in economic theory and the study of the interest rate in the successive steps of his typology.

Yurovsky's last synthesis

For Yurovsky, the *theory of static equilibrium prices* (A) found a perfect expression in Walras and Pareto's theory (i.e. their exchange equations, together with the notion of general equilibrium). However, his adoption of this theory is not without reservation, especially concerning the notion of marginal utility. Yurovsky is not optimistic about the commensurability of utility, but believes that the theory loses nothing if it does not have such a standard of measurement. In contrast, Yurovsky remarks that the hypothesis of continuous (vs discrete) goods could severely reduce the practical significance of the theory.

Yurovsky used the example of 100 million Russian peasants each holding 0.1 tractors according to the theory of marginal utility. There should be, with continuous goods and by aggregating all individual possessions, ten million tractors in the country. In practice, however, there would be no tractors.

More generally, Yurovsky advocates the Walrasian concept of equilibrium, which is at the foundation of his attempt to introduce dynamics into economics and move from static to dynamic equilibrium: first in the stationary economy, then in the evolutionary economy and finally leaving the field of equilibrium for crises and cycles.

In the field of static economics, short run supply and demand determine equilibrium prices. And Ricardo had already perfectly defined the *theory of dynamic equilibrium prices* (B1), or long run prices, with his theory of costs of production. Yurovsky had not explicitly expressed his intention of building a synthesis between Walras and Ricardo, but his theory of static and dynamic equilibrium prices expresses nothing less than such an attempt. Moreover, his vision of progress in economic science supports this view.

Indeed, for Yurovsky, too much emphasis had been laid on opposing schools of thought in political economy, while in fact they only applied different focuses to the various parts of his typology. For instance, Ricardo essentially worked in the field of economic dynamics (B), stressing the role of costs of production (B1), and examining issues of growth related to the relation between value and distribution and issues of machinery and population (B2). For his part, Walras formulated the developed version of the theory of economic statics (A), and made some attempts in economic dynamics. Yurovsky congratulated Walras for his attempts to introduce dynamic considerations in section VII of the *Éléments d'économie politique pure*, with the '*marché permanent*' (B1) and the '*société progressive*' (B2). In that direction, however, Yurovsky noted that Schumpeter's attempt seemed more promising.

Most economists and schools were therefore working on different aspects of the 'same building', but for most of their work, they were using the same concept – equilibrium – and the same tools – mathematics and reasoning at the margin. Yurovsky evoked in this respect Thünen, Cournot and Ricardo's theory of rent. There is almost no need for a synthesis: history of economic thought follows a continuous line, according to Yurovsky's reconstruction.

Yurovsky called for an evolution of economic research: from static and dynamic equilibrium (A and B1) to evolution and cycles (B2 and B3). Incidentally, his *Essays on Price Theory* (1919) went on to play such a role in the Soviet Union: it closed the chapter on the Russian synthesis, ended the studies on static and dynamic equilibrium prices, and announced the research agenda of the 1920s and 1930s: the study of dynamics, monetary fluctuations, crises and cycles. For Yurovsky, the task of economic science moved, at the beginning of the twentieth century, from statics to dynamics.

In the Soviet Union of the 1920s, Kondratiev's Institute of Conjuncture would symbolise this change and go beyond the Russian synthesis, but its spirit had not disappeared completely. It would continue to survive in Kondratiev's Institute.[18] Kondratiev's own research programme was based on Tugan-Baranovsky's theory of crises. Moreover, Shaposhnikov and Slutsky were Kondratiev's very close collaborators in the Institute, and most Soviet economists were educated with Tugan-Baranovsky's textbook and read the works of the protagonists of the Russian synthesis.

It is interesting to note in this respect that Shaposhnikov never returned to 'static' issues, as in his previous investigations. He worked on related but dynamic subjects – like the influence of the velocity of money on the dynamics of price – and never returned to his synthesis. The same applies to Slutsky and other members of the Institute.

Yurovsky's *Essays on Price Theory* (1919) inaugurated several transitions in the history of Russian economic thought. It was the last state-of-the-art Russian volume on marginalism in which the author could show such a positive appraisal for a long time. It represents the transition point from static to dynamic approaches in Russian economic thought. At the same time, it is also the last explicit attempt at a synthesis between marginalism and the classical theory, and in this sense represents the last attempt within the 'Russian synthesis'. With this last attempt, many concerns of the Russian synthesis disappeared.

First, Marx disappeared from the scene. Barnett searched through the whole *Essays on Price Theory* and found only one reference to Marx: 'Apart from one mention in a footnote of little significance, Marx is nowhere to be found.'

(Barnett 1994, 64) I performed the same exercise with Walras, and counted 23 references of greater significance. It means that, for Yurovsky, the classical theory of value *is* Ricardo's costs of production theory, as if Ziber never wrote a line on Ricardo.

Second, value disappeared. Even if he frequently uses the expression 'value and prices', it is only, for Yurovsky, to highlight that the concept of evaluation is important. In contrast, there are many notions of prices in his work: market prices, static equilibrium prices, and dynamic equilibrium prices (in a stationary, evolutionary or cyclical framework).

Third, there is no transformation problem left, nor is it at the origin of the investigation, since there is no value left to be transformed into prices. The different prices encountered in Yurovsky's typology denoted instead a progressive notion of dynamics.

Fourth, labour no longer plays any role in Yurovsky's theory of prices. This issue remains nevertheless open, since Yurovsky did not come to a decisive conclusion on the issue of distribution.

With these four points, Yurovsky's synthesis departed from Tugan-Baranovsky's original synthesis, and seemed to catch up with Marshall.

Yurovsky and Marshall

Yurovsky's last synthesis acted as a turning point for the Russian synthesis. There is still, in his work, the idea of a synthesis between the subjective and the objective theories, between the marginalist theory (Walras) and the classical theory of value (Ricardo). But his attempt at a synthesis is, in several significant aspects, more in line with Marshall's approach.

First, Yurovsky's static equilibrium prices (A) equate instantaneous demand and supply, without taking into account the possibility of supply adjusting with the new investments obtained through savings out of income. This recalls Marshall's market prices, in which supply is fixed in the very short period.

Second, Yurovsky's dynamic equilibrium prices (B1) incorporate income distribution and allow the possibility of supply adjusting to expected demand. This is akin to Marshall's short period position, where producers can adjust their supply 'with the appliances already at their disposal' (Marshall 1920, Book V, chapter 5, §6).

Third, Yurovsky's theory of economic evolution (B2), with income accumulation and investment, evokes Marshall's long period:

> In long periods on the other hand all investments of capital and effort in providing the material plant and the organization of a business, and in acquiring trade knowledge and specialized ability, have time to be adjusted to the incomes which are expected to be earned by them: and the estimates of those incomes therefore directly govern supply, and are the true long-period normal supply price of the commodities produced.
>
> (Marshall 1920, Book V, chap. 5, §7)

Fourth, Yurovsky's interpretation of the transition from classical political economy to marginalist economics is coherent with Marshall's *ceteris paribus* argument. Both considered that Ricardo and Jevons focused their attention on *partial* aspects of the phenomena, being perfectly aware of the other aspects affecting prices.

These four points undeniably initiated a process of catching up with Marshall's approach. Yet, there are still divergences between Yurovsky and Marshall. Most significantly, Yurovsky followed Walras's general equilibrium framework and not Marshall's partial equilibrium. Moreover, Yurovsky's emphasis on dynamics (B4) foresees another direction for research. The process of catching up was only starting.

The evolution of the Russian synthesis

> Tugan-Baranovsky was not the only Russian economist who attempted to reconcile the marginal utility theory with the labour theory of value. V. K. Dmitriev also tackled the problem. For him, however, it was a technicality related to price level determination rather than a philosophical or an ethical issue.
>
> (Makasheva 2008, 80–81)

Everything started with the Marxian transformation problem. From Tugan-Baranovsky's attempt, the Russian synthesis is a consequence of the debate on the transformation of labour value into prices of production.

First, Marx's labour theory of value was strongly appealing in a country where the link between labour and value was strongly felt. Second, an incompatibility between labour value and market prices was perceived as unsustainable after the positivist methodological approach gradually affected the Russian economic profession starting from the middle of the nineteenth century, but producing its full effect only at the turn of the twentieth century (see Zweynert 2008). Third, the simultaneous appeal of subjective theories in most areas of human knowledge, and especially of marginalism in political economy, made it possible for both theories to meet.

Despite Engels and Marx's English residence, the Marxian transformation debate was essentially a Continental affair. Since Engels's Prize Essay Competition, most attempts to guess, criticise, amend or defend Marx's transformation procedure had come from German-speaking countries (C. Schmidt, Lexis, Böhm-Bawerk, Bernstein, Hilferding and Sombart; see Dostaler 1978 and Alcouffe *et al.* 2009), from Italy (Loria, Croce, Pareto, etc; see Potier 1986), or from Russia.

In these countries, and for the period under investigation in this book, an interest in Marx *and* in the marginalist theories – be it critical or supportive – was not uncommon. There are many significant examples. For instance, the German economist and statistician Lexis was one of the first participants in the transformation debate (Jorland 1995, 69–73). He even, according to Jorland

(1995, 240), introduced his student Bortkiewicz to this issue. But at the same time, he was a lucid interpreter of the significance of the Walrasian pure mathematical system of equations (see Bridel 1996, 159–161, 175–181, 225). In the same country, Bernstein, the revisionist leader within the Social Democratic Party, proposed a reconciliation between Marx and marginalism (Dostaler 1978, chap. IV, A1) In Italy, where marginalism was widespread due to Pareto's influence, Croce's approach to Marx 'is explicitly located within the field of the revisionist critique': he studied marginalism 'for which he will manifest an almost exclusive interest' (Potier 1986, 156). And in Russia, a similar attitude is provided by Tugan-Baranovsky's synthesis.

This was seldom the case in France and England (with a few notable exceptions, like Wicksteed). In England, even socialists were Ricardian, while they were Marxists on the Continent. In France, the domination of the French liberal school certainly impeded some Marxist vocations (see Arena 1995).

The Russian synthesis

Unmistakably, there were several different Russian attempts at a synthesis between 1890 and 1920. However, a general pattern emerges from all of them. The *Russian synthesis* in the theory of value and prices is characterised, in all these attempts, by the inclusion in a general framework of value of two different theories: first, a classical theory, representing the objective side of economic life and depicting production relations; second, a marginalist theory, representing the subjective side of economic life and depicting exchange relations. It resulted, for all these authors, from a feeling that both theories were *incomplete*, with gaps needing to be filled. There was also a common will to fill the gap between value and prices, after Marx had separated them in the third volume of *Capital*. For this reason, the mathematicians' synthesis did not come out of the blue, but followed the established tradition initiated by Tugan-Baranovsky.

There were, however, notable differences between all these attempts. Tugan-Baranovsky's attempt was *started* along Marx and Menger's lines, while the mathematicians' attempts *started* along Ricardo and Walras's lines. Tugan-Baranovsky's attempt is constructed within a normative and positive political economic framework, while the mathematicians' attempts are conducted as a purely positive investigation. The former had in mind gravitation around ethical value, the latter along a system of simultaneous equations. The platform for reconciliation in the former attempt is economic planning, while that for the latter is based on improved forms of demand (Walras) and supply (Ricardo).

The Marxian transformation problem in particular, and the relation between value and prices in general, were subjected to two treatments. In the first synthesis (Tugan-Baranovsky's), value and prices are bound to diverge under capitalism, but a bridge may be established between the two until their reunification under the socialist flag. In the second synthesis (the mathematicians'), there is no reason to continue to distinguish value from prices: marginal utility and costs of production are reconcilable without any need to refer to *labour costs* (*labour value*, in Marx's terminology). Against all expectations, Russian economists of the second generation of the synthesis invariably continued to refer in one way or another to the notion of labour expended in production, with the notable exception of Yurovsky. This inevitably re-introduced a notion of value next to the category of prices. The justification of this re-introduction was not always clearly spelt out by Shaposhnikov and his contemporaries. The clearest of them on this issue, Bortkiewicz, saw in the system of labour value an explanation of the *existence* of profit, the determination of its *level* being provided by the system of prices (see Faccarello 1983, 137). For his part, Shaposhnikov is more concerned to show the superiority of the mathematical method by exposing the compatibility it allows between the classical and the marginalist approaches.

Tugan-Baranovsky's synthesis was intended as a reconciliation between labour and marginal utility (see line 1 in Table 6.3), or between Marx and marginalism, but it ended as a synthesis between costs of production and marginal utility (Table 6.3, line 2). With Shaposhnikov and the mathematical economists, there is a shift in the focus of the synthesis: Ricardo's costs of production are reconciled with marginal utility. But, at the same time, there is an attempt at a reduction of these costs of production into labour, with the notion of the total sum of the labour embodied in the production of a commodity under current technical conditions. This results in a return to the Marxian transformation problem, and puts a new focus on the synthesis between labour and costs of production (Table 6.3, line 3). For his part, Yurovsky abandons the claim of any link between labour and costs of production (Table 6.3, line 4). Table 6.3 summarises the evolution of the Russian synthesis at different stages: Tugan-Baranovsky's socialist synthesis (1), Tugan-Baranovsky's capitalist synthesis (2), Shaposhnikov and the mathematicians' attempts (summarised under the label 'Shaposhnikov'), and Yurovsky's last synthesis (4).

It has always been clear what the subjective side was in the Russian synthesis: first Menger, then Walras. In the latter case, it is better to refer to Walras's mathematical method and tools embedded in an Austrian terminology. In contrast, there was always an ambiguity about what was the objective side in the Russian synthesis: Marx or Ricardo? When Tugan-Baranovsky tried to reconcile Marx with Menger, he ended up, with his capitalist synthesis, in a reconciliation of Ricardo with Menger. And when Shaposhnikov tried to reconcile Ricardo with Walras, he introduced a procedure of transformation between Ricardo's costs of production and Marx's labour value. But in the background, and this

Table 6.3 Comparisons within the Russian synthesis

	Value	*Prices*	
1. Tugan-Baranvosky	Labour costs		Marginal utility
2. Tugan-Baranovsky		Costs of production	Marginal utility
3. Shaposhnikov	Labour costs	Costs of production	Marginal utility
4. Yurovsky		Costs of production	Marginal utility

clearly becomes apparent in Table 6.3, Ziber's influence is still present. Ziber provided an understanding of *a* classical theory of value encompassing Ricardo *and* Marx. And this reading of the classical theory of value, however transformed in the successive attempts at synthesis by Tugan-Baranovsky, Shaposhnikov and his fellow mathematical economists, is still very much present in the background. Only with Yurovsky does Ricardo get rid of every Marxist interpretation.

The Russian synthesis can finally be characterised as the series of attempts at synthesis between marginalism – Walrasian mathematical tools in an Austrian terminology – and a classical theory of value – inherited from Ziber's reading of Ricardo and Marx.

This Russian synthesis is the result of two legacies. First, the Marxian transformation problem is at the origin of the lines of research that led to these attempts at synthesis. Second, Ziber's reading of the classical economists is at the origin, conscious or not, of how Russian economists understood the transformation problem, how they read the marginalists, and, finally, how they produced their syntheses. In an ethical and normative framework, or within the mathematical school, notwithstanding the differences these imply, the Russian synthesis is singular and specific, in that it strives to maintain a strong link between labour, value and prices.

With Yurovsky's *Essays on Price Theory* (1919), the link between labour and value was broken, the notion of value disappeared, and the Russian synthesis lost its peculiarities, and began the process of catching up with Marshall.

Notes

1 Bukharin composed this book in 1913–1914 between Vienna and Lausanne. The manuscript was first lost, then retrieved and eventually published in Russian in 1919. It was further translated in German in 1925, in English in 1927 and in 1967 in French. The appendix in question was, however, already published in German in 1914 in *Die neue Zeit*, and it originated, as will be seen, in the early 1910s partly as a consequence of the teaching activities of Shaposhnikov.

2 On the Russian (and Soviet) school of mathematical statistics, see Eliseeva (2003) and Barnett (2011).

3 These scarce biographical elements are taken from Shaposhnikov's obituary essay (1914).

4 Dmitriev intended to write a second series of at least three further essays, on the theory of rent, on the theory of industrial crises and on the theory of monetary circulation (Nuti 1974, 30). This plan remained an intention.

5 It must be noted that although Dmitriev recognised Tugan-Baranovsky as a great economist, and globally reviewed the latter's *Principles of Political Economy* favourably, he had a bad opinion of his theory of costs of production and of profit. About costs of production, he wrote: 'we must recognise that, as a theory of price, this theory takes us back to the pre-Ricardian (and in some respects pre-Smithian) period' (Dmitriev 1909b, 116–117).

6 Barnett's translation of the table of contents has been used: for more details (including translation of sections within chapters), see Barnett (2011, 207–215).

7 Bilimovic, Alexandr Dmitrievich (1876–1963) was professor of political economy at the University of Kiev between 1909 and 1920. He lived thereafter abroad: at the

Universities of Ljubjana (1920–1944) and Berkeley in California (since 1948). For a general presentation on Bilimovic, see Sušjan (2010).

8 At the time of printing this book, Petr Kljukin, from the Higher School of Economics (Moscow), is preparing a volume of Shaposhnikov's collected works (in Russian).

9 The life of Shaposhnikov being not well known, this section uses all the scarce sources available (Shukov 1980; Barnett 1995, 415–416 and 2005, 70–71; Belykh 2007, 11; and Kljukin 2010b, 673–675), to which new bibliographic records from the National Library of Russia are added, as well as new archival material (letters from Shaposhnikov to Bortkiewicz).

10 The journal *Kritičeskoe Obozrenie* (Critical Review), published between 1907 and 1909, specialized in book and literature reviews on philosophy, politics, law, economics and natural sciences. Dmitriev was also an active contributor to the economic section of this journal.

11 Bukharin wrote a critique of Tugan-Baranovsky's theory of value for this seminar. The following year, he attended Böhm-Bawerk's lectures in Vienna. This was followed by a spell in Lausanne to study Walras and other mathematical economists at the University Library, while completing his book on Austrian value theory, *Economic Theory of the Leisure Class* ([1919] 1927), with the paper on Tugan-Baranovsky as an appendix.

12 The Institute published a periodical *Economic Bulletin of the Institute of Conjuncture* between 1922 and 1929 and an irregular series *Questions of Conjuncture* between 1924 and 1928. The former collected data, indicators computed by the Institute, and methodological and theoretical papers by the members of the Institute, including Kondratiev, Slutsky, Shaposhnikov, Konyus, Chetverikov…. The recent publication by Kljukin of a collection of the most interesting articles from these journals, together with a useful historical reconstruction, in one volume will hopefully contribute to a renewed appreciation of the highly interesting debates in the 1920s (see Kljukin 2010b).

13 In particular, he made use of this example: one cannot exchange a piece of bread for the equivalent in opera, because it is not possible to buy a ticket for less than the full event.

14 It is useful to remember that, for Dmitriev, the mechanism of competition does not lower prices to costs of production, but on the contrary costs of production are rising toward prices, due to rational overproduction and extra inventory. Shaposhnikov refutes this argument in his review of Dmitriev's work (Shaposhnikov 1905).

15 Shaposhnikov had a complex and not only scientific relationship with Tugan-Baranovsky. For example, his dissertation (*Theory of Value and Distribution*) was ready in 1912 in St Petersburg, but its defence took place only in 1913 in Moscow. In a letter to Bortkiewicz, dated 14 November 1912, he commented:

> I do not know what to do with my dissertation. Tugan-Baranovsky had a rather strange position towards me. During the summer, he promised to expedite the convening of my defence. But when, in autumn, I raised the subject again, he stated that he had no time to write his report on my book to the faculty, and that he could do it only during the second semester. But after Christmas, he probably won't be any longer at the university. The Minister [of National Education] allowed him to teach only until the holidays. I don't know how to react. To take back my book from the faculty and submit it to another university will probably generate undesirable rumours, and the prospect of Kistyakovsky as opponent at the defence does not make me smile either. In brief, the situation is very confusing.

16 His book *Currency Problems and Policy in the Soviet Union* published in 1925 in English in London, is an interesting blend of policy testimony and discussions of theoretical issues, such as the introduction of a new currency, the circulation of

parallel currencies and the problem of a moneyless economy (see Yurovsky 1925). On Yurovsky's Soviet years, see also Barnett (1994) and Goland (2008).

17 This work has already been discussed once in the English language. See Barnett (1994, 64–67).

18 On Kondratiev's Institute, see Barnett (1995) and Kljukin (2010b).

References

Alcouffe, Alain, Friedrun Quaas and Georg Quaas. 2009. 'La préhistoire du problème de la transformation'. In Alain Alcouffe and Claude Diebolt, eds, *La pensée économique allemande*, 309–337. Paris: Economica.

Arena, Richard. 1995. 'French Socialists and Themes of Value, 1872–1914'. In Ian Steedman, ed., *Socialism and Marginalism in Economics*, 188–202. London: Routledge.

Barnett, Vincent. 1994. 'The Economic Thought of L. N. Yurovskii'. *Coexistence*, 31: 63–77.

Barnett, Vincent. 1995. 'A Long Wave Goodbye: Kondrat'ev and the Conjuncture Institute, 1920–28'. *Europe–Asia Studies*, 47(3): 413–441.

Barnett, Vincent. 2005. *A History of Russian Economic Thought*. London: Routledge.

Barnett, Vincent. 2011. *E. E. Slutsky as Economist and Mathematician: Crossing the Limits of Knowledge*. Abingdon, UK: Routledge.

Belykh, Andrej Akatovich. 2007. *Istoriâ Rossijskih èkonomiko-matematičeskih issledovanij (History of Russian Mathematical-Economic Investigations)*. Second edition. Moscow: LKI.

Bilimovic, Aleksandr D. 1914. *K voprosu o rascenke hozâjstvennyh blag (On the Question of the Evaluation of Economic Goods)*. Kiev: Imperial University St Vladimir.

Bortkiewicz, Ladislaus von. 1890. 'Review of Léon Walras, *Éléments d'économie politique pure, ou Théorie de la richesse sociale*, 2e édition, Guillaumin et Cie, Paris'. *Revue d'économie politique*, 4(1): 80–86.

Bortkiewicz, Ladislaus von. 1906–1907. 'Wertrechnung und Preisrechnung im Marxschen System (I–II–III)'. *Archiv für Sozialwissenschaft und Sozialpolitik*, XXIII: 1–50; XXV: 10–51 and 445–488. Parts II and III translated into English by J. Kahane. 1952. 'Value and Prices in the Marxian System'. *International Economic Papers*, 2: 5–60.

Bortkiewicz, Ladislaus von. 1907. 'Zur Berichtigung der grundlegenden theoretischen Konstruktion von Marx im 3. Band des Kapital'. *Jahrbücher für Nationalökonomie und Statistik*, 34: 319–335. Translated into English: 'On the Correction of Marx's Fundamental Theoretical Construction in the Third Volume of Capital'. In Paul M. Sweezy, ed., *Karl Marx and the Close of His System*, 199–221, 1949. New York: Kelley.

Bortkiewicz, Ladislaus von. 1921. 'Objektivismus und Subjektivismus in der Werttheorie'. *Ekonomisk Tidskrift*, 23(12): 1–22.

Bridel, Pascal. 1996. *Le Chêne et l'architecte, un siècle de comptes rendus bibliographiques des Éléments d'économie politique pure de Léon Walras*. Geneva: Droz.

Bridel, Pascal. 2008. 'Bortkiewicz et Walras. Notes sur une collaboration intellectuelle avortée'. *Revue d'économie politique*, 118(5): 711–742.

Bukharin, Nikolay Ivanovich. 1914. 'Eine Ökonomie ohne Wert'. *Die Neue Zeit*, 22: 806–816 and 23: 850–858.

Bukharin, Nikolay Ivanovich. [1919] 1927. *Političeskaâ èkonomiâ rant'e (Economic Theory of the Leisure Class)*. London: Martin Lawrence.

Dmitriev, Vladimir Karpovich. [1904] 1974. *Èkonomičeskie očerki (Economic Essays)*.

Moscow: Rikhter. First essay published in 1898, Moscow: Moscow University. Second and third essays published in 1902, Moscow: Rikhter. English edition by Domenico Mario Nuti. 1974. London: Cambridge University Press.

Dmitriev, Vladimir Karpovich. 1908. 'Teoriâ cennosti. Obzor literatury na russkom âzyke (Value Theory. Review of the Literature in the Russian Language)'. *Kritičeskoe Obozrenie*, VII: 12–26.

Dmitriev, Vladimir Karpovich. 1909a. 'Teoretičeskaâ statistika. Obzor naučnoj i naučno-popularnoj literatury na russkom âzyke (Theoretical Statistics: Review of the Scientific and Vulgarisation Literature)'. *Kritičeskoe obozrenie*, VI.

Dmitriev, Vladimir Karpovich. 1909b. 'Novyj russkij traktat po teorii političeskoj èkonomii. M. I. Tugan-Baranovskij. Osnovy političeskoj èkonomii. Spb., 1909 (A New Russian Treatise in the Theory of Political Economy. Tugan-Baranovsky's Principles of Political Economy, 1909)'. *Russkaâ Mysl'*, 30: 102–125.

Dmitriev, Vladimir Karpovich. 1911. *Kritičeskie issledovanija o potreblenii alkogolja v Rossii (Critical Research on Alcohol Consumption in Russia)*. Moscow: Râbupinskij.

Dostaler, Gilles. 1978. *Valeur et prix. Histoire d'un débat*. Montréal: François Maspero, Presses Universitaires de Grenoble, Les presses de l'Université du Québec.

Eliseeva, Irina Ilinichna. 2003. 'Rossijskaâ statističeskaâ škola (Russian Statistical School)'. In Y. V. Yakovec, ed., *Rossijskie èkonomičeskie školy (Russian Economic Schools)*, 233–255. Moscow: IFK-MFK.

Frank, Semen L. 1900. *Teoriâ cennosti Marksa i eâ značenie. Kritičeskij ètûd' (Marx's Theory of Value and its Meaning. A Critical Study)*. St Petersburg: Vodovozova.

Faccarello, Gilbert. 1983. *Travail, valeur et prix: une critique de la théorie de la valeur*. Paris: Anthropos. Electronic edition, 2009, available at: http://ggjjff.free.fr/ (accessed on 16 July 2014).

Girshfeld, V. 1910. 'Teorema o proporcional'nosti predel'nyh poleznostej blag ih trudovym stoimostâm (Theorem of the Proportionality of the Marginal Utility of Goods with their Labour Costs)'. In Mikhail Ivanovich Tugan-Baranovsky and Pavel Isaakovich Lyubinsky, eds, *Voprosy obshchestvovedenija (Problems in Social Sciences)*, vol. 2. St Petersburg: Slovo.

Goland, Yury M. 2008. 'Leonid Naumovich Yurovsky. Portret na fone epohi (A Portrait of Yurovsky in Context)'. In Leonid N. Yurovsky, *Denežnaâ politika sovetskoj vlasti, 1917–1927, Izbrannye stat'i (The Monetary Policy of the Soviet Regime, 1917–1927, Selected Papers)*, 5–36. Moscow: Ekonomika.

Jorland, Gérard. 1995. *Les paradoxes du capital*. Paris: Odile Jacob.

Kljukin, Petr Nikolaevich. 2010a. 'Genetičeskij princip v issledovanii nasprediâ E. E. Sluckogo i ego osnovnye rezul'taty (The Genetic Principle in the Research Heritage of E. E. Slutsky and its Principal Results)'. In Evgenij Evgen'evič Slutsky, *Èkonomičeskie i statističeskie proizvedenie. Izbrannoe. (E. E. Slutsky's Selected Economic and Statistical Works)*, 17–91. Moscow: Eksmo.

Kljukin, Petr Nikolaevich, ed. 2010b. *Izbrannye trudy Kondrat'evskogo kon'junkturnogo instituta (Collected Works of Kondratiev's Conjuncture Institute)*. Moscow: Ekonomika.

Makasheva, Natalia A. 2008. 'Searching for an Ethical Basis of Political Economy: Bulgakov and Tugan-Baranovsky'. In Vincent Barnett and Joachim Zweynert, eds, *Economics in Russia. Studies in Intellectual History*, chap. 6, 75–89. Aldershot, UK: Ashgate.

Marchionatti, Roberto. 2007. 'On the Application of Mathematics to Political Economy. The Edgeworth–Walras–Bortkievicz Controversy, 1889–1891'. *Cambridge Journal of Economics*, 31: 291–307.

Marchionatti, Roberto and Raffaella Fiorini. 2000. 'Between Walras and Ricardo. Ladislaus von Bortkiewicz and the Origin of Neo-Ricardian Theory'. *Revue européenne des sciences sociales*, 38(117): 173–191.

Marshall, Alfred. 1920. *Principles of Political Economy*. Eight edition. London: Macmillan and Co.

Nuti, Domenico M. 1974. 'Introduction'. In V. K. Dmitriev, *Economic Essays on Value, Competition and Utility*, 7–28. London: Cambridge University Press.

Potier, Jean-Pierre. 1986. *Lectures italiennes de Marx. Les conflits d'interprétation chez les économistes et les philosophes (1883–1983)*. Lyon: Presses universitaires de Lyon.

Samuelson, Paul. A. 1975. 'Review: *Economic Essays on Value, Competition, and Utility*. by V. K. Dmitriev, D. M. Nuti, D. Fry'. *Journal of Economic Literature*, 13(2): 491–495.

Schütte, Frank. 2002. *Die ökonomischen Studien V. K. Dmitrievs*. Ph.D. diss., Technische Universität Chemnitz. Available at: http://monarch.qucosa.de/fileadmin/data/qucosa/documents/5136/data/start.html (accessed on 5 August 2014).

Shaposhnikov, Nikolay Nikolaevich. 'Letters from Shaposhnikov to Bortkiewicz (1910–1926)'. Uppsala Universitätsbibliothek, Sweden: Manuskript und Musikabteilung, Kapsel 7. Unpublished.

Shaposhnikov, Nikolay Nikolaevich. 1905. 'Svobodnaâ konkurrenci i cena tovarov. V. K. Dmitriev. Èkonomičeskie očerki (Free Competition and the Price of Goods. On Dmitriev's Economic Essays)'. *Russkoe Èkonomičeskoe Obozrenie*, 2: 76–90.

Shaposhnikov, Nikolay Nikolaevich. 1906. *Teorija pribyli Bem-Baverka (Böhm-Bawerk's Theory of Profit)*. St Petersburg: Senackij.

Shaposhnikov, Nikolay Nikolaevich. 1909a. 'Review of Tugan-Baranovsky's Principles of Political Economy (1909)'. *Kritičeskoe Obozrenie*, 5: 48–53.

Shaposhnikov, Nikolay Nikolaevich. 1909b. *Uchenie Tûnena ob estestvennoj zarabotnoj plate (Thünen's Natural Wage Doctrine)*. Jaroslav: Typography of the Provincial Government.

Shaposhnikov, Nikolay Nikolaevich. 1912a. *Teoriâ cennosti i raspredeleniâ (Theory of Value and Distribution)*. Moscow: Mysl'.

Shaposhnikov, Nikolay Nikolaevich. 1912b. 'Walras'. In *Novyj Ènciklopedičeskij Slovar' (New Encyclopaedia)*, vol. 9, 460–461. St Petersburg: Brockhaus and Efron. Original and French translation available at http://francois.allisson.co.

Shaposhnikov, Nikolay Nikolaevich. 1912c. 'Walras'. In *Ènciklopedičeskij Slovar' (Encyclopedia)*, vol. 7. St Petersburg: Granat.

Shaposhnikov, Nikolay Nikolaevich. 1914. *Pervyj russkij èkonomist-matematik Vladimir Karpovich Dmitriev, Doklad na zasedanii Obshchestva im. A. I. Chuprova, posvjashchennom pamjati Dmitrieva (The First Russian Mathematical Economist V. K. Dmitriev, Lecture at the A. I. Chuprov Society, Held in Memory of Dmitriev)*. Moscow: Lissner and Sobko.

Shaposhnikov, Nikolay Nikolaevich. 1915. *Protekcionizm i svoboda torgovli (Protectionism and Free Trade)*. Petrograd: Ministry of Finance.

Shaposhnikov, Nikolay Nikolaevich. 1917. 'O nauchnoj cennosti abstraktnoj teorii (Scientific Value of Abstract Theory)'. *Ûridičeskij Vestnik*, XVII: 134–143.

Shukov, N. S. 1980. 'Shaposhnikov'. In A. M. Rumjancev, ed., *Èkonomičeskaâ enciklopediâ (Economic Encyclopaedia)*, vol. 4, 415. Moscow: Sovetskaâ Ènciklopediâ.

Slutsky, Evgeny Evgenevich. 1910. *Teoriâ predel'noj poleznosti (The Theory of Marginal Utility)*. Master's Thesis, University of Kiev, Manuscripts section, National Library Vernadsky, Kiev, F. I, No 44850. Ukrainian published edition 2006. Kiev, KNEU. Russian first publication, edited by Petr Nikolaevich Kljukin, 2010. Moscow: Eksmo.

Slutsky, Evgeny Evgenevich. 1915. 'Sulla teoria del bilancio del consumatore'. *Giornale degli economisti*, 51: 1–26. English translation by Olga Ragusa, 1952. 'On the theory of the budget of the consumer'. In George J. Stigler and Kenneth T. Boulding, eds, *Reading in Price Theory*, 27–56. Homewood, IL: Irwin.

Slutsky, Evgeny Evgenevich. 1926. 'Ein Beitrag zur formal-praxeologischen Grundlegung der Oekonomik'. *Académie Ukrainienne des sciences, Annales socio-économiques*, 4: 238–249. English translation by Claus Wittich, 2004. 'An Enquiry Into the Formal Praxeological Foundations of Economics', *Structural Change and Economic Dynamics*, 15: 371–380.

Slutsky, Evgeny Evgenevich. 1927. 'Zur Kritik des Böhm-Bawerkschen Wertbegriffs und seiner Lehre von der Messbarkeit des Wertes'. *Schmollers Jahrbuch*, 51(4): 545–560. English translation by Roger Rosko and John Chipman. 2004. 'A Critique of Böhm-Bawerk's Concept of Value and his Theory of the Measurability of Value'. *Structural Change and Economic Dynamics*, 15: 357–369.

Stoliarov, Nikolay Aleksandrovich. 1902. *Analitičeskoe dokazatel'stvo predloženoj g. M. Tugan-Baranovskim politiko-èkonomičeskoj formuly: Predel'nye poleznosti svobodno proizvedennyh produktov proporcional'ny ih trudovym stoimostâm (Analytical Proof of the Politico-Economic Formulae Proposed by M. Tugan-Baranovsky: Marginal Utility of Freely Produced Goods Proportional to their Labour Costs)*. Lecture at the Physico-Mathematical Society of Kiev, 11 February 1902. Kiev: Kuk'ženko.

Sušjan, Andrej. 2010. 'Historicism and Neoclassicism in the Kiev School of Economics: The Case of Aleksander Bilimovich'. *Journal of the History of Economic Thought*, 32(2): 199–219.

Tugan-Baranovsky, Mikhail Ivanovich. 1909. *Osnovy političeskoj èkonomii (Principles of Political Economy)*. St Petersburg: Slovo. Reprint of the fourth edition, 1998. Moscow: Rosspèn.

Walras, Léon. 1988. *Éléments d'économie politique pure*, vol. VIII of *Auguste et Léon Walras, œuvres économiques complètes*. Variorum edition by Claude Mouchot. Paris: Economica.

Yurovsky, Leonid Naumovich. 1907. *Teoriâ političeskoj èkonomii. Kratkij kurs po lekciâm prof. Tugan-Baranovskogo (Theory of Political Economy. A Short Course Based on the Lectures of Prof. Tugan-Baranovsky)*. St Petersburg: Bezobrazov.

Yurovsky, Leonid Naumovich. 1910. *Der Russische Getreideexport: Seine Entwickelung und Organisation*. Ph.D. thesis, supervised by Lujo Brentano. Stuttgart: Münchener Volkswirtschaftliche Studien no 105.

Yurovsky, Leonid Naumovich. 1919. *Očerki po teorii ceny (Essays on Price Theory)*. Saratov, Russia: Saratov University.

Yurovsky, Leonid Naumovich. 1925. *Currency Problems and Policy of the Soviet Union*. London: Parsons.

Zalesky, V. F. 1893. *Uchenie o proiskhozhdenii pribyli na kapital. Otd. I. Uchenie o cennosti (Study on the Origin of Profit on Capital. First Part: Study on Value)*. Kazan, Russia: Univ. tip.

Zweynert, Joachim. 2008. 'Between Reason and Historicity: Russian Academic Economics, 1800–1861'. In Vincent Barnett and Joachim Zweynert, eds, *Economics in Russia: Studies in Intellectual History*, chap. 5, 57–73. Aldershot, UK: Ashgate.

Conclusion

This book offers the first history of the Russian synthesis. The theoretical context in which this synthesis took shape has been outlined in the first part of this book. After the basic concept of value and prices in Russian economic thought was defined (Chapter 1), it has been shown that in the 1870s Ziber already provided the basis for an interpretation of a classical theory of value embedding the legacies of both Ricardo and Marx (Chapter 2). It has further been argued that this only delayed the reception of marginalism in Russia, which entered the country only in the 1890s, first in its Austrian version, then in the mathematical Walrasian version. It has been shown that the marginalist theories were perceived as theories of exchange only and not as theories of production (Chapter 3). Once all constituting parts were laid down, the history of the Russian synthesis is carefully reconstructed in the second part of this book (Chapters 4 and 5 for Tugan-Baranovsky; Chapter 6 for Dmitriev, Bortkiewicz, Slutsky – and others – Shaposhnikov and Yurovsky).

It all started from the Marxian transformation problem

The starting point of the research programme into value and prices in Russia is the Marxian transformation problem. This debate encouraged some of Marx's supporters to find solutions outside the Marxist camp. Tugan-Baranovsky provided two answers. First, he offered to correct Marx with a numerical solution to the 'inverse transformation problem', suggesting transforming prices into value. Second, he proposed his 'no transformation' hypothesis with his attempt at a synthesis between marginal utility and the labour theory of value. There is no possible synthesis between value and prices in capitalism, while the synthesis becomes possible under socialism with a rational organisation of production through an 'economic plan'. In this case, prices are planned in order to follow ideal values. The transformation of prices into value is thought of as an historical (or utopian) process. The synthesis acts here as a reformulation of the transformation problem. It should be underlined, as it is rather uncommon, that in both solutions Tugan-Baranovsky proceeded from prices to value and not the other way round.

After Tugan-Baranovsky, in his own attempt at a synthesis, Shaposhnikov also tackled the transformation problem. Shaposhnikov tried to show the compatibility between labour values (quantities of labour time) and costs of production: wages, profits and rent. The issue of rent having been discarded, as Ricardo did in his time, the relation between profits and wages was still waiting for an explanation. It came from the transformation of capital into labour.

The idea of reducing several factors of production into one is not new. Specifically, the idea of reducing capital into labour, by considering capital as previous quantities of labour, was an idea developed several times earlier in the literature. It was revived by Marx and later on by Tugan-Baranovsky, who explained, without however demonstrating it, that there was no need to calculate an infinite historical regression to the very first capital good. It was enough to consider recursively, in the present day technical conditions, all the means of production necessary to produce the good in question *here and now*. This processing of capital as labour took over the mathematical formulation, first advanced by Dmitriev in 1898: the total amount of direct and indirect labour embodied in a commodity is given by a system of simultaneous equations with commodities producing other commodities by way of coefficients of production. The resulting labour value is eventually transformed into Ricardian prices of production, given that one good is taken as a numeraire. The rate of profit is obtained from the technical conditions of production in the wage goods sectors, together with the given real wage rate. This last result, obtained by Dmitriev and retrieved with amendments by Bortkiewicz, was severely condemned by Shaposhnikov. Like most Russian economists rejecting distribution theories, he saw here another limitation to theoretical economics, which was unable to explain the origin of profit without first taking a real wage rate as given. The theory of prices was compatible with a theory of value which could be reduced to labour, at the cost of settling *ex ante* the conditions of the theory of distribution.

The first ingredient of the synthesis: Marx and Ricardo

The transformation problem is not the whole story; it is only the starting point of the Russian synthesis. The latter was a combination of an objective theory of value depicting the conditions of production with a subjective theory of prices representing human needs.

For Tugan-Baranovsky, the objective theory of value is the classical theory of value. By 1890, he had not clearly distinguished the theory of Ricardo from that of Marx, and he considered that they had a *labour theory of value*. In his 'simple synthesis', with labour as the only explicit factor of production, this identification of Ricardo with Marx is simple enough to be managed. In his 'complex synthesis', however, there is a distinction between a costs of production theory in the historical economy (capitalism), and labour value (which he called labour costs) in the logical economy. Indeed, in a very Marxian fashion, costs of production are the mere appearance of the phenomena of labour value. But at the same time, and closer to Tugan-Baranovsky's interpretation of Kant than to Marx's, labour value conforms to the social ideal, in which the economy is only a means to achieve humankind's needs (vs capitalists' needs). Ricardo's costs of production *and* Marx's labour value have their own place in Tugan-Baranovsky's attempt at a synthesis.

For Shaposhnikov, the objective theory of value was also the classical theory of value, understood as Ricardo's costs of production theory. His synthesis was nevertheless accompanied by a concern to show that, regardless of moral considerations, labour could fit into his mathematical synthesis. The transformation (or reduction, in Bortkiewicz's terminology) of costs of production into dated labour showed that, once again, Marx and Ricardo were both present in this attempt at a synthesis.

This perceived indecisiveness in the Russian synthesis is perfectly understandable if one remembers that Ricardo and Marx were both introduced in Russia by Ziber in the 1870s. Ziber offered a – retrospectively confusing – interpretation of Ricardo and Marx that was very influential. According to this reading, there is homogeneity in the classical school: both Ricardo and Marx were supporting the same classical theory of value, which embodied both the social labour theory of value and the individual costs of production theory. There is therefore nothing odd in the attitude of Russian economists towards their classical theory of value, seen as represented by both Ricardo and Marx.

The second ingredient: marginalism

In addition to that singular Russian classical theory of value, the subjective theory of prices was borrowed from the marginalist theories. The first wave of marginalism was Austrian. It settled in Russia and imposed its own terminology. The second wave was Walrasian and was steeped in mathematics.

Accordingly, Tugan-Baranovsky's marginalism was Austrian, and was presented with the help of Menger's schemes. The subjective value is rendered for him by a system of determination of relative prices, which is restricted to the exchange of a number of goods, given with objective conditions. It should be remembered that Tugan-Baranovsky had no knowledge of Walrasian general equilibrium but that he interpreted the interdependence in the economy, through the Marxian notion of reproduction scheme, as a form of circular representation of the economy. For his part, Shaposhnikov used a Walrasian general equilibrium and the notion of interdependence as his method.

For all protagonists of the Russian synthesis (including this time even Yurovsky), the marginalist theory of prices was not self-sufficient. It could not explain prices without the help of the classical theory of value, since it expressed only the subjective side of economic life, and therefore overlooked production. Marginalism was perceived as filling the gap of the missing demand side. This clearly supports the idea that marginalism only brought change within continuity. In others words, the 'marginalist revolution' was by no means a revolution in Russia. It was not throwing away the old theories; it was only completing them.

Labour and distribution

Since the Russian synthesis involved a dialogue between marginal utility and costs of production, understood as the sum of wages, profits and rent, this implied that one expression of the classical theories of value, i.e. costs of production, had been selected, while the others, essentially the quantity of labour theory, had been rejected. It meant, significantly, that Marx's theory of distribution (surplus originates in the exploitation of labour) did not fit into this scheme.

This is where the dual understanding of the classical theory of value proved particularly useful. For Shaposhnikov, costs of production and labour value were interchangeable. For his part, Tugan-Baranovsky's attempt at a synthesis translated a desire to keep a strong normative content in the notion of value. Value in this case was thought of as an ideal price. He kept the two notions – costs of production and labour value – but assigned to them two different domains of application. The difference between actual prices and ideal value measured the degree of unethical behaviour, the degree of remoteness from socialism, eventually defining an empirical measure of exploitation.

The end of the Russian synthesis?

For his part, Yurovsky was neither interested in the Marxian transformation problem, nor in any link between labour and value. Nevertheless, as the last representative of the tradition of the Russian synthesis, he felt the need to combine classical political economy and marginal utility.

What distinguished the Russian synthesis from the Marshall approach is first and foremost the will to keep a strong link between labour and value, while stressing at the same time the need to reduce the gap between value and price.

Indeed, by starting with Marx, the Russian synthesis was designed never to become Marshallian; it was insulated from English marginalism for more than two decades after the introduction of marginalism in Russia in 1890. But, as in Western countries, the influence of Marshall seriously grew at the end of the 1910s, in spite of Walras's general equilibrium already being deeply rooted.

In actual fact, political circumstances prevented the confrontation of Walras and Marshall in the writings of Russian economists. From the 1920s onwards, immediately after Yurovsky's *Essays on Price Theory*, it became politically dangerous to bring marginalism and any conciliatory attitude towards this theory into the debates. Marginalism was banned, and the Russian synthesis was no longer on the agenda. But it did not signal the ultimate transformation of the Russian synthesis – its disappearance. The whole intellectual legacy that had accumulated in the Russian synthesis by the end of the Tsarist regime in Russia did not evaporate in 1917.

The Russian synthesis, as distinct from other European approaches on value and prices, failed to find its place in global economic thought. Only parts of it were considered theoretically and analytically convincing, and these parts are already well known: the contributions to the Marxian transformation problem, and those by Dmitriev and Bortkiewicz to the mathematical development of the classical theory of value and distribution. Retrospectively, this history of the Russian synthesis looks like the story of a failure.

This story has nevertheless much to teach. On Ricardo and Marx, for instance, the Russian synthesis did not help us to grasp their theories of value and prices, or to better understand the difference between them. But the ways these theories were read, modified and appropriated were an important step in the understanding of the future debates on planning: from Ricardo and Marx to planning through Ziber and the Russian synthesis. These future debates were also steeped in Austrian and Walrasian marginalism, which has been somewhat neglected. Some protagonists of the Russian synthesis participated in these debates, and their students kept the Russian synthesis in mind. The Russian synthesis thus survived both inside and, with emigration, outside the USSR.

Value and prices

The Russian synthesis was an attempt to bring the notions of value and prices closer together, first for ethical and practical reasons, then for logical reasons. For Tugan-Baranovsky, value always retained its own heuristic, it coexisted with price. For Shaposhnikov and the mathematicians, value merged with prices and lost its autonomy. This articulation between value and prices shows how related the Russian synthesis and the Marxian transformation problem are.

In the Russian synthesis, a system of prices exists with a system of value *at the same time*, and not according to a short period–long period articulation à la Marshall. Marginal utility and costs of production play a dominant role in the system of prices, while labour keeps playing a very important role in the value system. It is precisely this articulation between value and prices that allows this singular – Russian – connection between labour and value.

The very idea of keeping a link between labour and value disappears with Yurovsky's last synthesis, and thereby the Russian synthesis lost its particular identity. Behind the link between labour and value, on which the Russian synthesis was based, hides a conception of distribution which the Russian economists, while catching the train of marginal utility theory, were trying to pack in their suitcases.

Index

Page numbers in *italics* denote tables.

Croce, Benedetto (1866–1952) 104n13, 120, 124, 161–2

Danielson, Nikolai Frantsevich (1844–1918) 23, 25–7, 30n12, n14, 128n8
Diehl, Karl (1864–1943) 50n23
Dietzel, Heinrich (1857–1935) 19, 80, 116
distribution 2, 14, 17, 41–2, 45, 50n15, 54, 58–9, 63, 86, 90, 93–5, 97, 102, 145–9, 152–3, 155, 157–60, 171, 173–4; fall of the rate of profit 17, 50n24, 84, 87–8, *88*, 90, 111; profit 15–18, 34, 39–41, 45, 66, 89–90, 101, 104n13, 136–8, 142–3, 146, 151–3, 163, 164n5, 171; rent 26, 34, 66–7, 136, 151, 153, 157, 159, 164n4, 171; wages 15–16, 34, 39, 41, 45, 66–7, 79–84, 97, 120, 136, 146, 151, 153, 171
Dmitriev, Vladimir Karpovich (1868–1913) 1–2, 4, 7, 28, 47–8, 53, 57–62, 64–5, 67, 69n13, 114, 124, 126, 127n2, 128n8, 133–43, 145–7, 150–7, 161, 164n4–5, 165n10, n14, 170–1, 174; on the synthesis 135–8; on the transformation problem 17–18, 109; on Ziber 44
Dostoyevsky, Fyoror Mikhailovich (1821–1881) 79, 104n6

Edgeworth, Francis Ysidro (1845–1926) 59, 139, 156–7
Engels, Friedrich (1820–1895) 16–17, 19, 26, 29n5, n7, 30n14, 46, 49n6, 123–4, 161
ethics 1, 7n1, 76–7, 79–80, 82, 86, 91–2, 97–100, 104n6, 105n17, 110, 118, 120, 122–4, 129n18, 134, 155, 161–2, 164, 173–4
exploitation 15–17, 19, 39, 40, 47, 50n24, 82, 86–90, *88*, 93, 97, 102, 104n13, 121, 123, 173

Fireman, Peter (1863–1962) 16, 29n5
Frank, Semen Lyudvigovich (1877–1950) 4, 28, 91, 155; on the synthesis 144
freedom 93, 95–6, 100, 102–3
Frisch, Ragnar (1895–1973) 58
Fuks, Vladimir Aleksandrovich 26

Gelesnoff, Vladimir Yakovlevich (1869–1933) 4, 28, 146
general equilibrium 3, 13–15, 57, 59, 63–5, 67, 139–40, 158, 161, 172–3

Georgievsky, Pavel Ivanovich (1857–1938) 103n2
German historical school 22–8, 56, 60, 68, 77, 111
Girshfeld, Vladimir 125, 128n8, n10, 143, 155
Gosplan (State Planning Committee) 76, 148
Gossen, Hermann Heinrich (1810–1858) 25, 27, 54–6, 68n3, 77, 82, 111, 127n3, n5, 133, 137, 145, 149, 156
Greig, Samuil Alexeevich (1827–1887) 126–7

Hegel, Georg Wilhelm Friedrich (1770–1831) 2, 22, 36, 49n6
Hildebrand, Bruno (1812–1878) 80
Hilferding, Rudolf (1877–1941) 17, 161

industry in Russia 6, 23–5, 34, 56, 75, 91, 123–4, 148

Jevons, William Stanley (1835–1882) 13, 19–21, 27, 54–5, 58, 111, 127n5, 145, 156–7, 161

Kant *see* neo-Kantianism
Kautsky, Karl (1854–1938) 19, 35, 46
Kistyakovsky, Bogdan Aleksandrovich (1868–1920) 165n15
Klejnbort, Lev Naumovich (1875–1950) 35, 76
Knies, Karl (1821–1898) 46, 49n7, 50n16, 80
Kondratiev, Nikolay Dmitrievich (1892–1938) 6, 77–8, 104n5, 128n8, 148, 159, 165n12; Conjuncture Institute 148, 159, 165n12, 166n18
Konyus, Aleksandr Aleksandrovich (1895–1990) 165n12
Kropotkin, Pyotr Alexeyevich (1842–1921) 91, 93, 96

labour: abstract versus concrete 39; complex versus simple 19, 97; division of 39–41, 43, 45, 95; importance in Russia 3, 47, 152, 161, 173–4; total amount of 17, 103, 113, 135–7, 143, 151, 171; *see also* value
Legal Marxists 5, 24–5, 28, 30n15, 36, 48, 87, 91, 127n6, 144; *see also* revisionism
Lenin, Vladimir Ilich (1870–1924) 24, 27, 35–6, 75, 91; on Ziber 36
Lexis, Wilhelm (1837–1914) 16, 116, 147, 161

eBooks
from Taylor & Francis
Helping you to choose the right eBooks for your Library

Add to your library's digital collection today with Taylor & Francis eBooks. We have over 50,000 eBooks in the Humanities, Social Sciences, Behavioural Sciences, Built Environment and Law, from leading imprints, including Routledge, Focal Press and Psychology Press.

Free Trials Available
We offer free trials to qualifying academic, corporate and government customers.

Choose from a range of subject packages or create your own!

Benefits for you
- Free MARC records
- COUNTER-compliant usage statistics
- Flexible purchase and pricing options
- All titles DRM-free.

Benefits for your user
- Off-site, anytime access via Athens or referring URL
- Print or copy pages or chapters
- Full content search
- Bookmark, highlight and annotate text
- Access to thousands of pages of quality research at the click of a button.

eCollections
Choose from over 30 subject eCollections, including:

Archaeology	Language Learning
Architecture	Law
Asian Studies	Literature
Business & Management	Media & Communication
Classical Studies	Middle East Studies
Construction	Music
Creative & Media Arts	Philosophy
Criminology & Criminal Justice	Planning
Economics	Politics
Education	Psychology & Mental Health
Energy	Religion
Engineering	Security
English Language & Linguistics	Social Work
Environment & Sustainability	Sociology
Geography	Sport
Health Studies	Theatre & Performance
History	Tourism, Hospitality & Events

For more information, pricing enquiries or to order a free trial, please contact your local sales team:
www.tandfebooks.com/page/sales

www.tandfebooks.com